MW00966133

Histories, Cultures, and National Identities

Histories, Cultures, and National Identities

Women Writing Spain, 1877–1984

Christine Arkinstall

Lewisburg
Bucknell University Press

Associated University Presses
2010 Eastpark Boulevard
Cranbury, NJ 08512

The paper used in this publication meets the requirements of the American National Standard for Permanence of Paper for Printed Library Materials Z39.48-1984.

Library of Congress Cataloging-in-Publication Data

Arkinstall, Christine.
Histories, cultures, and national identities : women writing Spain (1877–1984) / Christine Arkinstall..
p. cm.
Includes bibliographical references and index.
ISBN 978-0-8387-5728-4 (alk. paper)
1. Spanish literature—Women authors—History and criticism. 2. Spanish literature —20th century—History and criticism. 3. National characteristics, Spanish, in literature. 4. Politics and literature—Spain. 5. Women in literature. 6. Spain—Civilization. I. Title.

PQ6055.A86 2009
860.9'92870904—dc22

2008022706

PRINTED IN THE UNITED STATES OF AMERICA

For my parents, Judy and Brian,
and for John Kronik, mentor par excellence

Contents

Acknowledgments

This book, in its various incarnations, has accompanied me for a long time. It would not, however, have reached print without the contributions of many along the way: my family and friends, who have kept me healthy in body and soul, and ensured that I enjoy a life beyond the books; my students at the University of Auckland, whose passion for the subject matter always rekindled my own; colleagues, office staff, and Roberta Wilson, for their continued support. As always, I owe special gratitude to Mercedes Maroto Camino, who never once faltered in her meticulous critique of the many drafts. The dedicated focus that the final writing stages required was made possible through Glenn.

I also thank the University of Auckland for the sabbatical leaves that have periodically fed the manuscript, enabling me to conduct vital archival research in Spain. The personnel at the National Library in Madrid warrant special mention for their invaluable assistance during these periods. Essential contributions have also been made by Macrino Fernández Riera and José Bolado, whose scholarship on Rosario de Acuña has been indispensable for my work.

Great appreciation is due Professor Greg Clingham of Bucknell University Press. I also wish to acknowledge the anonymous first reader of the manuscript, whose evaluation was exceptional for its rigor and constructive commentary. As before, it has been a real privilege to work with the production team of Associated University Presses.

Material from Part 1 appeared in "Writing Nineteenth-Century Spain: Rosario de Acuña and the Liberal Nation," *Modern Language Notes* 120, Hispanic Issue (March 2005): 294–313. Other selected sections from Part 1 were previously published in "Configuring the Nation in Fin-de-Siècle Spain: Rosario de Acuña's *La voz de la Patria*," *Hispanic Review* 74, 3 (Summer 2006): 301–18, and have been reprinted by permission of the University of Pennsylvania Press. Material from Part 2 first appeared in "Rhetorics of Maternity and War in Angela Figuera's Poetic Work," *Revista Canadiense de Estudios Hispánicos* 21, 3 (Spring 1997): 457–78. Sections from Part 3 were published in "Painting History: Ekphrasis, Aesthetics and Ethics in Rosa Chacel's *Barrio de Maravillas* and *Acrópolis*," in *Revista de Estudios Hispánicos* 39, 3 (2005): 489–514. I am very grateful to all the journals for permission to reprint here.

I thank Editorial Postermil and the Fundació Lluís Carulla for their generosity in granting copyright permission to reproduce on the jacket cover the poster by C. G. Zunzurren (1935), published in *La Guerra Civil en 2000 carteles* by Jordi Carulla and Arnau Carulla (Barcelona: Postermil, 1997), vol. 1, 102, fig. 219.

Histories, Cultures, and National Identities

Introduction: Women Writing Spain?: The Politics of Historical, Cultural, and National Identities

PUBLISHING ON CULTURAL AND POLITICAL MATTERS HAS TRADITIONALLY been considered the province of men. Indeed in Western European patriarchal representations, the nation is conceived of in gendered terms as a feminine entity, domesticated, civilized, and molded according to the desires of its male creators. When women have participated in the construction of national and cultural paradigms, they have invariably been cast in masculine histories as minor players or exceptions to the rule. Woman has served as the nation's ideal and monument, but rarely as its protagonist.

The ensuing study proposes to address the literary production of three women writers whose works articulate their configurations of history, culture, and nation in modern Spain, from 1877 to 1984. These writers are Rosario de Acuña (1850–1923), Ángela Figuera (1902–84), and Rosa Chacel (1898–1994). The dates that constitute the temporal parameters of my discussion refer to the publication in 1877 of the first drama that I examine by Acuña, *Amor á la patria* [Love of the Nation], and to 1984, when Chacel publishes her novel, *Acrópolis* [Acropolis].[1] The period to be examined, therefore, is that of modernity, which, as Matei Calinescu notes, was predicated on a specific appreciation of time that, beginning in the mid-nineteenth century, was envisaged as a "*human time* and sense of history as experienced and valued culturally" (1987, 9).[2] Until the end of the Spanish Civil War in 1939, this period also saw the rise of the Spanish liberal nation amid more conservative nationalist visions, facets of which are conveyed in Acuña's work from the late nineteenth century. From 1939 until 1975, under the Franco regime, the history of liberalism was one of repression, dissidence, and contestation, as evident in Figuera's poetic work. As for Chacel's retrospective reconstructions of liberal Spanish cultural life during the first three decades of the twentieth century, they intersect with concerns and aspirations facing post-Franco Spanish society from 1975 onward, in its rapid transformation from dictatorship to democracy, and from a modern to postmodern nation.

Departing from the premise that history, culture and politics are, at all times, underpinned by gender,[3] I will seek answers to the following important questions: What difference does it make when a female writer ventures into the traditionally masculine domains of history writing, culture, and politics? What kinds of history and culture does she underline and from whose perspectives? In what terms does she consider the nation? How does her particular envisioning of a cultural and political community mesh with those paradigms offered by her male counterparts? Crucial to my analysis are the entangled concepts foregrounded in the title of this study: culture, history, nation, and identity.[4] All these notions stand in interdependent relationships with one another, as identities, far from being predetermined, are formed and reformed historically in constant negotiation with sociocultural and political factors. Vital for the constitution of identities is representation, as highlighted by Stuart Hall when he maintains that "identities are about questions of using the resources of history, language and culture in the process of becoming rather than being . . . Identities are therefore constituted within, not outside representation." Furthermore history is fundamental for the formation of identities, in that, Hall continues, these need to be understood "as produced in specific historical and institutional sites within specific discursive formations and practices, by specific enunciative strategies" (1996, 4). It is this embedding of sociocultural and political identities in specific historical circumstances that will be privileged when I address the literary works of Acuña, Figuera, and Chacel.

Moreover Hall argues, it is impossible to separate identities from differences: "[I]dentities are constructed through, not outside, difference. . . . The unity, the internal homogeneity, which the term identity treats as foundational is not a natural, but a constructed form of closure" (1996, 5). Fashioned on the culturally arbitrary boundaries established by discourses, differences attest to the policies of acceptance and rejection that shape sociocultural and political bodies and identities. It is therefore at the borders of difference that identities are constantly recreated. As Homi K. Bhabha asserts, difference "is not so much a reflection of *pre-given* ethnic or cultural traits set in the tablets of a 'fixed' tradition as it is a complex ongoing negotiation . . . *not so much the teleologies of tradition as much as its powers of iteration, its forms of displacement and relocation.*" The articulation of differences as imaginary in-between spaces enables, Bhabha affirms, the elaboration of "strategies of selfhood and communal representations that generate new signs of cultural difference and innovative sites of collaboration and contestation" (1994, 269–70). These premises are enacted in the histories written by Acuña, Figuera, and Chacel. Their representations reveal identities as made, not innate, and introduce differences into more established cultural and political discourses, thus creating the potential to initiate progressive change.

Throughout my study I will be primarily concerned with the ways in which works by Acuña, Figuera, and Chacel imagine and engender the Spanish nation, in a process that avows the inseparability of literary and sociopolitical representations. The concept of the invention or symbolic construction of a nation through discourse has been developed by many scholars, notable among whom are Benedict Anderson in *Imagined Communities* (1991) and Eric Hobsbawm, who emphasizes "the element of artefact, invention and social engineering which enters into the making of nations. . . . Nations do not make states and nationalisms but the other way round" (1997, 9–10).[5] Likewise similar concepts are foregrounded by E. Inman Fox in *La invención de España* (1998), which addresses the construction of the Spanish liberal nation and national identity from the mid-nineteenth century to 1939. Significantly among the writers and intellectuals whom Inman Fox examines not one woman is mentioned. Yet many of the male writers and intellectuals featured by Inman Fox, such as Francisco Giner de los Ríos, Modesto Lafuente, and José Ortega y Gasset, constitute the foils with and against whom writers like Acuña and Chacel fashion their visions of Spanish cultural and national identity. By way of contrast, my discussion will stress that women writers have also and always participated in the elaboration of concepts pertaining to nation, culture, and history, in critical dialogue with other sociocultural and political discourses.

The forms of identity debated by Acuña, Figuera, and Chacel in their works are those considered to emerge in the period of modernity itself: nationality, sexuality, class, and "race" (Martín Alcoff 2003, 5).[6] The political lens through which the writers view these issues is liberalism, with all three embracing variants of Republican thought. Republican ideals are important for women's histories because they stress the agency of individuals in constructing political and cultural identities.[7] Hence, as Ross Poole remarks on differentiating between republicanism and nationalism: "For the republican, the relationship is ideally one of *agency*: citizens *form* the State through their political activity. For the nationalist, the relationship is one of *mimesis*: citizens *recognise* themselves in the State" (2003, 276). It is this relationship of agency that is underscored in the works that I examine by Acuña, Figuera, and Chacel, who eschew repetition of the already given. For them, created histories become sources for reflection, speculation and the elaboration of more dynamic sociopolitical narratives, in which women almost invariably occupy significant positions.

Undoubtedly it is the foregrounding by classical liberalism of the theoretically natural equality of all human beings due to their capacity for reason, of equal rights for all, and of the ideal of liberty or autonomy, that renders liberal thought extremely attractive to women who live and create within masculine histories and cultures. At the same time, however, liberal philosophy, in its stress on the inherent equality of all human beings, tends to elide engendered differences, for reasons which Linda Martín Alcoff explains as follows: "Modern liberalism harbored a serious paradox . . . and one that has not yet been resolved in either its political institutions or its political thought. Political and moral rights are based on what all persons necessarily share in common; differences are considered merely contingent and therefore either politically irrelevant or actual obstructions" (2003, 6). Nevertheless equal political and civil rights were contingent on the ownership of property, which few Western European women held independently (Voet 1998, 31–32). This situation was exacerbated by the rise of capitalism, which removed economic production from the household, bringing about the demarcation between public and domestic spheres. The public realm was considered proper to men and the language of reason, while the domestic realm was assigned to women and the language of sentiment (Phillips 1998, 4). It is with these gendered dichotomies, disadvantageous to women and their ability to participate in cultural and political life, that Acuña, Figuera, and Chacel will each engage in ways specific to the differences inherent in their respective contexts.

In a study that spans just over a century of Spanish cultural politics, the selection of these three writers warrants justification. My choice of Acuña, Figuera, and Chacel is motivated by the following considerations. First, although they are already excentric figures in terms of their positioning as women writers in patriarchal societies, they also create bodies of work that critique liberal thought and that demonstrate an acute awareness of gender politics. Any number of female authors might well have illustrated currents of cultural politics applicable to each period, such as Emilia Pardo Bazán in Acuña's context, Mercedes Salisachs in Figuera's, and María Zambrano in Chacel's. However, as I hope to render evident in the course of my discussion, it is the differences underscored in the production of Acuña, Figuera, and Chacel that interrogate the cultural politics informing national identities in their respective contexts, to thus provide fascinating insights into the nuances of those politics and the writers' negotiation of engendered sociopolitical limits.

Secondly, the literary genres for which Acuña, Figuera, and Chacel are best-known are arguably those most associated with the ethos of their respective eras. During the last three decades of the nineteenth century, the context in which Acuña was producing her dramas, theater was among the most popular forms of public entertainment (Jover and Gómez-Ferrer 2001a, 628). More important still for Acuña's liberal orientation, literature, and especially theater, was viewed by liberals as the ideal medium for mentoring and illuminating the Spanish people with respect to its past, present, and future.[8]

Regarding Figuera's contestatory remembering of the liberal politics associated with the Spanish Second Republic (1931–39) and the Republican struggle during the Civil War (1936–39), her poetic corpus can be considered to continue the spirit of the *Romancero* or collection of ballads composed by soldiers during that Civil War, according to which poetry was conceived of as a weapon in the struggle against fascism. Indeed it was during the Civil War, when "literature went to war, and poetry more than any other form of expression" (Salaün 1985, 10), that verse became the preferred vehicle for registering accounts by the Republican left of that national tragedy. Consequently, in the ongoing climate of war that prevailed during the repression of liberalism under the Franco dictatorship, poetry constitutes a most appropriate genre for Figuera's denunciation of the regime and her reclaiming of officially banished histories.

As for Chacel, the trilogy that she published between 1976 and 1988 captures the aesthetic legacy of Spanish philosopher Ortega y Gasset with regard to creating a "new novel" on a par with the best of European literature. As I expand on below, the first two of Chacel's three novels revive the stellar decades of twentieth-century Spanish modernisms, as represented by the so-called Generations of 1898, 1914, and 1927. Narratives of memory, they also intersect with efforts by official bodies in the post-Franco period to recover an erased or marginalized liberal cultural heritage, so as to lend historical weight to Spain's reemerging democracy and full integration into Europe.

Thirdly, like the histories that they seek to recover and revindicate, the status of Acuña, Figuera, and Chacel within Spanish literary history has been, until recently, one of relative marginalization, if not oblivion. With regard to Acuña, due to her radical political orientation, embracing of freemasonry, and unconventional lifestyle, she became an increasingly notorious and repudiated figure within conservative literary and social circles from the mid-1880s onward. Although, as a defender of ideals associated with the Spanish First Republic (1873–74), Acuña and her work received limited acknowledgment during the Second Republic,[9] she was subsequently forgotten during the Franco dictatorship, for which feminism, freethinking, and freemasonry were anathema. However, since the consolidation of democracy in the 1980s, subsequent to Franco's death in 1975, Acuña's memory has been progressively honored, especially from the 1990s onward.[10] The author of an impressive body of work, in the form of both drama and essays, she has yet to receive appropriate recognition in the annals of literary history, with few studies existing on her works. Despite being hailed as "the pioneer of women's literature within Spanish freethinking" (Simón Palmer 1989, 7), Acuña has received most attention from historians interested in the association of nineteenth-century Spanish liberalism with freethinking and freemasonry.[11] Yet closer examination of her production reveals a writer deeply immersed in contemporary currents of liberal thought, which she opens up to penetrating critique.

Of the three writers, Figuera's work is possibly the least known.[12] Initially well-received by the literary establishment of the Franco dictatorship, due to her apparent embracing of Francoist norms of femininity, Figuera's poetic production became increasingly denunciatory of the regime from the late 1950s onward, at a point when Spain began to free up its economy and the general Spanish population was endeavoring to put behind it the Civil War and its aftermath. Figuera's work, therefore, is engaged in a process of determined remembrance when many were wishing simply to forget.

In contrast, Chacel is undoubtedly the best-known writer, with her cultural "recovery" from within Spain by writers, intellectuals, and scholars beginning in the mid-1960s and growing in momentum after 1975, with the demise of the Franco dictatorship.[13] Her acceptance into a literary canon, however, has been, at best, partial.[14] Conspiring against Chacel's full incorporation are a multitude of factors, such as the androcentric environment of early twentieth-century modernism, her decades of exile in South America after the Civil War, prejudices on the part of literary critics, and the challenging complexity of her avant-garde literary production, which does not lend itself to being on best-seller lists.

Fourthly, and carrying the greatest weight in determining my selection of writers, the emphasis in works by Acuña, Figuera, and Chacel on liberal histories associated with Republican ideals contributes to throwing light on the history of Spanish democracy and the ways in which this history has shaped competing concepts of national and cultural identity for well over a century. According to Juan Pablo Fusi, the first Spanish revolution in the name of democracy was the anti-Borbonic revolution initiated by radical liberals in 1868. Known as the *Gloriosa* or Glorious Revolution, it produced the shortlived First Republic, the ideals of which underlie the sociopolitical aspirations expressed in Acuña's work. Spain's second experiment in democracy was that period known as the Second Republic, terminated by the victory of the Nationalists in the Spanish Civil War in 1939 and the ensuing Franco regime. It is from within the confines of this dictatorship that Figuera's poetry reclaims dissident histories identified with the vanquished Second Republic. The third, and finally successful, period of democracy in Spain began after Franco's death in 1975 and continues to this present day (Fusi 2001c, 801–2). From this later context Chacel's works remember and revindicate the cultural liberalism to which not only the Second Republic was indebted but also the consolidation of democracy in post-Franco Spain. Although these diverse contexts and biographical information pertaining to the authors will be addressed more specifically within the respective Part on each writer and her works, I now turn to outline the principal features of these contexts and to position accordingly my reading of the literary production of Acuña, Figuera, and Chacel.

It was the nineteenth century, a dramatic and tumultuous period in Spanish history, that witnessed the birth of modern Spain in the sense of a national consciousness (Álvarez Junco 2004, 144; Tusell, 1999, 99). Emerging from the so-called War of Independence against the French (1808–14), this embryonic consciousness of a nation based on collective sovereignty gathered strength with the growing importance of liberalism as a sociopolitical force, made manifest in the 1812 Cádiz Constitution. Hence, as Tusell declares: "The nation in the nineteenth century was born linked to the exercise of national sovereignty and accompanied by the liberal revolution, to the extent that one cannot be understood without the other. . . . Moreover, the Nation was conceived of, in accordance with these liberal underpinnings, as a contractual reality, derived from the exercise of collective sovereignty, the sum total of individual desires" (1999, 88). The bitter conflict between an old order of divinely ordained power and a new order conceptualized according to the ideal of popular sovereignty is evident in the repression of liberalism under the restored monarchy of Fernando VII (1814–33). It was not until Fernando's death in 1833, which brought to a close what was known as the Ominous Decade of despotic rule and heralded the return to Spain of exiled liberals, that liberal thought, in league with Romanticism, began to make greater impact on the direction of Spanish political life. Even then, its evolution was chequered, punctuated by the Carlist wars (1833–39, 1846–49), ideological divisions within liberal ranks and numerous military uprisings to "protect" the nation's freedom.

The model of liberalism predominant throughout most of the nineteenth century was that upheld by the Moderates. Moderate liberalism considered the unity of the Spanish nation as inseparable from Catholicism, as inscribed in the 1812 Constitution, and was characterized by a patriotic rhetoric that nostalgically looked back to the past in search of liberal roots (Tusell 1999, 101). In contrast with this more conservative Moderate paradigm, which sought a limited bourgeois revolution in the interests of an elite, the other broad strand of liberalism was the Progressive ideal, founded on industry and commerce, the advancement of the working classes and a secular society (Inman Fox 1998, 38).[15] This liberal model came to the fore briefly in the period 1854–56, to reach its greatest moment of political clout with the Glorious Revolution and the First Republic, only to be ousted with the restoration of the monarchy in 1875. It is in keeping with the ideals of Progressive liberalism that Acuña's dramatic corpus and essays participate in fashioning a specific construct of the nation in late nineteenth-century Spain that contrasts with that upheld by the restored monarchy. Consequently Acuña's representations invariably hinge on the alliance of an illustrated lower- or upper-middle class with the lower classes, and emphasize forms of interclass solidarity born from freedom of association, scientific education and religious and political tolerance. Also shaping Acuña's sociopolitical stance are the liberal ideals associated with the philosophy of Karl Krause (1781–1832) and the *Institución Libre de Enseñanza* (Free Institute of Education).[16]

Nevertheless within Moderate and Progressive liberalisms there existed a welter of political variants, such as Radicals, Democrats, Unionists, Federal Republicans, and Republicans. As I will develop, Acuña's position can best be aligned with federal republicanism: the great hope, never realized, of the First Republic. Federal republicanism constitutes an attempt to reconcile the liberal goals of national unity and sovereignty by the people with regional independence, and to replace state centralization with alliances between the government and regions.[17] The tensions inherent in this political orientation come to the fore in Acuña's early work, while the recognition by federalism of diversity within unity renders it significant for the paradigms of gender, "race," and class with which Acuña's work grapples.

In Part 1 I unravel questions regarding how Acuña's vision of late nineteenth-century Spain serves to perpetuate but also to question myths of national identity. To a certain degree, Acuña works within mainstream liberalism, which perceived historiography and literature as vital for forging an ideal national unity as yet unrealized in the Spanish context. Liberal histories of the time, therefore, looked back to the past so as to rewrite selectively historical events in accordance with contemporary goals.[18] Such a history, as Bernard Lewis has noted, was prevalent in the Romantic period and the genre of the historical novel. Seeking to embellish and "correct" the past, historical fiction often resorted to foundation myths to validate political and cultural claims (1975, 56–59).

For nineteenth-century Spanish liberalism, the dominant foundation myth on which it substantiated its formulations of the nation was the so-called War of Independence. In this conflict, the Spanish people was retrospectively cast as affirming its sovereign will by expelling the French invaders from national soil. It is this legend that Acuña takes up in 1877 in the first work that I address, *Amor á la patria.* Drawing on the concept of nation as family, Acuña's drama presents conflicting notions of patriotism and nation to stress the tensions informing a desired national unity, far from becoming a reality.[19] Portrayed as revealing a greater sense of patriotism than their male counterparts, Acuña's female characters argue for women's superior self-awareness and ethical stance in their participation in politics.

A second foundation myth for nineteenth-century liberalism used by Acuña was the early sixteenth-century uprising of the *Comuneros,* the leaders of Castilian communities who rebelled against Charles V. This history constitutes the subtext for Acuña's focus in *Tribunales de venganza* [Tribunals of Vengeance] (1880) on a practically contemporaneous revolt that emphasizes to a greater degree issues of class and "race": the uprising of the Valencian *Germanía* or brotherhood of guilds. As a result, Acuña's play advocates the recognition of racial and religious others, national sovereignty based on a collective social contract inclusive of the lower classes, and the Progressive liberal ideals of the nation as republic and federation.

It is with the fin-de-siècle myth of Spain's backwardness that Acuña interacts in *El Padre Juan* [Father John] (1891). Such an invention was common to both traditionalists and liberals, who represented Spain as a comparatively primitive agricultural society, isolated from northern European advancements and inadequate as an imperial power (Ringrose 1996, 15–24). While Acuña's *El Padre Juan* partially conforms to this historical paradigm, it also attributes Spain's ills to rampant consumerism, negligence in using scientific knowledge, and an educational system straitjacketed by religious dogmas. In particular, it is Acuña's critique of the religious question that differentiates her position from other strands of liberalism. That difference is also manifest when she assigns part of the cause for the nation's sociocultural penury to prejudices among the very proponents of liberalism, unable to divest themselves of conservative attitudes toward class and gender.

The context within which Acuña lived and wrote bears comparison with the first of three phases identified by Czech historian Miroslav Hroch as important in the process of nation formation. Scholars have explained this phase as characterized by the presence of an active body of intellectuals dedicated to the discovery of the history, culture, and language of the nation, but with scarce repercussions on national life as a whole. The context of the Second Republic crucial to the poetry of Ángela Figuera could be considered to parallel the third of Hroch's phases: one that sees a well-articulated political project that succeeds in attracting the support of important sectors in society, to become a mass political movement. In between these two contexts, and remembered by Chacel's post-Franco novels, there exists a second phase, which in Spain would encompass the so-called Generations of 1898 and 1914, in which patriotically minded intellectuals, from the middle and lower-middle classes in particular, critique the state of the nation and endeavor to foster a sense of national consciousness and civic community (Guibernau 1999, 96–97; Tusell 1999, 124).

Acuña's context witnessed the hopes and dreams of a partially successful liberalism, with all the fissures that accompany the desire for national unity and the need to recognize diversity and plurality. Figuera's context saw the demise of the liberal project in the post-World War I years (Romero Salvadó 1996), its contested resurrection in the form of the Second Republic and the defeat of that Republic by the Nationalists, representative of an old, traditional Spain and its sociopolitical structures. If, during the Civil War, Republican Spain has been described as a nation in "virtual disintegration," Nationalist Spain constituted "a coherent state in formation" (Richards 1996, 206–7). The latter's systematic, ruthless deployment of violence was dedicated to its alleged reconquest of liberal Spain, which was aided, in turn, by policies of economic and cultural autarky during the first two decades after the Civil War. In contrast with the Republican ideal of human agency in constructing the nation, Francoist Spain relied on an essentialist, mimetic vision of national identity and history.

Figuera's poetic work engages directly with the political extremes that can result from nationalist movements, exemplified by the National Catholicism of the Franco regime (1939–75). A dictatorship pushes to its furthest consequences the concept of a nation-state, whereby the state "has the monopoly of what it claims to be the legitimate use of force within a demarcated territory and seeks to unite the people subject to its rule by means of cultural homogenization" (Guibernau 1999, 14).[20] Such a quest for homogeneity, however, belies the presence within a given territory of social, cultural, ethnic, and political groups whose differences challenge the state and that therefore must be violently expelled or suppressed for the nation-state to achieve its aims. On the victory of the right-wing Nationalists in the Civil War, those defending Republican ideologies and movements arguably became part of what Guibernau defines as a "nation without a state," in that the defeated did not identify with the state into which their physical, and I add, conceptual, territory was forcibly assimilated. In such a situation, Guibernau asserts, the state is regarded as foreign and those stateless persons contained within it "maintain a separate sense of national identity . . . and the explicit wish to rule themselves," in accordance with principles of democracy and popular sovereignty, fed by memories of a self-governing past (1999, 16, 24–26).

In Part 2 it is the notion of history as fissure and trauma within the context of the Civil War and ensuing Franco dictatorship that is paramount in my study of Figuera's work. Inserting her corpus firmly into its sociohistorical context, I read her poetry against the official discourses, imagery, and symbolism dominant during the Franco regime. The history performed by the dictatorship has been described as a practice of therapy and amnesia, designed to "correct" historical narratives perceived as detrimental to a militaristic, totalitarian concept of the nation (Boyd 1997, 232–301). Working against such a history of amnesia, Figuera's poetry challenges the Francoist erasure of liberal histories by recasting the dictatorship's paradigms of time, based on the liturgical calendar. Especially important in Figuera's recovery of dissident histories are dates. Whereas the regime deploys dates for purposes of legitimation and triumphalist commemoration, in Figuera's compositions these same markers of time function to infuse the present with its denied historical conflicts. As well as these temporal sites of memory, Figuera's poetry foregrounds material sites that record the repression effected by a totalitarian power within national space. Her critique of the Franco dictatorship relies on a constant revisiting of the Civil War, in order to underscore the continuation of that conflict on a psychological level in her contemporary present.

Figuera's contestation of the regime is at its fiercest from the late 1950s to the early 1960s, making her part of what Fusi calls the "counterculture of critique" that emerges at that same moment (2004, 112). In particular, Figuera's attack on the dictatorship from within Spain is based on undermining the very foundations of Francoist rhetoric. The regime's principles of triumphalism, autarky, and totalitarian exclusivity are subverted by Figuera's rewriting of the symbolic cornerstones of Franco's National Catholicism, the figures of the Virgin and Christ. A blend of Falangist and Catholic doctrines, National Catholicism founded the political and religious integrity of the Spanish nation on the paradoxical ideal of the mother as virgin, with the Francoist state dedicated to an intensive process of Marianization. The image of Christ resurrected was similarly cast as synonymous with the Nationalist Crusade and its "Liberation" of Spain from Republican values, to which the alleged disintegration of the Spanish nation was imputed.

Of fundamental importance in Figuera's undermining of a monumental history that seeks to impose closure on Spain's liberal past is her recourse to the symbol of the wound, allusive to Spain's internal trauma and divisions. On the very border between inside and outside, the self and the other, the wound allows Figuera to develop symbols and images of hybridity, which create spaces of mediation disallowed by the Manichean politics of the dictatorship. This mediating principle comes to be embodied in the fusion that Figuera progressively effects of Christ and Mary, both of whom bear Spain's burden of history, in a dual process of atonement and national rebirth. Such hybrid images and symbols bring together in imaginary dialogue opposing histories and sociopolitical positions, and, by so doing, open up prospective paths for a divided Spain's future reconciliation and peace.

The Franco regime, as Fusi has affirmed, put paid to the extraordinarily rich cultural worlds that Spain enjoyed in the first three decades of the twentieth century (2004, 107). It is from the post-Franco years of 1976 to 1988 that Chacel remembers and reconstructs those milieux, when she publishes, subsequent to the death of Franco and the end of the dictatorship in 1975, her trilogy of *Barrio de Maravillas* [The Maravillas District] (1976), *Acrópolis* (1984), and *Ciencias naturales* [Natural Sciences] (1988). This period constituted a context in which burning concerns for Spain were reestablishing and consolidating a democracy, privileging open debate, recognizing diversity, and forging a European culture and economy. In this process governmental cultural entities sought to recover and celebrate the memory of those writers, artists, and intellectuals associated with the ill-fated liberalism of the Second Republic through public homages, exhibitions, and catalogues.[21] Silvina Schammah Gesser has described such policies as part of a "recuperation industry," which aimed "to reconcile the 'two Spains' at home and to re-invent the image of Spain as a modern and civilized nation abroad."[22] In effect, just as the Second Republic considered culture to be the pivotal force that would create its new Spain from 1931 onward (Fusi 2001b, 681), so, too, did culture arguably perform a similar role in the early post-Franco years.

At the same time, the success of the so-called Transition to democracy was ensured through an official pact of amnesia, which precluded raking over the embers of the Civil War and reigniting divisions still smouldering from the dictatorship.[23] The flight from representing contentious political histories that such a pact encouraged throughout the seventies and eighties was also reinforced by postmodernism, which, José Antonio Gabriel y Galán denounces, tends to manufacture a *light* history and which results, according to Juan Carlos Onetti in 1989, in "a conscious abandoning of memory and truth as ethical suppositions underpinning all creative acts" (quoted by Rodríguez Puértolas 1995, 273).[24]

Privileging the recovery of early twentieth-century modernist cultural histories and particularly those relating to her own avant-garde Generation of 1927, Chacel's trilogy largely avoids the more politicized issues that the official post-Franco pact of amnesia was anxious to avoid. Nevertheless her narratives constitute what David Herzberger has identified as novels of memory, which foreground establishing a dialogue between present and past (1995, 85). Paramount in novels of memory, which Herzberger defines as "those fictions in which past time is evoked through subjective remembering," is their engagement with and exploration of a neglected or misrepresented history. Thus, Herzberger explains, "[t]he past that is explored . . . is the past largely eschewed or appropriated by historiography under Franco, the lived past of the Civil War and the strains of dissent that anticipate the conflict and persist in its aftermath. . . . [H]istory does not stand outside of individual consciousness as a form imposed, but rather impinges upon the consciousness of characters and forces its way into their considerations" (1995, 66, 68).

Memory, however, is selective and often inaccurate, and its narratives, at best, can only bring back a fragmented experience. Consequently sociologist Maurice Halbwachs insists, remembering the past is pure representation, "a reconstructed picture, . . . a description created long afterward by a writer. . . . We compose it anew and introduce elements borrowed from several periods which preceded or followed the scene in question" (1992, 60–61). With regard to Chacel's trilogy, it is important to realize that its production was a gradual process that took place over decades and hence is, effectively, a representation of the past from diverse contemporary perspectives. Chacel conceived of parts of the trilogy in Rome in the 1920s, and from 1955 onward repeatedly refers to drafting sections in her diaries.[25] Yet she did not write these novels in any consolidated fashion until she returned to Madrid in 1974, as if remembering were contingent on her once again inhabiting the settings that constitute their places of memory.[26]

Part 3 centers on Chacel's first two novels in her trilogy, *Barrio de Maravillas* and *Acrópolis*, which privilege, like Acuña's works, the role of education and culture in the formation of a liberal Spain. Consequently the attempt to render a high culture responsive to Spain's pressing social needs, form public opinion, and foster innovative change are themes of primary importance in Chacel's *Barrio* and *Acrópolis.* These texts reveal the tensions of a democracy in the making in which all must theoretically participate, but in which many lack the means to do so. Therefore, although, of the three writers, Chacel's sociopolitical philosophy is often the least explicit in her creative work, I will argue that close examination of her narratives, in conjunction with her extensive body of essays, reveals a sharp awareness of class and gender inequalities.

Drawing on the theories of French cultural historian Pierre Nora, I posit that Chacel's representations of the overlapping literary generations of 1898, 1914, and 1927, corresponding to variants of early, high, and late Spanish modernism, function as sites of memory for modalities of generational consciousness committed to a liberal transformation of the nation. As in Acuña's works, Chacel's texts take issue with the engendered separation between domestic and public spheres, represented by the key modernist spaces of home and city. As a consequence, her narratives will argue for the incorporation of cultural practice into the home and for reformulating the city as embodied spaces in which all its citizens are granted full recognition and sociopolitical rights. In this process special emphasis is accorded to transforming a dynamics of distanced seeing, premised on the preservation of class and gender privileges, into one of approximation to and understanding of feminized others. With regard to Chacel's *Barrio* and *Acrópolis,* I will also maintain that her avant-garde aesthetics are invariably linked to sociopolitical concerns. These narratives premise culture not only as a valuable heritage that invites the nation to critique and learn from its historical pasts, but also as a sociopolitical forum for working through dilemmas current in the present.

The relevance for the twenty-first century of the visions of history, culture and national identity elaborated by Acuña, Figuera, and Chacel is taken up in the conclusion. There I discuss the extent to which their liberal narratives have been materialized in present-day Spain, now a democracy, "federation," and European nation. In this context, the dialogue that the writers open up between past and present and their interrogation of cultural and national identities are pertinent for the issues of historical memory, "race," and nation with which Spain wrestles today. Through my study, I hope to contribute to existing cultural histories of Spain by showing how works by women writers can offer different perspectives on accepted paradigms of Spain's cultural and national identities. In so doing, they complicate and enrich these frameworks, rewriting their figurative borders.

Part 1
Representing the Nation in Nineteenth-Century Spain: Rosario de Acuña and the Liberal Debate

¡*Justicia* y *libertad* los pueblos gritan,
. . . .
y al paso de los siglos se adelantan,
coronándose reyes en la historia
con el lauro inmortal de la victoria[!]
—Acuña 1880, 54

[*Justice and freedom* the peoples shout,
. . . .
and as the centuries pass, they take the lead,
crowning themselves kings in history
with the immortal wreath of victory!]

Introduction

Throughout the nineteenth century, history writers in Spain selectively recovered and refashioned narratives of the past to nurture a fledgling national unity, pursue contemporary goals, and forge ideals for the future. The process of constructing a liberal national identity was inseparable from the creation of a national history, culture, and literature. Although women writers and intellectuals were engaged in this enterprise, it is principally their male counterparts who have been acknowledged for their contributions.

Symptomatic of such exclusion is Rosario de Acuña, playwright, poet, essayist, freethinker, and prominent freemason. Although

Acuña was almost an exact contemporary of the canonically inscribed Emilia Pardo Bazán, her considerable literary corpus has not yet received the recognition it deserves, on account of the controversy provoked by both the writer and her works. In contrast with Pardo Bazán's Catholicism, Acuña was fiercely anticlerical. Writing historical theater, a genre considered off-limits to women due to its engagement with the public sphere,[1] Acuña there addressed contentious sociopolitical issues. She also maintained a strong presence in the liberal press, contributing regularly to the freethinking weekly, *Las Dominicales del Libre Pensamiento,* between 1884 and 1891.[2] Acuña defended working-class interests and, once resident in Gijón from 1909 onward, was instrumental in the founding of the nondenominational school, the Escuela Neutra Graduada, in 1911. An active advocate of women's rights and education, her outspokenness on these issues led to her going into exile in Portugal from 1911 to 1913, due to the political scandal that erupted from the publication of a letter of hers to Luis Bonafoux in *El Internacional* in Paris and *El Progreso* in Barcelona.[3] Granted political amnesty in 1913 due to the efforts of influential Asturian liberals, Acuña spent her remaining years in Gijón, accompanied by her companion, Carlos de Lamo Jiménez. Continuing to be heavily involved in workers' associations, she died of a stroke in 1923.[4]

Acuña's combative political profile was, without doubt, unusual for an upper-middle-class woman writing in late nineteenth-century Spain. In a context that discouraged women from participating in the literary sphere, the sanctioned model of femininity was that of the silent, compliant "Angel in the House," a paradigm that Acuña's works contend.[5] Women who did write were encouraged to dedicate themselves to literature that reflected the private self, specifically poetry. This was the path initially followed by Acuña herself, who began, with considerable success, as a poet and writer of minor essays on noncontentious subjects.[6] Nevertheless by adhering to sociocultural mores as to the genres that they should cultivate and the content of their work, women writers ran the risk of being called mere *literatas,* their work discredited and marginalized. A woman whose writing was considered as good as a man's was described as *varonil* [manly or virile].[7] Both these epithets were used with regard to Acuña's work (Simón Palmer 1989, 8, 26). That Acuña herself was aware of the social censure attached to women who dared to write on subjects prohibited to their sex is evident in her frequent proclamations of self-modesty, in which can be glimpsed both doubt as to her literary worth and also her subtle satirizing of paradigms denigratory to women.[8]

My discussion of Acuña's work opens with an analysis of the second and third of her five plays, *Amor á la patria* (1877) and *Tribunales de venganza* (1880). Unlike the better-known *Rienzi el Tribuno* [Tribune Rienzi] (1876) and *El Padre Juan* (1891), these dramas have not been republished. Neo-Romantic pieces, they deal with two of the founding myths of Spanish liberal nationalism: the War of Independence fought against the French, and the uprising of the Valencian Germanía in 1519 and 1522. Acuña's *Amor á la patria* probes contrasting paradigms of patriotism, with particular weight given to those models upheld by female characters. Specifically these women embody principles of independence that bring together Acuña's feminist beliefs, republican ideals, and the Progressive liberal dream of the nation as a federation of autonomous states.

The goals of republicanism and federalism are given greater prominence in Acuña's *Tribunales de venganza*, which debates the contested transformation from nation as dynasty to nation as brotherhood, in the sense of an alliance among equal citizens established through civil fraternity.[9] Fundamental for such a transformation is the concept of the nation as an imagined community, formed voluntarily through commonly held ideals and systems of sociopolitical and cultural association. Foregrounded in this process is Acuña's negotiation of issues pertaining to estate, class, and "race," through reformulations that mark the transition from older, closed sociopolitical systems, considered unviable, to more open, modern models premised on the liberal social contract.

The importance attributed to religion in conservative and liberal models for Spain is at the crux of Acuña's *El Padre Juan*. Of particular significance for her envisioned transformation of the nation are the cultural politics associated with Krausist thought and the Institución Libre de Enseñanza, premised on a gradual evolution of the people through a secularized, scientific education.[10] Here Acuña's analysis of obsolete and viable forms of national governance serves not only to vindicate liberal thought but also to critique it, exposing the gendered premises that underpin liberalism itself.

Defining the Liberal "Family": Kinship and National Unity in *Amor á la patria*

Contemporary Spanish nationalism, José Álvarez Junco has argued, is born with the popular uprising against the Napoleonic forces in 1808. This date marks the beginning of what came to be mythified as the War of Independence: the conflict during which the Spanish people successfully rebelled against the imperial, foreign invader. Whether the war was later represented as the people's affirmation of national sovereignty, according to the liberals, or as proof of the people's loyalty to inherited tradition, as stated by the conservatives, such renditions constituted inventions that belied the war's complexity.[11]

This conflict was both an international one fought by France, England, and Portugal, and also a civil war in which those foreign powers were supported by different sectors of the Spanish population. With allegiances divided among the elite groups, most of the general Spanish population aligned itself with England and Portugal: a position, however, more marked by xenophobia against the French than by any clear sense of national unity. Conversely support for the French by Enlightenment reformers can be construed as patriotic, in that they perceived the administrative and cultural models of France as crucial to strengthening the Spanish monarchy and remedying Spain's declining international prestige (Álvarez Junco 2004, 120–22).

Acuña's *Amor á la patria*, a one-act tragedy in verse, is set in Zaragoza on July 2, 1808.[12] Depicting the attempt by the town's inhabitants to defend it against the French, the play aligns itself with a liberal sociopolitical perspective, in which, as Inman Fox notes, "the people becomes an active political subject" (1998, 36).[13] The people are primarily represented through the characters of Inés and her daughter, María, who, reminiscent of the French symbol for Republican revolution, Marianne on the barricades, are preparing to blow up their home to prevent the advance of the French. In the midst of this activity Inés's son, Pedro, reappears. Now a captain in the French army besieging Zaragoza, he had abandoned the family home nine years earlier to seek opportunities not present in Spain. Engaging in an argument with Pedro as to what constitutes patriotism, Inés entreats her son to leave the French army and defend the Spanish cause. On surprising Pedro in French uniform with her mother and not recognizing him as her brother, María fires on him and kills him. The play ends inconclusively with the women continuing to prepare for the imminent arrival of the French.

In Acuña's play, Zaragoza marks a space that is both regional and national. The competing definitions of patriotism associated with this place allow Acuña to open up a debate regarding Spanish national identity. At the time, the War of Independence was fed by a patriotism that was local rather than national. The reality was not that of a nation united—the goal of liberals of all persuasions—but of a state formed of competing *patrias* or regions, each with its own interests. The recasting of the war as a national conflict only emerged retrospectively with the liberal establishment in 1812 of the *Cortes* or Parliament of Cádiz and its Constitution, intent on legitimating a new nation built on collective sovereignty and consensus rather than on royal privilege (Álvarez Junco 2004, 129–30).

Regional patriotism is suggested in Acuña's play by María's exclamation to Inés: "¡como si sangre tuya no tuviera / y no fuese Aragon la patria mia!" [as if I were not of your blood / and Aragon not my motherland!] (Acuña 1877, 9),[14] as well as by repeated references to the legendary heroine of the defense of Zaragoza, Agustina of Aragón. Indeed Inés sees María as another Agustina:

> ¡No en valde á la Agustina Zaragoza
> has visto combatir; la patria mía
> no ha de rendirse nunca al extranjero
> mientras albergue tantas Agustinas!
> (12)

> [You have not seen Zaragoza fight / like Agustina in vain; my motherland / will never have to surrender to foreigners / while it shelters so many Agustinas!]

Yet on other occasions, the "patria" represented by Zaragoza and Aragón becomes identified with Spain, as in Inés's following admonition to Pedro:

> . . . ¿y sin fuerzas desde entónces
> para vender como traidor tu pátria,
> . . . .
> no juraste verter tu sangre toda
> por defender la libertad de España?
> (21)[15]

[and without strength since then / to sell off, like a traitor, your *patria,* / . . . / did you not swear to shed all your blood / defending Spain's freedom?]

To a certain extent, this slippage between the local and national reflects the fact that, within the context of the War of Independence, Aragón and Spain were not opposed terms. Rather, as Álvarez Junco notes, "to revindicate all that was Aragonese was, in 1808–14, one of the ways of proclaiming oneself Spanish" (2004, 86). Within Acuña's context of 1877, Aragón arguably stands for a patriotism that is simultaneously distanced from and equated with Spain, and that suggests both the Progressive rejection of the Restoration monarchy and the advocation of Spain as a federation made up of autonomous regions, members of the national family.

Competing definitions of patriotism are further explored by Acuña in the diverging perspectives of Napoleon offered by different characters. For Inés, he is not the epitome of liberal revolution and freedom from antiquated sociopolitical structures, but the patriarchal, feudal "verdugo de la tierra" [executioner of the land] (Acuña 1877, 13), who desires to enslave Spain as a satellite of imperial France: "¡[L]a Francia quiere que tu patria / en repugnante feudo esclava viva!" [France wants your *patria* / to live as the slave of a repugnant feudal system!] (10). Such a portrayal of Napoleon, however, is undercut through Pedro, for whom, as for Spanish Enlightenment reformers, Napoleon embodies the progressive spirit of the French Revolution, offering democracy to a Spain subject to a backward monarchy:

¡Napoleon, al fragor de sus cañones
y en los sangrientos campos de batalla,
enseña al pueblo á conquistar derechos
que un bárbaro egoismo le negaba!
(24)

[Napoleon, to the din of his cannon fire / and on the bloody battlefields, / teaches the people to win rights / denied them by a barbarous egoism!]

These shifting parameters of patriotism are underscored by an important dialogue between Pedro and Inés, which constitutes the dramatic kernel of the play. Pedro is uncertain as to what constitutes his *patria,* given that it still lacks a tangible presence: "¿Dónde la pátria está, que no la veo?" [Where is the *patria*, which I cannot see?] (29). In contrast, Inés retorts that *patria* is inseparable from the place where one is born, grows up and dies:

> ¡Está donde nacieron tus sonrisas,
> . . . .
> donde meces la cuna de tus hijos
> y guardas las cenizas de tus deudos[!]
> (29)

> [It is where your smiles were born, / . . . / where you rock your children's cradle / and keep your relatives' ashes!]

For Pedro, *patria* is a changeable concept, defining that place where ambitions can best be realized. Conversely, according to Inés, it is an immutable entity that lies at the very core of one's identity. Her vision thus resembles the original meaning of "nation," explained by Timothy Brennan as "both the modern nation-state and . . . something more ancient and nebulous—the '*natio*'—a local community, domicile, family, condition of belonging" (1990, 45).

The relationship between subject and nation, however, is not a natural given but a cultural construct, as Raymond Williams's following distinction elucidates: "'Nation' as a term is radically connected with 'native.' We are *born* into relationships which are typically settled in a place. This form of primary and 'placeable' bonding is of quite fundamental human and natural importance. Yet the jump from that to anything like the modern nation-state is entirely artificial" (1985, 180). It is the relationship between the given placing of national subjects, on the one hand, and their consciously willed sociopolitical construction of the nation, on the other, that Acuña's drama presents as vital for the elaboration of alternative national visions.

The cultural construction of the nation rests on tropes of kinship, on which Acuña draws to equate the nation with mother.[16] Such a formulation was characteristic of nineteenth-century Spanish liberalism, which identified the ideal nation of social equality with a motherland that all were obliged to defend.[17] Consequently, in Acuña's play, mother and *patria* are interrelated concepts, as intimated by María: "Madre y patria: guardando estos dos nombres / el alma siempre vivirá tranquila" [Mother and nation: honoring these two names / the soul will always live in peace] (Acuña 1877, 10).

This fusion of mother and *patria* is embodied in Inés, who, due to her motherhood, conforms to the traditional, allegedly natural destiny for women.

At the same time, Inés is also a widow and hence possesses an independence that would have been legally impossible should she still have been married. In this sense, Inés allows Acuña to avoid the problems that married women presented to liberal theory, which argued, on the one hand, for women's equality and, on the other, for their supposedly natural subjection to male authority (Brennan and Pateman 1998, 94–95). Inés's seemingly contradictory states make her the ideal symbol for the liberal Spanish nation, as both mother of all its people and also autonomous and self-governing. Although, as mother, Inés partially conforms to essentialist norms of femininity, these same attributes also stand as guarantors of the inviolability and continuity of the nation against imperial aggression and opportunistic betrayal, represented by Napoleon and Pedro respectively.

The opposition created between Acuña's female characters, on the one hand, and Pedro on the other, refracts national sentiment with gender. Here it is women, not men, who are repeatedly seen as embodying true patriotism. Not only are Inés and María prepared to destroy their home, strategically placed at the entrance to the town, rather than have it captured by the French and used as a fortification against their cause.[18] They are also willing to sacrifice their lives, and even souls, for the freedom of their *patria*, with Inés exclaiming:

> ¡¡Por la patria mia,
> . . . .
> . . . por conquistar su libertad bendita
> y mirarla temible y poderosa,
> la vida, es poco, el alma perdería!!
> (Acuña 1877, 8).

[For my motherland, / . . . / . . . to win her blessèd freedom / and see her powerful and inspiring awe, / life is but naught, I'd sacrifice my soul!!]

Indeed Inés's patriotism is taken to an extreme when she places love of country before love of her son, repudiating Pedro for his support of Napoleon: "¡tú no has nacido, no, de mis entrañas!" [no, you haven't come from my womb!] (26). Although Acuña partially presents Inés as an unnatural mother who rejects her own son, Inés's lack of sentimentality also emphasizes her reason and shows that women can make hard decisions in the interests of the nation, to which their primary allegiance is due.[19]

These manifestations of patriotism work on several levels. First, they concur with the more general purpose of sacrifice—to shape and confirm national sovereignty—as noted by Jean Bethke Elshtain: "Only a preparedness to forfeit one's own life rounds out, or instantiates in all its fullness, devotion to the political community" (1992, 146–47). Secondly, and more specifically, they also reveal how during the War of Independence, as Álvarez Junco explains, patriotism became identified with those who "fought against the French, which also meant sacrificing oneself for the collective body and fighting for freedom" (2004, 134).

While the patriotism of Acuña's female characters confirms certain tenets of liberalism, the writer's depiction of Inés and María critiques the liberal division of society into public and domestic spheres. In *Amor á la patria* it is the home that becomes the political arena within which decisions that will affect a larger community, beyond the domestic sphere, are debated and made. Furthermore Inés and María stand for an alternative model of femininity that moves away from essentialist concepts pertaining to Woman's weakness and dependence to embody what Ursula Vogel describes as the kind of Romantic "self-reliant femininity" proposed by Friedrich Schlegel. Such an ideal, Vogel elucidates, exalted "deviations from the accepted norms of female propriety. . . . in Sparta's women who took part in masculine exercises and were, as mothers, willing to sacrifice the most 'natural' feelings to the demands of patriotism, he [Schlegel] discovers a lost history of independent womanhood" (1986, 36). Schlegel's contestatory paradigm, like Acuña's, challenges essentialist notions of femininity in the interests of national good.[20] It is this model of autonomous femininity that Acuña will develop further in *El Padre Juan*, through her portrayal of the female coprotagonist, Isabel.

Consequently both Inés and María serve as models for patriotic emulation. Just as Inés constitutes, María affirms, her ideal—"aprendiendo de tí con entusiasmo / á ser noble y á ser buena patricia" [learning from you with enthusiasm / to be noble and a good patriot] (Acuña 1877, 10)—María in turn inspires courage in her beloved, Tomás, who declares:

[¡]Y yo con el recuerdo idolatrado
de mujer tan amante como fiera,
si ántes con entusiasmo peleaba,
como un leon me lanzaré en la guerra!
(17)

[And I, with the hallowed memory / of a woman as loving as she is fierce, / if before I fought with enthusiasm, / now like a lion I'll throw myself into battle!]

Acuña thus casts women not only as heroes in their own right but also as the physical and figurative mothers of heroes of both sexes, ensuring the transmission and continuity of national virtues identified with feminine principles: "¡ . . . de tan bravas hijas / héroes no más, es justo que nacieran! ... " [and to such brave daughters / it is only fitting that heroes are born!] (17).

Furthermore Acuña's representation of Inés underscores that the Progressive liberal concept of the nation was firmly equated with national sovereignty rather than with entrenched class privileges, even though this was an ideal still to be realized.[21] Inés's identification with the common people is patent in her having embraced their lot by choice. Originally of noble birth, Inés, María tells us, loses her reputation, class and family when she falls in love with and marries an artisan:

tú, la heróica mujer, buena entre todas,
de estirpe noble, poderosa y rica,
que por unir tu suerte á un artesano
perdiste nombre, posicion, familia;
tú, la madre del alma idolatrada,
que entre el humilde pueblo confundida
diste siempre el ejemplo de virtudes[.]
(9)

[You, heroic woman, good above all others, / of noble, powerful and wealthy lineage, / who, through casting in your lot with an artisan / lost reputation, status and family; / you, dear, idolized mother, / who, one with the common people / was always a paragon of virtue.]

By marrying for love and marrying down, Inés flies in the face of aristocratic conventions that premised marriage on rank, family, and old money. Her rejection by her family suggests the social opposition to women's desire for independence and autonomy. By exercising choice with regard to her marriage partner, Inés revindicates the liberal premise of the autonomous individual who can freely enter into a social contract. As Wendy S. Jones indicates, "if a woman was free to choose her spouse, she was by implication a trustworthy adult, capable of other significant choices and actions" (2005, 37). By renouncing her class privileges out of love for a member of the common people, Inés represents the Progressive ideal, to which Acuña adhered, of a virtuous upper class prepared to act as moral leaders for the future good of Spain. Once again, the play privileges voluntary alliances over and above relationships determined by birth and place, at the same time as it charges an enlightened upper class with driving sociopolitical change.

Nation as Voluntary Association and Civil Fraternity in *Tribunales de venganza*

A more pronounced foregrounding of members of an artisan or lower-middle class as effective agents for overturning traditional hierarchies of power emerges in Acuña's following drama, *Tribunales de venganza,* first performed in Zaragoza in 1878 and published in 1880. Although Acuña now addresses a more remote period in Spanish history, the theme of revolution by artisan groups behind a common cause serves as an allegory for radical liberal aspirations. As in *Amor á la patria* and *El Padre Juan,* the political events in *Tribunales de venganza* are played out within a family. However, the concept of the family as a natural unit established through birth and verifiable bloodlines is countered through the stress now placed on the obscurity of family genealogies and on the role played in its formation by sociocultural alliances, such as voluntary adoption and associationism.

The drama opens in Valencia in 1519 when the Moor Asail, the unrecognized, adoptive elder brother of the protagonist, Guillen Sorolla, a member of the Valencian Germanía, betrays him by allowing the noble, Luis Cabanillas, to abduct Sorolla's wife, Andrea. In return, Asail hopes for information from Cabanillas that might identify his own mother's murderer. As for Cabanillas, he aims to satisfy his lust for Andrea and use her to convince Sorolla to abandon the Germanía and thus stifle the rebellion. Although Andrea remains steadfast in her loyalty to Sorolla and refuses Cabanillas, Sorolla is captured and eventually executed in Játiva two years later. Within such a plot, Andrea clearly invites interpretation as a chaste national body disputed by opposing political interests: on the one hand, by an abusive nobility, and on the other, by a revolutionary lower-middle class. Andrea's faithfulness to the latter, represented by Sorolla, can be read as indicative of Acuña's political alignment with more radical liberal concerns.

It is important that the historical events of which the Germanía is protagonist evoke the almost contemporaneous uprising of the Comuneros, who rebelled against Charles V's perceived abuse of Castilian law. The significance of the Comuneros for nineteenth-century Spanish liberalism and its push for decentralization is stressed by Rafael Altamira in his *Historia de España y de la civilización española* (1899–1906), where he describes the Comuneros's political program, which granted relative autonomy to its city communities, as groundbreaking for its time.[22] Lasting barely a year, from May 1520 to April 1521, the rebellion of the Castilian Comuneros was motivated, on the one hand, by the desire of a group of urban nobles to preserve the independence of the Cortes and, with it, the traditional powers of the Castilian towns. On the other hand, it was fuelled by the people's xenophobia toward the rule of Charles V, seen as a foreign king who was subjecting Spain to excessive taxation to finance his European interests. As the conflict dragged on, it began to assume the vestiges of a civil war that challenged the power of the aristocracy, now increasingly alienated from the Comuneros (Elliott 1970, 151–55). Among those few nobles who continued to support the Comuneros's cause was Rosario's ancestor, Antonio de Acuña, bishop of Zamora.[23]

It is into this family tradition of opposition to established power that Acuña inserts herself when she chooses for her drama the theme of the uprising by the Valencian Germanía, who saw the Comuneros as forerunners of their own struggle. Nevertheless the causes of each attempted revolution were different. Whereas the revolt of the Comuneros was primarily due to political reasons, that of the Germanía was social in origin, revolving around two main factors: first, the arming of the guilds in 1519 against feared raids on the Valencian coast by Turkish galleys; and secondly, an outbreak in Valencia of the plague, attributed to immorality, from which the nobility, perceived as the most sinful social group, fled. The result was the formation of the Germanía, an urban movement made up of armed artisans, whose initial intention was to make Valencia a republic. Like the rebellion of the Comuneros, the uprising of the Germanía was unsuccessful, being put down some months later in October 1521. Sorolla's unhappy end resembles that of its leader, Vicenç Peris, executed in March 1522 (Elliott 1970, 156–59).

Acuña bestows historical authority and legitimacy on her dramatic rendition of these events by taking her key characters, as acknowledged in her manuscript, from real-life figures privileged by the liberal historian, Modesto Lafuente. In his account of the revolt of the Germanía in his monumental *Historia de España*,[24] Lafuente describes Sorolla, a wool weaver, as one of the thirteen artisans in the revolutionary Junta, whose self-proclaimed mission was to protect the Valencian kingdom against the Moors and abuse by the nobles. As the Junta took control of settlements in the kingdom, Sorolla, Lafuente specifies, was named governor of Paterna, Benaguacil, and La Pobla. Unlike Acuña's unqualified exaltation of Sorolla, Lafuente's appraisement of this figure is mixed, oscillating between depicting him as an "audacious youth," with "abilities superior to those of his fellows," and casting him as a liar who spreads false rumors to obtain his ends (Lafuente 1888, 8:137–42).

With regard to Cabanillas, governor of Valencia, he is portrayed by Lafuente in neutral tones, while Acuña's character, Asail, is probably drawn from Lafuente's reference to Sorolla's eventual betrayer, "a Moorish servant of his." These negative connotations attached to the Moorish "race" in Lafuente's history are reinforced by his reference to the two thousand Moors in the region who came out in armed support of the rebellious nobility (1888, 8:148, 143). Conversely Acuña's representations of Asail, as I will develop below, are not as Manichean as Lafuente's.

The variations between Acuña's and Lafuente's accounts highlight differing visions of the liberal project and the weight afforded to specific national constituencies in bringing these visions to fruition. Undoubtedly the more conservative approach is represented by Lafuente, who sees the uprising of the Germanía as a revolution without direction and doomed to political failure, with recent parallels in unsuccessful federal experiments in eastern and southern Spain. His repeated references to the Germanía's inability to control the "plebe" or common people, and to the anarchy prevailing among the population (1888, 8:141, 145), indirectly critique the contemporary liberalism of the Federal Democrats, uneasily poised, as I will expand on below, between their alleged commitment to a common people and their fear of the demands made by increasingly politicized lower classes. In contrast, in her condemnation of the Spanish monarch and Cabanillas, and her privileging of the Germanía, Acuña can be seen to revindicate the late nineteenth-century radical liberal agenda, which sought to create a federated Spain with socialist underpinnings. That ideal had come close to realization just four years prior to the first performance of *Tribunales* with the First Republic (1873–74), a consequence of the Glorious Revolution of 1868 and the abdications of Isabel II and her successor, Amadeo of Savoy, in 1868 and 1873 respectively.

Crucial, therefore, for understanding Acuña's dramatic use of the Germanía are the events that unfolded in Spain between 1868, which saw the Glorious Revolution, and 1874, which marked the demise of the First Republic. It was the provisional government of that revolution that legalized the right of association, considered intrinsic to the freedom of all Spanish citizens. This right gave great impetus to the development of working-class movements, fuelled by propaganda from foreign internationalists. While socialism developed rapidly in Madrid, the growth of anarchism in eastern and southern Spain brought the national workers' congress, celebrated in Barcelona in 1870, to declare in favor of workers appropriating privately owned means of production and constituting themselves as a "free federation of free workers' associations" (Artola 2001, 357).

The tensions provoked by the liberals' commitment to principles of individual freedom and their fear of the consequences for national unity from those very working-class movements that they had helped bring into existence engendered dissension and splits within Republican ranks between 1870 and 1871. One faction were the above-mentioned Federal Democrats, who supported a republic founded on a federal pact that would guarantee its unity, and who favored sociopolitical transformation through constitutional law. Another more revolutionary group were those Republicans who maintained that the current political order had to be destroyed by force. Called the intransigents due to their opposition to a monarchy, they insisted on the need for a political program of social reforms in order to retain the loyalty of the working classes, increasingly attracted to the First International. However, they were neutralized when the Federal Democrats agreed to work with Ruiz Zorrilla's ministry (Artola 2001, 353–54). It was within this fluid, rapidly shifting scenario of liberal allegiances that the First Republic was proclaimed in 1873.

The struggle of the Germanía depicted in Acuña's drama can be read as an allegory of events in 1873, when the newly inaugurated First Republic, initially under the presidency of federalist Francesc Pi y Margall, and subsequently under the more conservative Salmerón, debated its Constitution, which defended the concept of Spain as a federation provided that the unity and integrity of the nation were not compromised. Impatient at this slow-moving theoretical discussion, federalists in Alcoy, Cartagena, Valencia, and Andalucía proclaimed these areas independent cantons, intersecting with federal interests among the First International and working-class socialism. With a political solution that might recognize the cantons stymied, and in order to prevent further civil disorder, Salmerón called in the army under General Pavía to squash the Cantonalist uprisings.

Alarmed at the perceived disintegration of the nation, the Republicans decanted toward more conservative positions. Throughout 1873, radical liberals, influenced by the increasing apprehension of the bourgeoisie, joined forces with conservative federalists to form the United Republican Party. While its manifesto defended the rights granted by the 1869 Constitution, it broke definitively with federalism, which allegedly threatened social order, freedom, and progress. On January 2, 1874, Pavía's coup d'état brought in an authoritarian, nonconstitutional Republic, first under Serrano and then under Sagasta, with the entire country in a state of emergency. With the First Republic in tatters, there remained no other option but the restoration of the monarchy in 1875, in the form of Alfonso XII (Artola 2001, 365–68). In summary, then, the events that unfolded between 1868 and 1874 foreground the tension between two fundamental liberal premises: on the one hand, the defense of individual civil liberties, on which federalism was founded, and, on the other, the upholding of the unity of the nation, vital for guaranteeing freedom to all.

In Acuña's *Tribunales* the federal vision of a pluralistic, decentralized nation is still a dream. Spain suffers under the absolutist rule of the Catholic Charles V, who favors imperial policy in Europe over the need to resolve internal injustices:

> Son tantos los desmanes que sufrimos,
> es tanta la justicia que queremos,
> que ese rey ambicioso de victorias
> tuviera que olvidarlas mucho tiempo:
> . . . .
> Valencia, esta Valencia de los Cides
> gime oprimida por feroces dueños ...
> (Acuña 1880, 9)

[Such are the abuses that we suffer, / such is the justice that we want, / that that king desirous of victories / would have to forget about them for a long time: / . . . / Valencia, this Valencia of Cids / moans oppressed by ferocious masters]

Here the monarchy is represented as increasingly dissociated from the interests of the nation and as no longer responding to the needs of an oppressed Spanish people, symbolized by a subjugated, feminized Valencia. Nevertheless Valencia's problems are not attributed so much to the king as to the nobles' appropriation of rights held to belong to the people: "Un pueblo entero sus lamentos lanza / pidiendo al trono hispano los derechos / que una nobleza estúpida le arranca" [An entire people cries out in lament / asking the Spanish throne for their rights / usurped by foolish nobles] (18). Through Acuña's sociopolitical lens, the corrupt nobles symbolize the perceived contemporary decadence of the Spanish upper classes, dedicated to self-gain, while the king presents the monarchy as an unresponsive and unviable system of government, incarnate in Acuña's contemporary context in Isabel II, Amadeo of Savoy, and the lackluster Restoration monarchy.

In terms of the larger family or nation, Asail, Sorolla's unknown adoptive brother, occupies an ambiguous position and thus serves to focalize some of the sociopolitical issues specified above. A *morisco* or Moor who has converted to Christianity, Asail declares to Andrea, however, that he is Christian not by choice but "por mandato expreso / del rey de vuestra raza" [by express order / of the king of your race] (24). The resentment produced by his forced religious conversion overrides any feelings of loyalty toward Andrea and Sorolla, who have taken him into their home and given him work, and by extension, toward Christian Spain. Such a breakdown of sociocultural relations mirrors the historical context of the kingdom of Valencia, progressively paralyzed by the Moorish problem, which brought about the imposed conversion of its Moors to Christianity between 1520 and 1525 (Inman Fox 1998, 45).[25] By foregrounding in *Tribunales* such elements of religion and "race," Acuña critiques policies of forced integration into a nation of diverse peoples and draws attention to the importance of voluntarism in establishing the communal social contract necessary for the desired unity of the nation (Martínez 2004, 14). She argues for respect for other cultures within her contemporary national context, while indirectly revindicating the liberal ideal of freedom of worship briefly made reality by the 1868 Revolution.

Of noble Moorish descent, Asail's account of his early years casts the Valencian Arabs as an independent, peace-loving people, at one with the fertile land that they cultivated:

> En los fértiles llanos de Valencia
> de árabe raza y sin feudales dueños
> una pequeña aldea se veía
> blanca paloma entre frondoso huerto.
> (Acuña 1880, 21)

> [On the fertile plains of the kingdom of Valencia / of the Arab race and free from feudal masters / a tiny village could be seen / a white dove in a luxuriant orchard.][26]

In contrast to this Edenic picture of civilized self-governance and material well-being, the pole of barbarity is assigned to the "condales señores" [counts] who, within a narrative of imperial conquest, pillage Asail's village, and rape and murder his mother: "De condales señores vil cuadrilla, / seguida de jayanes y escuderos, / como feroces tigres de la Nubia" [Composed of counts a vile band, / with an entourage of ruffians and squires, / like ferocious Nubian tigers] (22). During the course of these atrocities the twelve-year-old Asail is separated from Sorolla, his adopted two-year-old brother, whom he presumes dead also. It is his memories of these events that fuel his promise to his dying mother to avenge her dishonor, caused, unbeknown to him, by Cabanillas: "¡Borrar esas memorias! ¡Más valdría / que pidiérais al sol matar su fuego[!]" [Erase those memories! It would be simpler / to ask the sun to extinguish its fire!] (24).

Through Asail's story, Acuña undercuts dichotomized historical renditions derived from that other founding myth of Spanish nationhood, the Catholic "Reconquest"; narratives that present the Arabs as aggressive, barbaric hordes and the nobility as paragons of Christian virtue. As Sorolla's adoptive elder brother, Asail reminds Acuña's contemporary audience that the Moors, cast out of the Spanish nation, have an earlier historical claim and should be acknowledged as a legitimate part of Spain's tradition and heritage. As a victim seeking revenge for his mother's murder at the hands of Cabanillas, Asail revindicates the claims of all others wronged by continued quasifeudal policies.

However, as his adoptive brother's betrayer, albeit unwitting, Asail also exhibits negative attributes that cast him as other to a nineteenth-century Spain anxious to shake off its representation by northern European countries as the exotic, barbaric other to their civilizations. Liberal internalization of this kind of image was exemplified in the attitude of regenerationist Joaquín Costa, for whom, according to María Dolores Gómez Molleda, "the Spaniard still wore his African turban under his tophat and his world was one of hunger, malnutrition, lack of culture, superstition, brutishness, the flick-knife, oligarchy and caciquism" (Gómez Molleda 1966, 344). The negative facets of Asail's portrayal, therefore, can be seen as partially revelatory of liberal aspirations to dissociate the country from a perceived inferiority and decadence, rendered all the more acute by the progressive disintegration of its Latin American empire. Within this context Africa became the focus for Spain's renewed imperial pretensions, critiqued perhaps in Acuña's play through her censure of the marauding nobles. The ambiguities inherent in Asail's character and story, then, suggest both criticism effected by Progressive liberals of official Spanish colonial policies in Africa and also their desire to distance Spain from Africa through Europeanization.[27] Not coincidentally, Asail's ambivalent characterization as, on the one hand, a brother to the Spaniard and, on the other, as deceitful traitor, echoes similar representations of the Arab in discussions on colonial policy in the Restoration years (La Porte 2003, 482–85).

Within Acuña's drama paradigms relating to Africa are redeployed to denounce a contemporary history of internal colonization in Spain, radicated in the struggle between a closed, hierarchical stratification of society upheld by interlocking principles pertaining to "race" and estate, and a more flexible model that permits social mobility, premised on class. The narration of this history is initially channeled through Asail, who tells Cabanillas the fable of a caged Nubian lion that, haunted by memories of its homeland, escapes, to regain temporarily its lost freedom:

> Ruge el leon de Nubia prisionero
> con rudo esfuerzo de su hercúlea garra;
> logra por fin reconquistar un dia
> la hermosa libertad que ambicionaba;
> . . . .
> y aspira el aire cálido que enciende
> en su pecho recuerdos de la patria[.]
> (Acuña 1880, 42)

[The Nubian lion roars, imprisoned / with the brute force of his Herculean claws; / he at last succeeds in recovering one day / that beautiful freedom long-desired; / . . . / and he breathes in the warm air that kindles / in his breast memories of the *patria*.][28]

Likening the lion's escape to uprisings by the Spanish populace, Asail lapses into the stereotype of the wily Moor to remind Cabanillas that such rebellions are passing and do not unduly compromise the aristocracy's continued subjection of the uneducated masses:

> La imbécil muchedumbre que te espanta
> compárala con el leon de Nubia:
> fiera brava que ruge y despedaza:
> hartándola de sangre un solo dia,
> lo ménos por un siglo vive esclava.
> (42–43)

[The imbecilic masses that terrify you / compare them with the Nubian lion: / a fierce beast that roars and rips to shreds: / quenching its thirst for blood on a single day, / it lives a slave for at least a century more.]

Nevertheless, given that the lion is the traditional symbol of a strong, centralized Castile and Spain under monarchic rule, Acuña's description is subversive. For those in power, the latent strength of the people must be contained, like the imprisoned lion, lest it fragment the centralized state: "fiera brava que ruge y despedaza" [a fierce beast that roars and rips to shreds].[29] What makes Spain akin to Africa, Acuña's Asail suggests, is not its repudiated Moorish heritage but the continued denial of basic rights to its weaker subjects by the aforementioned "feroces tigres de la Nubia" [ferocious Nubian tigers] (22), repeatedly associated with Cabanillas and the aristocracy.[30] The contention that exists in *Tribunales* over concepts of estate and class, symbolized by the tiger and the lion, marks a debate between predetermined national configurations, such as dynastic orders, and self-determining alternatives in which the people are sovereign.

Hence the discourses of African colonialism used by Spanish liberals from the mid-nineteenth century onward to foster national unity, despite pressing internal problems, are reshuffled in Acuña's drama to highlight contemporary class issues. The tiger, a frequent marker in fin-de-siècle representations of the alleged exoticism and ferocity of the Moorish world, is now no longer outside but within the Spanish nation, epitomizing an upper class that preys on a common people.[31] Nuances of this discussion may be traced, I propose, in Acuña's confusing use of the term *raza* [race], which refers on some occasions to social estate and on others, to class. The first usage is highlighted when Andrea tells Cabanillas that the "señores" [lords], whom he represents, are a "raza envilecida" [degenerate race], an estate doomed to extinction, in contrast with a "pueblo," the working classes with whom she identifies, who are rebelling against their oppression:

> Crimen sin nombre, bárbaro, inhumano
> levantó de mi pueblo los clamores,
> y hoy su poder inmenso y soberano
> hace temblar de espanto á los señores.
> Viértase nuestra sangre por tu mano;
> provoca nuevamente sus furores,
> y se hundirá tu raza envilecida
> de Dios y de los hombres maldecida.
> (39–40)

[An indescribable crime, barbaric and inhuman / caused an uproar among my people, / and today their immense, sovereign power / makes the lords tremble in fear. / Shed our blood, / reawaken their fury, / and your degenerate race will vanish / cursed by God and all humanity.]

Similar notions are echoed by Sorolla when he describes Cabanillas and his kind in archetypal terms as a "raza vil cuyos andrajos / jamás esconden del honor la llama" [vile race whose rags / will never hide the flame of honor] (45). Affirming that their "rags" or moral impoverishment cannot obscure the flame of national honor borne by himself and his political "brothers," Sorolla embodies the ethos of the Progressive liberals of the 1868 Revolution, whose rallying cry was "Long live Spain with honor!" (Aranguren 1981, 108).[32]

Acuña's second usage of the term *raza,* equated with class, can be observed in her description of the aristocracy as "¡[v]erdugos de las razas desvalidas, / de la razón, del pueblo y de las vidas[!]" [executioners of defenceless races, / of reason, the people and lives!] (Acuña 1880, 44). The nobles therefore represent a rigidly stratified social system seen as antithetical to reason and to developing a defenceless people, identified with the "razas desvalidas," into a sovereign nation or "pueblo." The layered meanings attributed to *raza* in *Tribunales,* therefore, articulate competing class interests within Acuña's Spain and forecast the demise of sectors in society unfairly privileged by blood and birth.

Aspects of the gradual and contested transformation that occurs in the second half of nineteenth-century Spain, from a society based on social estates to one founded on class (Jover and Gómez-Ferrer 2001f, 386; Ringrose 1996, 21), are also visible in Sorolla. Through her protagonist, Acuña suggests that the potential to shift oxidized power hierarchies rooted in the supremacy of the nobility and Catholic monarchy lies with a lower-middle or artisan class that might bridge working and upper classes. On the one hand, Sorolla is partially representative of the lower classes in that, as a *pechero* or taxpayer, he is oppressed by an unjust socioeconomic order that exempts the nobility, incarnate in Cabanillas, from taxes.[33] On the other hand, as an artisan, Sorolla also symbolizes a self-made class that has acquired what it has through work and not birth, with reputation contingent on an untarnished name:

> pobre artesano soy, sin más riquezas
> que las escasas que al trabajo debo,
> ni la fama se ocupa de mi vida
> ni más blasones que mi nombre tengo.
> (Acuña 1880, 8)

[I am a poor artisan, without greater riches / than those few acquired through my work, / nor does fame concern my life / nor do I have blazons other than my name.]

The intimated rejection of the legitimacy of rights through birth is further evident in Sorolla's unknown origins and his adoption by Asail's father, a rich merchant from Játiva, who bequeaths him an inheritance in recognition of his humility, loyalty, and hard work. Having invested half this money in studies (16), Sorolla stands for a new kind of nobility premised on the cultivation of intelligence and spiritual wealth. Notions such as these run counter to the importance placed by the upper and upper-middle classes in Acuña's context on material wealth, whether inherited, as with the aristocracy, or acquired through business and trade, as with the bourgeoisie. Sorolla incarnates the values of a professional and intellectual lower-middle class, in opposition to the landowning and financially powerful oligarchies of the Restoration. Thus when Sorolla asks Vicente, a fellow "brother," how he can contribute to the Germanía without fame and an inherited title, the latter responds: ". . . Guillen, tú puedes mucho, / tu vasta ilustracion, tu gran talento ... " [Guillen, you can do a lot, / with your vast learning, your great talent] (8).

In contrast, more privileged classes are portrayed as motivated purely by *honra* or wealth, sacrificing their honor for material gain. The result, Sorolla exclaims to Cabanillas, is a nation of bastards and monsters, engendered through the calculated prostitution of women and values:

> Sin amor vuestras mujeres
> se venden como esposas por el oro
> . . . .
> halagadas de bárbaros poderes
> les venden su virtud por su tesoro
> dando ser á unos hijos sin conciencia,
> . . . .
> monstruos de monstruos viles engendrados[.]
> (46)

[Without love your women / sell themselves as wives for gold / . . . / flattered by barbarous powers / they sell them their virtue for riches / shamelessly conceiving children, / . . . / monsters by vile monsters engendered.]

Through such a representation, Acuña may be seen to take umbrage with the unbridled materialism of a bourgeois society, which resulted in rampant corruption within the administration associated with Isabel II and the more conservative liberalism of the Moderates. The hope for Spain's regeneration, Acuña clearly proposes, lies with a hard-working, educated lower-middle class, as embodied by Sorolla.

As intimated by the surname of Sorolla, meaning "brother," Acuña further posits that a nation must be constructed according to a fraternal contract governed by reason, or what Andrea describes as "el pacto fraternal que nos impuso / la ley de la razon" [the fraternal pact imposed on us / by the law of reason] (20). Rather than national affiliation being predetermined through birth, Acuña's envisioned nation is premised on a voluntary coming together of subjects in the name of common ideals. As Carole Pateman observes, within civil society "[f]raternity is seen as a free union, and . . . implies the existence of communal bonds that are civil or public, not confined to assignable persons, and that are freely chosen" (1988, 78). Such an association of like-minded individuals is symbolized in the "gran Germanía valenciana" [great Valencian brotherhood] (Acuña 1880, 7), depicted by Sorolla as "esa noble hermandad" [that noble brotherhood] (8) and seen as continuing the "guerra sagrada" [sacred war] of the Comuneros (10).

The importance of associationism for the development of alternative sociopolitical formations that might challenge and change existing power structures cannot be underestimated in the formation of the liberal nation.[34] It was the nineteenth century that provided Spain with the sociohistorical conditions that permitted the rise of associationism, premised on the return of the emigrant liberals after the death of Fernando VII, the consolidation of the middle and lower-middle classes, and the growth and industrialization of urban centers. Such centers facilitated the exchange of information and knowledge, and the creation and institutionalization of sociocultural spaces for this purpose (Guereña 1999, 25–26).

Nevertheless it is important to remember that during most of the nineteenth century associationism was illegal and not officially sanctioned until 1887 (Jover and Gómez-Ferrer 2001e, 337). Even during the period 1868–74, dominated by the Progressive liberals, associationism was permitted only within clearly defined limits that protected bourgeois property rights. Although numerous associations were indeed created, they were intended to counteract working-class associationism, identified with the First International, instill bourgeois values in the lower classes, and give them the basic education required for industrialization. The restoration of the Bourbon monarchy in 1875 produced a crackdown on associations that revindicated working-class concerns.[35] In 1878, when Acuña's *Tribunales de venganza* was first peformed, the right to freedom of political association of all classes would still have constituted an unfulfilled dream. Its illegality would thus have permitted even stronger parallels to be drawn between the situation of the persecuted Germanía and that of certain contemporary groups.

In *Tribunales de venganza,* as in *Amor á la patria,* Acuña's rewriting of founding myths of Spanish liberalism is faithful to the latter's aim of recovering the history of a people represented as common. The purpose of writing such a history is, as Sorolla points out, to provide models for emulation so that the downtrodden might eventually defeat a seemingly cyclical history of tyrannical oppression:

> ¡Ay! Si la historia relatase un dia
> con lenguaje imparcial sus grandes hechos,
> acaso el mundo estremecido viera
> quien de virtudes le enseñó el ejemplo.
> ¡Ignorados plebeyos de mi patria
> ni ellos mismos tal vez se conocieron
> y acaso rompan la fatal cadena
> que forjan los tiranos en sus reinos!
>
> (Acuña 1880, 12)

[Ay! If one day history were to relate / in impartial words their great deeds, / perhaps the awe-struck world would see / who showed it the meaning of virtue. / Unrecognized workers of my motherland / perhaps they did not even know one another / and yet perchance break the fatal chain / forged by tyrants in their kingdoms!]

Although the responsibility of history, the verses declare, is to relate events in impartial terms—"con lenguaje imparcial"—Acuña's play reveals that her proclamation of objectivity is a purely rhetorical device designed to grant legitimacy to radical liberalism, committed to the "ignorados plebeyos" or unrepresented working classes.

Acuña lends still greater legitimacy to her sociopolitical enterprise when she describes national sovereignty as the inevitable consequence of a natural process that will see the figurative ice age of dynastic monarchies replaced by the dawn of new civilizations, in which formerly subjugated classes will declare themselves sovereigns of their historical destiny:

Brillante luz de un sol que sobre el cielo
han de mirar los siglos del mañana,
tal es la aurora que rompiendo el hielo
alumbra ya nuestra conciencia humana:
. . . .
¡*Justicia* y *libertad* los pueblos gritan,
. . . .
y al paso de los siglos se adelantan,
coronándose reyes en la historia
con el lauro inmortal de la victoria[!]
(54)

[The brilliant light of a sun in the heavens / that future centuries must surely see, / such is the dawn that, breaking the ice, / already enlightens our human consciousness: / . . . / *Justice and freedom* the peoples shout, / . . . / and as the centuries pass, they take the lead, / crowning themselves kings in history / with the immortal wreath of victory!]

Reconciling, however, such imaginings with Spain's contemporary reality is well-nigh impossible, as the denouement of *Tribunales* makes clear: Cabanillas emerges triumphant, Sorolla and his "brothers" are eliminated through betrayal, and Andrea, although unsullied and ever faithful to Sorolla, must survive alone after her husband's execution.

The sociopolitical settings for Acuña's *Amor á la patria* and *Tribunales de venganza* depict worlds in transition between old and new orders, and offer up for scrutiny the concepts of estate, class, and nationhood that underpin the material and ideological foundations of these orders. Ostensibly the dramas focus on the historical beginnings of Spanish liberalism, rewriting its legends to grant the contemporary liberal project authority and authenticity. Nevertheless the plots also foreground the tensions inherent in key premises of liberalism: namely, national unity and individual liberty. Whereas *Amor á la patria* posits that the desired freedom of the nation is dependent on the unity of its social actors, such an argument can no longer be sustained in *Tribunales de venganza*, dominated by divided families and broken dreams. Here national unity is portrayed as highly unstable and as ultimately constructed on suspect alliances that have betrayed the more radical liberal ideals of Spain as republic and federation, which premise national unity on the constitutional recognition and interdependence of all its peoples.[36] In terms of gender, the very real historical exceptionality of women like Inés and María, and the comparatively minor, if important symbolic, role granted to Andrea, reveal the patriarchal nature of bourgeois liberalism and its fraternal contract in Acuña's Spain, with women's inclusion in liberal civil society largely reduced to embodying masculine ideals.

Acuña's examination of the issues and challenges facing the liberal project for Spain comes to the fore with greater intensity in her 1891 play, *El Padre Juan*, which portrays in unequivocal terms the imperative need to transform Spain into a liberal society on a par with northern European countries. In *El Padre Juan* Acuña moves away from the possibility of a revolution effected by the lower classes to endorse a sociocultural revolution initiated by an illustrated upper class. As the ensuing pages will develop, *El Padre Juan* further highlights the dilemmas faced by Progressive liberalism, torn between the need for national unity, for a realistic acknowledgment of social differences and for viable solutions to the conflicts that arise from the principle of political self-determination.

Setting the Scene for *El Padre Juan*: Spain's Landscapes of History

By 1891, the year that saw the sole performance of Acuña's most controversial drama, *El Padre Juan*, the writer was, for conventional social circles, a figure of undeniable notoriety. Not only had Acuña dared to separate from her husband on account of his infidelity, but she had also publicly embraced freethinking and freemasonry, in 1884 and 1886 respectively.[37] Such actions struck at the core of upper-middle-class society of the time, undermining the feminine ideals of forbearing silence and dependence, and the institution of the Catholic Church. Marginalized by the influential sociocultural circles in which she had previously moved,[38] from the mid-1880s Acuña resided principally in her birthplace, Pinto, a village on the outskirts of Madrid, where she could practice her beliefs in the regenerative powers of nature. Apart from travels in Europe and on horseback throughout Spain, there she would remain until 1891, when she established herself in Cueto, Cantabria, before finally moving to Gijón in 1909.

The polemic aroused by the one performance of *El Padre Juan* and its immediate closure is not surprising.[39] Its attack on the Catholic Church, its manifest advocation of Progressive liberalism, freethinking, and freemasonry, and its critical evaluation of Spain's past and present would have hit conservative society hard. The action, set in a remote Asturian village, revolves around the intention of a young, freethinking millionaire, Ramón, to demolish a Church hermitage, the focal point of the village *romería* or religious festival, and replace it with a series of edifices for public education and health. These plans meet with consolidated opposition from the villagers, spurred on by the pronouncements of the priest, Padre Juan. Crucial to Ramón's undertaking is the support of his friend, Luis, and his beloved, Isabel, whom he means to marry in a civil ceremony. Ramón's defiance of all sociocultural norms and his determination to ignore village hostility lead to his being murdered by youths, with Isabel remaining to denounce religious fanaticism and keep alive the spirit of their enterprise.

Acting as preface to the publication of *El Padre Juan* is Acuña's "Dedicatoria" [Dedication], where she contemplates the landscape at sunset from the Evangelist mountain in the Asturian European Peaks.[40] From her vantage point, on the very summit, Acuña proceeds to provide a panoramic vision of Spanish history:

> Llegó el momento en que, vencida la imponente ascensión, mis arterias golpeaban con *ciento veinte pulsaciones* por minuto. A nuestras plantas se extendía un océano de montañas, cuyas crestas, como olas petrificadas, se levantaban en escalas monstruosas a 1.000 y 1.500 metros sobre el nivel del mar. Al sur, las dilatadas estepas de Castilla, con sus desolados horizontes de desierto, iban perdiéndose en límites de sesenta leguas, entre un cielo caliginoso, henchido de limbos de oro y de destellos de incendio. Al norte, un inmenso telón límpido azul . . . era el mar. . . . Después el pensamiento recorrió, con su rapidez inmedible, los estrechos horizontes de la patria. (Acuña 1989b, 133–34)

> [The moment arrived when, having triumphed in the impressive ascent, I felt my arteries pounding at *one hundred and twenty pulsations* a minute. At our feet lay an ocean of mountains, the peaks of which, like petrified waves, rose up to monstrous heights of 1000 and 1500 meters above sea level. To the south stretched away the Castilian plains with their desolate desert horizons, to vanish gradually sixty leagues away into a misty sky, swollen with golden halos and fiery sparks. To the north, an immense clear, blue curtain . . . was the sea. . . . Then my thoughts reviewed, with immeasurable speed, the narrow horizons of the nation.]

The description offered bears a striking resemblance to Caspar David Friedrich's 1818 painting, *Wanderer above a Sea of Fog*, in which a young man surveys a mountain landscape similarly enshrouded in fog and cloud, with the sea in the distance. Like Acuña's own self-positioning, he is placed ambiguously within time and space, as it is uncertain whether he faces the terrain traversed or that still to be explored. Compared by John Lewis Gaddis in *The Landscape of History* to the historian, who must "advance bravely into the future with . . . [his] eyes fixed firmly on the past," the wanderer conveys both "mastery over a landscape and the insignificance of an individual within it" (Gaddis 2002, 2, 1). Such contradictory emotions are also present in Acuña's account. On the one hand, she has conquered the mountain, having "vencida la imponente ascensión" [triumphed in the impressive ascent] (Acuña 1989b, 133); on the other, the scene emphasizes the human "pequeñez de átomos" [atom-like smallness] (134).

Exploring the symbolic import of mountain conquest for Romantic thought, Marlon Ross contends that this is a masculine trope of self-empowerment and the space of the poet-prophet: "It is from mountains that prophets proclaim their truths; . . . the mountain symbolizes the necessary solitude of the leaders of men and the necessary stance of truth—its transcendence, its elusiveness, and its immense might" (1988, 44). Read against Ross's argument, Acuña's account of her ascent becomes a metaphysical quest, where the grandiose landscape invites thought and imagination to take risks beyond the ordinary: "Sentíamos la felicidad de aquella elevación espantable, y el arriesgado propósito que teníamos de pasar la noche sobre aquellas cumbres" [We felt the happiness derived from that horrifying height, and the risks inherent in our intention of spending the night on those peaks] (Acuña 1989b, 134). Such a topography conveys the liberal ideals of freedom from oppression and tradition, as Malcolm Andrews clarifies: "Pictures of wild scenery . . . appeal largely *because* they dramatize that landscape's own untrammeled liberty. Such landscapes constitute a gesture of defiance to what is felt to be an oppressive, expansionist civilization, and are therefore infused with political meaning." Wilderness connotes "liberty from the historical past, from tradition" (1999, 156, 159). Significantly similar tropes were frequent in discourses of freethinking, as exemplified in Acuña's letter of affiliation to the premises of freethinking, "Valiosísima adhesion," published in the weekly, *Las Do-*

minicales del Librepensamiento, on December 28, 1884. There she describes her quest for freedom of thought and truth in terms of ascending a mountain: "Ahora entremos con resolución en el camino de la Verdad, estrecho y orlado de precipicios. Al verme en él tiemblo, sin vacilar" [Now let us step out resolutely on the path of Truth, narrow and bordered with precipices. When I see myself there, I tremble but do not hesitate] (Acuña 1992e, 69).

Audaciously venturing into a conceptual and physical territory gendered as masculine, Acuña's emphasized self-positioning on the very mountain top—"Estábamos sobre la misma cumbre, en el remate mismo de la crestería de piedra" [We stood on the very peak, on the very ridge of the stony mountain top] (Acuña 1989b, 133)—bestows on her discourse an aura of exceptional height, distance and objectivity, and hence, intellectual and historical authority. With reminiscences of Francisco de Quevedo's "Salmo XVII," where he contemplates the ruinous city walls of his once-strong nation (Quevedo 1980, 318), Acuña judges that Spain's capacity to project forward into a modern future is restricted by past and present ills. Whereas her thought is described as without limits or "inmedible," the horizons of the *patria* are represented as narrow or "estrechos" (Acuña 1989b, 134).

Reviewing the constraints that supposedly hinder the Spanish nation, Acuña sees its peoples to the east as diminished by their Moorish heritage, because, she states, their reason has been stymied by fanciful literature: "Los pobladores de Levante, achicados con la herencia númida, de imaginación tan llena de colores y de fantasías" [The inhabitants of the East, diminished by their Numidian heritage, with such colorful imaginations, so full of fantasies] (134). Here Acuña may well be referring to *aljamiado* literature. Prohibited since the sixteenth century, these writings drew on the supernatural and on magic (Perry 1999, 43), which Acuña would have considered antithetical to her dream of a Spain founded on reason and science. As for northern Spain, there recent history has been disfigured by the bloody Carlist wars: "[E]l septentrión, sombreado por las hecatombes civiles, cuyo vaho de sangre, aún caliente, marca en la historia rasgos de ferocidad inconcebible" [The north, darkened by civil catastrophes, where the stench of blood, still warm, traces on history's pages signs of inconceivable ferocity] (Acuña 1989b, 134–35).[41] Echoing Goya's print, *The Sleep of Reason Produces Monsters* (1797–99), Acuña's description suggests that all Spain sleeps in ignorance, its reason destroyed by envy, social conventions, and religious superstition: "Alrededor, los pueblos todos de la patria, dormidos en noche de ignorancias . . . el odio latiendo a impulsos de la envidia y acribillando la integridad de la conciencia racional con las garfiadas de la rutina, de la superstición y de la impiedad" [All around, the peoples of my nation, asleep in a night of ignorance . . . with hatred beating to the rhythm of envy and destroying the integrity of rational consciousness with the claws of routine, superstition, and impiety]. Through the lens of Darwinian theory, Acuña portrays the Spanish state and society as entities that have not yet attained full rationality, halfway between ape and man: "tipos intermediarios entre el mono y el hombre" (135).[42]

Acuña's account of contemporary Spain conforms to the historical paradigm current at that time of evaluating negatively Spain's present so as to bring about its regeneration. For traditionalists, exemplified by Marcelino Menéndez y Pelayo, the hope for Spain lies in resurrecting a glorious past: "Spain, *if it was to continue existing,* had to be, to a large extent, *what it had been.*" In contrast, for Progressive liberals, such as the Krausist founder of the Institución, Francisco Giner de los Ríos, Spain's survival depends on forging new paths: "Spain, if it was to continue existing, had to be also, to a large extent, *what it had not been*" (quoted by Gómez Molleda 1966, 112–13). For Krausists, history was set within an Enlightenment paradigm of humanity's ascent toward the truth of reason, equated with progress and godliness (Gómez Molleda 1966, 93, 96), and producing freedom of thought and tolerance toward others; all features embraced by Acuña and evident in her work.

Religion and Reason in Late Nineteenth-Century Spanish National Identity

By the beginning of the 1890s, when Acuña wrote and staged *El Padre Juan,* anticlerical feeling among many liberal intellectuals was fierce.[43] Her work was not alone in voicing opposition to the Catholic Church and proposing alternative ideals. In 1876 Benito Pérez Galdós, whom Acuña greatly admired,[44] published the novel *Doña Perfecta,* whose protagonist, Pepe Rey, like Acuña's Ramón, represents a freethinking Spain misunderstood by a backward people (Simón Palmer 1989, 31). A similar plot is also evident in Galdós's 1878 work, *La familia de León Roch,* where the eponymous Krausist hero must struggle for his ideal amid a conservative, intransigent society. Moreover an exact decade after Acuña's *El Padre Juan*, Galdós's anticlerical drama, *Electra*, was performed.[45] Religion, then, as Raymond Carr insists, was "the prism through which all other conflict was refracted; more than this, it meant that the claims of the Church on society were a prime source of division in themselves" (1982, 464).

The battlelines between Catholic and reformist camps, generally representative of diverging visions for the Spanish nation, were clearly drawn from 1875 onward. It was then that a group of university professors and secondary school teachers, rejecting the government's demand that state education respect both the Catholic faith and the liberal Constitution,[46] left their employment, whether voluntarily or by ministerial order, to teach in the Institución Libre de Enseñanza, a private body founded in 1876 by Giner de los Ríos and others.[47] Under Giner's mentorship, the aim of the Institución was to transform gradually Spanish mentality through far-reaching reforms in the education system, so as to create a "pueblo" (both civilian mass and nation), able to think critically for itself (Boyd 1997, 36). Furthermore, considering that the Catholic Church hampered scientific progress and the full incorporation of Spain into the modern world, the Institución privileged a broad religious framework, "in which there was no room for small-minded differentiations between reason and faith" (Jiménez 1948, 170). The intention was to offer a third way forward for Spain based on sociocultural evolution, to counteract the two Spains of conservative tradition and radical revolution (Gómez Molleda 1966, 7). Crucial to this project was the secularization or, more precisely, "deseclesialización" of Spanish society, whereby it was envisaged that exclusive, hierarchical religions would give way to tolerance toward different creeds and to belief in their underlying unity. Rarely did such a stance imply an advocation of atheism; rather, it tended to be deistic, finding God in a plurality of religions and in nature (Gómez Molleda 1966, 91–107).

Such are the attitudes consistently evinced throughout Acuña's work. Although she was an acknowledged freethinker and freemason, such factors do not mean, as the black legend surrounding her would have it, that she was atheist. On the contrary, as she explains in her "Carta a un soldado español," she is pantheist, rejecting dogmatic religions and believing God to be found in natural scientific laws and in the *patria*: "De la religión que tengo te diría, a decir verdad, que es la del sol y la de la patria, si el amor a estas dos cosas pudiera llamarse religión. Dogmática no profeso ninguna . . . Las leyes de la naturaleza, catalogadas por las ciencias, . . . son las que deben constituir la única religión de los hombres" [As for the religion that I espouse, to tell the truth, I would say that it is a religion of the sun and nation, if love for these two things could be called religion. I am not dogmatic about any religion . . . The laws of nature, inventoried by science, . . . must constitute the only religion of humankind] (Acuña 2000a, 62). Similarly, in her will or "Testamento," written in 1907, Acuña unequivocally affirms her belief in God alongside her rejection of the Catholic Church, which she perceives as the greatest hindrance to the development of human reason (Acuña 1992b, 46, 50).

The religious question, and all that it implied for the ideological direction and formation of the Spanish nation, was also inevitably at the crux of the continued resistance to the Institución by conservatives. While liberal reformists considered the Catholic Church to be a divisive force in the nation, for their opponents, representative of the majority of public opinion, Catholicism had been, and was, the primary force that ensured Spain's cohesion, and indeed, was affirmed in the 1812 liberal Constitution, as previously mentioned. To refute its principles constituted, in Gómez Molleda's words, a "denial of the history of the nation, with the ensuing rift in national consciousness" (1966, 126–27). Religion thus played a crucial role in conservative political programs, as demonstrated by the founding in 1881 of the Catholic Union, of Carlist leanings. Formed under the leadership of Alejandro Pidal y Mon as a consequence of the Vatican's injunction that Catholics support the most suitable political party in the interests of the Church, in 1883 the Union allied itself with Cánovas's conservative liberal ministry (Carr 1982, 354).

Despite differences of opinion among more traditional and more liberal opponents of the Institución, they spoke with one voice when it came to defending religious education. Catholic intellectuals approached the challenge of the Institución not only through attempts to reaffirm orthodox education, but, more importantly, to reform it in line with Christian principles and the demands of a modern age. As a result, new organizations, centers of study, Catholic conferences, and journals proliferated to influence public opinion and defend the Catholic position (Gómez Molleda 1966, 159–61).[48]

It is this confrontation between the status quo and revolutionary alternatives, between the dogmatism of the Catholic Church and the kind of philosophies espoused by the Institución, that is at the heart of Acuña's *El Padre Juan.*[49] Within the drama characters portray a range of attitudes toward the Catholic Church that convey the complex social reality of the time. An examination of these attitudes helps to elucidate Acuña's position and the degree to which she aligns herself with, or reevaluates, liberal principles synonymous with the Institución and freethinking.

The degree of adherence to the Catholic Church is presented in the play as inflected as much by generation as by social class, gender, and political leanings. It is the older generation, represented by fifty-year-old doña Braulia, sixty-year-old Tía Rosa, and don Pedro de Morgovejo, Isabel's father, who profess most fervently their Catholic faith. This paradigm holds in spite of the differences in education between the liberal, worldly, and wealthy don Pedro, and the uneducated, conservative, rural women. While Isabel accuses her father of observing church practices purely out of habit, for don Pedro religion provides a positive model of conduct that prevents social discord among an uneducated majority and develops their reason: "Un ejemplo: un motivo edificante que evita el escándalo aquí, en estas aldeas pacíficas, donde casi todos los habitantes no usaron aún de su razón para discernir el bien del mal sin la ayuda de las creencias religiosas" [An example: a means of edification that avoids scandal here, in these peaceful villages, where almost none of the inhabitants has yet used reason to distinguish right from wrong without the aid of religious beliefs] (Acuña 1989c, 149).

Gender also plays a significant role in religious belief. With the exception of Isabel and doña María de Noriega, Ramón's mother, all the women proclaim their faith. Indeed these female characters manifest the greatest intransigence, equating Catholicism with "la verdadera religión" [the true religion], as conveyed by Consuelo's following words to Isabel: "¿Quieres saber por qué ni nosotras ni ninguna familia de esta cristiana aldea, admitiríamos el parentesco con Ramón? . . . porque es un hereje, impío, blasfemo, ateo, hijo de satanás, según tiene su alma de empedernida, y cerrada a la verdadera religión ... " [Do you want to know why neither we women nor any other family in this Christian village would recognize Ramón as kin? . . . because he is a heretic, impious and blasphemous, an atheist and son of Satan, such is his obstinate soul, closed to the true religion] (145). The women's faith confirms them as one of the primary bulwarks of the Catholic Church, due to their lack of education and unquestioning acceptance of ideals of femininity that privileged conformity to tradition and authority.[50]

A position initially between the unquestioning religious faith of the elders, especially Braulia and Tía Rosa, and the freethinking of educated characters—doña María, Isabel, Ramón, and Luis—is occupied by Diego, a well-to-do farmer of twenty-seven years. He exemplifies the fact that, during the Restoration years, religious belief and practice diminished not only in cities but also in rural areas, being most evident among younger men from both middle and working classes (Jover and Gómez-Ferrer 2001f, 396). While Diego questions if religion still exists—"¿Aún hay religión?"—Tía Rosa considers that the Catholic Church is as strong as ever: "¡A Dios gracias, y a esos buenos frailes que han avivado nuestra fe!" [Yes, thanks to God and to those good priests who have rekindled our faith!] (Acuña 1989c, 154). Diego criticizes the hypocrisy of reputed Catholics in the village, such as doña Remigia, seen by Tía Rosa as "una santa y una sabia" [a saint and wise woman], who always socializes with members of the clergy, but who is separated from her husband because of her adultery (153). Although he eventually concurs in seeing Ramón and his mother as "una familia de endemoniados" [a family possessed by the devil], he also defends the latter against criticism by village women, praising her charity and her compassionate care of the poor and ill (157). With his own religious sentiment one of mere observance of appearances, Diego's rejection of Ramón and Luis is presented as due more to differences in education and class than to religious reasons. Moreover it is implied that Diego's envy of Ramón is caused, at least partially, by the condescension with which he perceives Ramón treats him: "[E]n cuanto a tratar conmigo, siempre lo hace desde alto a abajo, y esto sería menester ser un bodoque para no conocerlo. . . . ya sé muy bien que él es un señor sabio, muy leído, etc.: pero, ¡qué diablo! no nos vamos tan lejos, sino porque él tuvo monises para embucharse de libros" [In his dealings with me, he always treats me with condescension, and you'd need to be a simpleton not to see it. . . . I do indeed know that he is a learnèd gentleman, very well-read, etc.: but, damn him! we're not so different except that he had the wherewithal to stuff himself with books] (151–52).

The figures around whom positions become most polarized are, significantly, Ramón and Padre Juan. Not appearing physically on stage until the very last scene, the priest embodies what one of the founders of the Institución, Manuel Pedregal y Cañedo, described as the invisible power of the Catholic Church, unable to be fought through violent means.[51] For the villagers as a whole, Padre Juan is a "santo varón, que nos lleva desde el confesionario por el camino del cielo" [a saintly man, who takes us from the confessional along heaven's path] (156). In contrast with the priest's image of sanctity, however, the discourse that he deploys and that is conveyed through the mouths of his parishioners is one of hatred and exclusivity. Thus Ramón, his family, and friends are "endemoniados que, como dice el Padre Juan, han caído sobre la aldea para probarnos" [possessed by the devil and, according to Father Juan, have descended on the village to test our faith] (154), while doña María's charity is judged as "caridad del Diablo, que corrompe al que la recibe y hunde más en los infiernos a quien la hace" [the Devil's charity, which corrupts those who receive it and sends further into hell those who give it] (157).

It is through the freethinking characters of María, Isabel, and Ramón that Acuña channels her criticism of a Catholic Church equated with fanaticism, as implied by María's following remark: "Esta aldea, poblada de criaturas ignorantes, sin más entendimiento que el de la astucia y la malicia, era terreno fértil para desarrollar la epidemia moral del fanatismo" [This village, inhabited by ignorant creatures, whose intelligence is limited to cunning and malice, was fertile soil for spawning the moral epidemic of fanaticism]. Likewise Isabel highlights the Catholic Church's greed: "Nuestros pueblos son un semillero de rencillas, cuentos, calumnias, pequeñas maldades, e ínterin los bienes conventuales aumentan . . ." [Our villages are a hotbed of quarrels, gossip, slander, and petty wrongs, and all the while the wealth of the religious orders increases] (166–67). Indeed it is such avariciousness that has contributed to the controversy over the hermitage, given that the Catholic Church has secretly agreed to sell it to Ramón (186). As for the corruption of the Church, it is indicated through Isabel's censure of Padre Juan, described as "impío" [impious] and as perverting "la noción del bien y del mal" [notions of good and evil] (150). Similarly through María it is revealed that Padre Juan's sanctity is pure façade; unbeknown to

Ramón, he is Ramón's natural father, a don Juan who seduced and abandoned an adolescent María.

The Catholic Church's self-interest and decadence, however, are represented as relatively recent occurrences. Prior to the Carlist wars, the resurgence of an inquisitorial spirit and the dominance of the Jesuits,[52] the Catholic Church allegedly propagated an ethos of love and nonviolence, as implied by Isabel's following statement: "Bajo la influencia de nuestro cura párroco, cuya máxima era sencilla, amar al prójimo, se contenían los odios, las envidias, las soberbias y la evolución a la nueva edad, acaso, acaso se hubiera hecho sin grandes violencias ... " [Under the influence of our parish priest, whose maxim was simple, love thy neighbor, hatreds, envies, and arrogance were reined in, and perhaps, perhaps the evolution to the new age might have taken place without excessive violence] (166). Here Acuña appears to suggest that before fanatical religious positions took hold in Spain, there might have existed the hope of working with the Catholic Church in national transformation, and not against it.

Whereas Acuña's drama portrays the Catholic Church and religion as fomenting hatred, exclusive divisions, and an immovilist mentality in Spain, it promotes reason, science, and education as vital for the emergence of a modern nation. Thus *El Padre Juan* constitutes a veritable exposition of the premises of Progressive liberalism and freethinking. In place of the Catholic religion, the character of Ramón represents the religion of rationalism, or what Acuña calls "la nueva Iglesia (cuyo dogma será la razón ilustrada por la ciencia), luchando contra la vieja Iglesia" [the new Church (governed by reason enlightened by science), fighting against the old Church] (Acuña 1989a, 235). It is on the site of the church hermitage that Ramón intends to build a school, hospital and model farm, to be known as "Villa Isabel" (Acuña 1989c, 158):

> Nuestra población rural está sumida en la ignorancia más espantosa, en un atraso moral repugnante. Creo de necesidad que la Escuela, la Granja modelo, el Instituto industrial con el Hospital y el Asilo, se levanten en nuestros campos como templos benditos, donde el pueblo español empiece a comulgar en la religión del racionalismo ... (185)

> [Our rural population is afflicted by the most terrible ignorance, by a repugnant moral backwardness. I believe it imperative that the

> School, model Farm and industrial Institute with the Hospital and Refuge, rise up in our fields like holy temples, so that the Spanish people may begin to commune in the religion of rationalism][53]

Ramón's portrayal as a freethinker is reinforced by Pedro's reference to him as a "librepensador" [freethinker] (150), who is suspect for "[¡]su ateísmo completo! ¡su libertad absoluta de pensar! ¡su falta, de fe!" [his total atheism! his absolute freedom of thought! his lack, of faith!] (149). That Ramón threatens those conservative forces of society represented by Catholicism, family, and monarchy is patent in his depiction of himself as "*Ateo,*" "*Bastardo,*" and "*republicano*" [an Atheist, Bastard, and Republican] (201).

Ramón's self-definition as a republican associates him with those Progressive liberal groups who supported the 1868 Revolution and the First Republic. According to Iris Zavala, laws approved during this period brought in universal male suffrage, albeit temporarily,[54] the academic freedom to teach and conduct research outside church jurisdiction, education for working classes and women, freedom of press, and, most importantly for the context of Acuña's play, freedom of worship and to express publicly antireligious sentiments. Major contemporary thinkers, such as Bergson, Comte, John Stuart Mill, and Marx, were the subject of press articles, while the German philosophers, especially Heine, Kant, Hegel, and Krause, were considered to offer viable frameworks for the intellectual construction of a liberal Spain (Zavala 1972, 182–98).

The desire on the part of Progressive liberals to meet the needs of the lower classes is suggested in Ramón's attitude toward the village *romería*; he does not attend it because of religious belief, but because he sees it as a custom that, because it originates in the people, is in keeping with his republican beliefs: "[Y]o no acudo a la romería sino por lo que tiene de popular; se olvida usted que soy un buen republicano" [I only go to the *romería* because it is a popular festival; you forget that I'm a good republican] (Acuña 1989c, 189). Acuña's characterization of Ramón, therefore, revindicates Progressive principles, seen as having been diluted or sacrificed by subsequent Restoration governments.

Also instrumental in the development of political liberalism and republicanism was freemasonry, which had entered Spain legally with the French in the War of Independence (Ferrer Benimeli 2001, 74–75, 105). Theoretically open to men of all nationalities, races, and creeds, freemasonry affirms that all are equal before the law. Its mission is to combat ignorance and stimulate ideas that are useful for the family, nation, and humanity, in a progressive, rational sense (Álvarez Lázaro 1998, 91–99). In the late 1880s and throughout the 1890s, Spanish freemasonry, whose members largely came from the middle and upper-middle classes, defended the equal participation of the working classes in the resources and responsibilities of the nation.[55] The movement thus upheld the right to freedom of association, peaceful demonstration, universal male suffrage, a secular state and education, civil marriage, and civil cemeteries (Álvarez Lázaro 1998, 104–5). This strand of liberalism is also apparent in Ramón, who has links to freemasonry through his adoptive father, described as "el condenado masón de su padre" [that cursèd mason, his father] (Acuña 1989c, 155). Indeed it may be argued that the three main principles of freemasonry, Equality, Freedom, and Fraternity (Ferrer Benimeli 2001, 28), identical to those of the French Revolution, are embodied in Acuña's play by Isabel, Ramón, and Luis, respectively.[56]

Despite these points of union between freemasonry and freethinking, one important difference is that, whereas the former advocates religious freedom, the latter is theoretically against all religions. Such a distinction frequently led freemasons to see adamant freethinkers as being as fanatical as the most die-hard Catholics. However, fruitful cross-fertilizations between freemasonry and freethinking did take place, as seen in certain figures and publications, such as Rosario de Acuña and *Las Dominicales del Librepensamiento* (Álvarez Lázaro 1985, 107–8, 179).

Critiquing Liberal Thought: Capitalist Individualism versus a Cooperative State of Nature

One of the central premises defended by liberalism is individualism. Yet, taken to an extreme, individualism and rampant economic development without heed of social impact prove detrimental to community interests. A dominant theme in *El Padre Juan* is the perceived harmful effects of capitalism and excessive material progress, encapsulated in Acuña's reworking of the traditional town/country dichotomy. Her discussion of town and country reveals these loci to be powerful symbols with which she formulates her thoughts on Spain's advancement and backwardness, civilization and barbarity. Acuña's representations of the country also swing between two poles, as she either collapses that space into the supposedly corrupt politics of the city or has it function as pure ideal.[57] In this way, the country reveals itself, on the one hand, as contaminated by the inequities of class structures reinforced by capitalism and, on the other hand, as an open space where collective ventures might begin to bring down social barriers.

In *El Padre Juan* opposition to Madrid, the Spanish capital and seat of government, is presented through Isabel and Ramón. Isabel describes the city as ill with a feverish greed and as poisoning the social body: "Cuando volvimos [de Madrid] tenía fiebre: en Madrid no la notaba. Allí, padre, deben tener todos fiebre, sin que ninguno lo note. . . . Madrid es un veneno demasiado activo para tomarle de pronto" [When we returned (from Madrid) I had a fever: in Madrid I wasn't aware of it. There, father, they must all have a fever without knowing it. . . . Madrid is too virulent a poison to be taken all at once] (Acuña 1989c, 147).[58] Undoubtedly at the time, Madrid was a hub of innovative ideas, with many opportunities for sociopolitical success (Jover and Gómez-Ferrer 2001f, 404). Nevertheless for Acuña the capital is equated with a betrayal of Progressive liberal ideals, committed to decentralization, in return for material gain for those in positions of influence and power.

Couched in still more forceful terms is Ramón's following denunciation of Madrid, where he alleges the urban environment has produced a citizenship obsessed with spectacle and rotten to the core: "¡[E]se medio es la causa de nuestra asfixia moral y física! ¡el ciudadanismo moderno, deslumbrante al exterior, por dentro agusanado!" [That environment is the cause of our moral and physical asphyxia! Modern civil society, dazzling on the outside, but wormeaten inside!] (Acuña 1989c, 184). The ruthless struggle for existence by the city's inhabitants, Ramón continues, has turned civil society into a jungle ruled by empty conventions, where reason and ideals are betrayed by self-interest: "Cogidos por el engranaje de esa vertiginosa máquina llamada gran ciudad, miles de seres han formado una sociedad de convencionalismos, donde la lucha por la existencia pierde su carácter de racional para convertirse en pugilato de fieras disfrazadas con máscara de virtudes ... ese medio donde las grandes ideas se achican por el interés del lucro! ... "

[Caught in the cogs of that dizzying machine called a great city, thousands of beings have formed a society ruled by convention, where the struggle for survival loses all rationality to become a contest among wild animals disguised by masks of virtue ... that environment where great ideas become small because of interest in profit!] (184). Consequently through Ramón, Acuña critiques a concept of liberal individualism that, as Mary G. Dietz explains, turns on "the notion of the rational man as a competitive individual who tends naturally to pursue his own interest and maximize his own gain." Such a paradigm is at odds with a communitarian liberalism that privileges the cultivation of virtuous reason and knowledge as restraining forces for the unprincipled pursuit of wealth (1998, 381–82).

In consonance with this ideal, Acuña proposes embracing an active life in the country that would enable the cultivation of both land and mind, and effect the recovery of a so-called state of nature. The liberal concept of a state of nature, which held that both sexes were inherently free and equal individuals, was founded on the collaborative participation of men and women in socioeconomic production and the social contract. With the rise of capitalism, that interdependent economic relationship altered, and women either competed with partners for wages, in the case of the working classes, or became men's economic dependents, as with the upper and middle classes. Such a development, Teresa Brennan and Pateman note, was a tragedy, because "at one and the same time, and as part of the same social process, liberal individualist ideas emerged that held out a promise of freedom and equality for women, yet socioeconomic changes denied that promise and reinforced patriarchy" (1998, 97).

The nuances of Acuña's critique of capitalism and modes of socioeconomic production, as evident in *El Padre Juan,* are present more fully in two substantial essays from 1882, "Influencia de la vida del campo en la familia" [Influence of Country Life on the Family] and "El lujo en los pueblos rurales" [Luxury in Rural Villages]. While in "Influencia" Acuña stresses the importance of a country environment for the development of reason and women's participation in the social economy (Acuña 1882c, 8–10), in "El lujo" she initially draws little or no distinction between the city and the rural town. Both are seen as in the thrall of a culture of consumption and driven by an immoral pursuit of luxury that, like an invasive cancer, destroys "pueblos," in the sense of both rural town and nation: "Esta carcoma, este mal invasor, repugnante siempre en los grandes centros de las naciones, y mucho más en los hogares del agricultor, es el lujo . . . esa *enfermedad moral* que aqueja á nuestros pueblos . . ." [This cancer, this invasive evil, always repugnant in the great cities of nations, and even more so in the homes of those who work the land, is luxury . . . that *moral disease* that afflicts our towns and nations] (Acuña 1882b, 141–42).[59]

Nevertheless, Acuña claims, it is in rural areas that the desire for luxury proves especially negative, because it reinforces social classes and damages the common interests of a nation that should be united behind shared goals: "[E]se lujo que como barrera infranqueable se alza entre los padres y los hijos, entre los hermanos, entre los amigos, aislando los intereses . . . y dividiendo en clases ... ¡terrible palabra tratándose de pueblos y de aldeas agricultoras! . . . deduciendo las consecuencias funestas que acarrea á los intereses de la nación . . ." [That luxury that, like an insurmountable barrier, divides parents and children, siblings, and friends, sidelining common interests . . . and producing class divisions ... what a terrible phrase when talking about towns and agricultural villages! . . . deriving in fatal consequences detrimental to the nation's interests] (142).[60] The vain emulation by rural inhabitants of affluent city dwellers has led, Acuña maintains, to the devaluing of agricultural work, the exploitation of the soil, and the neglect of Spain's superlative natural resources (148–54). Inappropriate cultivation of the land is rendered synonymous with the lack of culture within the nation. As a consequence, the nation is not self-sufficient, neither in terms of agricultural products nor literature, having to import the former from its colonies and the latter from foreign countries (154, 163).

Hope for the nation, Acuña asserts, can only lie in "el pueblo alejado de la capital" [the village far away from the capital], which should ideally represent "el perfecto estado de gracia de la existencia" [the perfect state of grace in existence]. There humanity, learning from nature's example, may reach "las cumbres de la racionalidad" [the heights of rationality] and agriculture might fulfil its potential with the aid of science: "[E]l poder del trabajador incansable, que estudiando en las veladas del invierno . . . los libros de agricultura que la experiencia y la observación entregan á la publicidad, realizara en sus heredades las mejoras que le ofrece su aprendida ciencia" [The power of the untiring worker, who, by studying in long winter evenings . . . books on agriculture that experience and observation bring to the public's notice, might effect on his property the improvements suggested by his acquired knowledge] (146–47).[61] By removing the "pueblo," both village and nation, from capitalism and the effects of state centralization (meanings inherent in "capital"), Acuña arguably seeks to empower a socioeconomic sphere equated by Hegel with civil society and which does not fit easily into either the public or domestic realm. As Susan Moller Okin elucidates, within the distinction between state and society, civil society is categorized as private, but within the differentiation between nondomestic and domestic life, it is seen as belonging to the public sphere (1998, 117). Similar premises pertained to the place of nature within liberal thought. On the one hand, nature underwrote the equality of all human beings, regardless of their sex; on the other, it was often seen as standing in opposition to civil society (Pateman 1988, 82, 101), to be traditionally associated with Woman. As I will develop in the concluding section of my analysis, it is the inequalities inherent in the ambiguities that accompany the liberal division between the public and domestic realms that Acuña's work endeavors to address.

Throughout "El lujo," Acuña is careful to state that she is not recommending that society retreat to an imagined bucolic era nor is she idealizing absurd virtues (1882b, 159). On the contrary, an enlightened attitude toward agricultural work, together with the general relinquishing of luxury by both men and women, will bring national prosperity.[62] Increased agricultural growth, in harmony with nature, will result, Acuña optimistically heralds, in the opening up of better internal and external markets, an improved national economy, a more equal distribution of wealth, and the ultimate incorporation of a marginalized Spain into an allegedly civilized northern Europe: "[Y] repartiéndose la riqueza, se suprimirán los pobres con la disminución de los ricos, y cuando avanzando á las primeras líneas, de las cuales marchamos tan distantes, nos vean aparecer en el concurso universal de la civilización, nos harán sitio . . ." [And, with a more equal distribution of wealth, poverty will vanish as the number of rich decreases, and when we advance to the forefront, from which we are currently so distant, and other nations see us appear in the universal gathering of civilizations, they will make room for us] (1882b, 162–63). In short, it is necessary to leave behind a society of excessive consumption and petty provincialism if Spain is to win recognition by foreign countries and enter the coveted annals of civilized history: "Para lograr la honrosa calificación de nación culta en los pueblos extraños y en las páginas del historiador, es menester que se olviden esos alardes irrisorios . . . de riquezas imaginables" [In order to merit the honorable title of cultured nation among foreign nations and in the historian's pages, we must forget those ridiculous displays . . . of imaginable riches] (161–62).

In *El Padre Juan*, the liberal perception that Spain was generally isolated from major European developments and significantly inferior to northern European powers is conveyed by the extreme isolation of the village. Described as situated "a quince leguas de la primer [*sic*] carretera, y a más de veinticinco del primer ferrocarril" [fifteen leagues from the nearest road, and more than twenty-five from the nearest railway], it effectively lies "al fin del mundo" [at the ends of the earth] (Acuña 1989c, 154). Although such isolation did reflect the reality of most Asturian mountain villages, it functions for Acuña more as a symbol than as a faithful representation of Asturias at the time, which was enjoying strong economic growth and modernization due to its coal mining and manufacturing industries (Ringrose 1996, 240–42).[63] Nevertheless, as stated earlier, in an age in which possession of an empire constituted the major measuring stick of a Western nation's worth, Spain was perceived as the prime example of racial, or national, decadence among the Latin countries (Álvarez Junco 2004, 500–505).

These issues pertaining to national inferiority color, I suggest, the reasons why Acuña situates her play near Covadonga and casts Isabel as descended from Pelayo (Acuña 1989c, 132, 143). One of the last Visigoth kings, Pelayo was credited with initiating the Catholic Reconquest of Moorish Spain in the early eighth century, through his victory against the Arabs in the battle of Covadonga.[64] Personage and place, then, bear highly conservative meanings as major sources of Catholic tradition and nationhood, with characters in *El Padre Juan* describing the village as "esta cristiana aldea" [this Christian village] and Asturias as "tierra bendita" [holy land] (145, 152). During the nineteenth century, however, the Visigoth world was idealized not only by traditionalists but also by liberals for supposedly beginning the political, religious, and legal unification of Spain (Cirujano Marín, Elorriaga Planes, and Pérez Garzón 1985, 92). Moreover the term *goda* or Visigoth became identified with Spanish patriotism and the nation's struggle for freedom when it was used to refer to those Spaniards who opposed French invasion in the War of Independence.[65] These nuances are implicit in Acuña's allusion to Isabel as a "mujer de raza goda" [woman of the Visigoth race] (Acuña 1989a, 234).[66]

The intersecting concepts of national independence and unification associated with Pelayo and the Visigoths, together with their provenance from northern Spain and northern Europe, respectively, render them attractive symbols for Acuña. By identifying them with Isabel, they are not so much vehicles for a conservative nationalism as harbingers of a liberal cultural reconquest and renaissance based on an idealized northern European culture.[67] In *El Padre Juan* the subtext of the Moorish expulsion becomes equated with curing the Spanish nation of its perceived intellectual poverty and decadence, which make it akin to Africa.[68] A necessary component in such regeneration is the equal participation of all classes and both sexes in the social contract. It is to this question that I now turn in my final section concerning Acuña's work.

Of Reason, Emotion, and the Social Contract: Redressing the Domestic and Public Spheres

Social contract theory is fundamental to liberal thought. As Pateman remarks, the notion that all social relations should be based on contract was truly groundbreaking, given that it affirmed the natural equality of all human beings and their right to withhold or consent to the exchange and use of their property and person without coercion and informed by reason (1988, 39, 56). Nevertheless Pateman contends that classic contract doctrine was patriarchal, as it also insisted that women were born subjected to men and that women freely consented to their alleged natural subjection in exchange for men's protection (1988, 41). Notions regarding women's "natural" subordination to men pervade Spanish law in fin-de-siècle Spain, which expressly prohibited single women, together with deviants, minors, and foreign nationals, from legally representing others and from participating in local or national administration and government. As for the married woman, she was considered "a dependent being, but free and rational" (Scanlon 1986, 123–27); a turn of phrase that renders evident the inability of liberal thought to reconcile conservative prejudices pertaining to women with its premises of freedom and equality based on natural reason.[69]

In *El Padre Juan* Acuña examines different configurations of the social contract and its liberal corollaries—the relationships between reason and emotion, and the public and domestic spheres—through her portrayal of Ramón and Isabel. Far from representing material realities, however, Isabel and Ramón are models yet to be realized, as underlined in Acuña's "Apuntes" or notes to the play, where she states, with regard to Isabel, that "mujeres como ésa no las hay, pero así deberían ser todas" [women like her do not exist, but all women should be like her]. Similarly Ramón is "ideal, abstracto, de carne y hueso no hay ningún Ramón, pero lo habrá" [an abstract ideal; no flesh-and-blood Ramón yet exists, but one will]; Ramón is the "hombre ideal" [ideal man] and the "doctrina también ideal" [equally ideal doctrine] (Acuña 1989a, 234–35). Notwithstanding their proclaimed common function as ideals, Isabel and Ramón also serve as contrasting foils that permit Acuña to expose incongruities in liberal thought and debate the manner in which envisaged changes in Spanish society and the nation might best be wrought.

Ramón can be read as embodying an Enlightenment-inspired revolution of Spanish culture and society from "on high," as suggested by his following patronizing proclamation to the villagers: "Con la dulzura del apóstol, con la serenidad del mentor, [yo] llevaba a vuestros hogares el aura fecunda de la libertad, y . . . os sacaba de las estrechas sendas del instinto para llevaros a las cumbres de la inteligencia ... " [With an apostle's sweetness, a mentor's serenity, I brought into your homes freedom's fertile breath, and . . . I drew you away from the narrow paths of instinct to lead you to the heights of intelligence] (Acuña 1989c, 201).[70] What this meant for political liberalism in Acuña's time was not only transforming the nation through the education of the individual, as advocated by Giner de los Ríos, but effecting a simultaneous revolution of state structures, as recommended by Joaquín Costa. Both these options were present at the same time, and especially from 1881 onward with Sagasta's government, when the Institución brought greater influence to bear on political organizations (Gómez Molleda 1966, 420–23).

The notion of needed structural change is implicit in Ramón's intention to demolish the hermitage, raising in its stead edifices for social education and health. In order to implement his vision, Ramón is prepared to contract members of a politicized working class, in the form of laborers from Gijón, a socialist stronghold, who are described as "avanzados" [advanced] (Acuña 1989c, 218).[71] The play warns, however, that radical change, if effected prior to an adequate process of education to smooth the way, will be perceived as an act of violence by a conservative community and will provoke conflict. Ramón's tenacious pursuit of his ideals at all costs is inherently antagonistic, as suggested when he repeatedly describes his proposed undertaking using metaphors of war and assault: "¡Oh! todas las almas firmes en un carácter progresista, debieran unirse para ofrecerla [a la Iglesia] la batalla! ... " [Oh! All souls steadfast in progressive thinking should unite to do battle with it (the Catholic Church)!] (185) and "[u]n muro de granito se derrumba con el hierro y con el fuego" [a granite wall collapses with iron and fire] (221). Consequently when Luis learns of Ramón's determination to proceed with his plans in the face of social opposition, he qualifies his attitude as extremist, declaring: "¡Y tú hablas de violencias ajenas!" [And you talk about the violence of others!] (221). Ramón is thus represented as a figure that encapsulates both the flaws and virtues of freethinking. On the one hand, his uncompromising intransigence runs counter to Giner's thesis of nonviolence, intended to offset fanatical anticlericalism. On the other, his connection with socialism anticipates the strategic union of liberal intellectuals like Acuña with the working classes that began to manifest itself toward the beginning of the twentieth century (Gómez Molleda 1966, 426–27).[72]

In contrast to Ramón, Isabel can be seen as symbolizing more faithfully the spirit of Giner's more gradual transformation of the nation through education. Consequently she implores Ramón to delay the demolition of the hermitage, so as to allow mentalities to adjust: "La transición será suave: primero se cierra la ermita, después se derriba" [The transition will be gentle: first, close the hermitage, then demolish it]. Whereas for Ramón, "[t]oda parada, es . . . un retroceso" [any halt is . . . a retreat], for Isabel "[d]etenerse, no es renunciar al avance" [to pause does not mean abandoning the advance] (Acuña 1989c, 220). Similarly when Isabel warns him of the violence that his course of action is provoking—"¡Ramón . . . tú no sabes la agitación que hay allá abajo ... !" [Ramón . . . you're unaware of the social turmoil that exists down there!]—Ramón responds: "¡Isabel! ... ¡O a mi lado o enfrente de mí!" [Isabel! ... You're either with me or against me!] (222). Evidently what Acuña criticizes is Ramón's inability to find a reasonable compromise in accordance with a given context.

That the position that Acuña promotes as more feasible is Isabel's is not only suggested by the fact that Ramón's actions lead to his murder by Diego and other village youths, as Ramón and Luis prepare for the demolition of the hermitage. It is also intimated by her observation that the character of Isabel is "el papel más importante de la obra" [the most important role in the play] and that she is "la personificación de la mujer del porvenir, de la mujer ideal" [the personification of the woman of the future, the ideal woman] (Acuña 1989a, 233); in short, the New Woman for the new century.[73] Such a revindication is closely connected with Acuña's categorical belief that women must be included and acknowledged as full participants in the building of a liberal nation and society, as evident in her following declaration from "Valiosísima adhesion": "¡Defender la libertad de pensamiento sin contar con la mujer! ¡regenerar la sociedad y afirmar las conquistas de los siglos sin contar con la mujer! . . . ¡Imposible!" [Defend freedom of thought without counting on women! Regenerate society and affirm the victories of the centuries without counting on women! . . . Impossible!] (Acuña 1992e, 63). The reason why the type of woman that Isabel represents does not yet exist is due, Acuña states, to the contradictions at the heart of the liberal intellectual, who is a freethinker in political and cultural circles, but a conservative Catholic within his own home: "Y de aquí también esas inconcebibles contradicciones de hombres libre-pensadores en el foro, en los ateneos, en los congresos, en las profesiones, en las cátedras, en el libro: hombres libre-pensadores *intelectual*, y socialmente, y católicos fervorosos en el seno de la familia; hombres hechos *dos*" [And consequently also those inconceivable contradictions in men who are freethinkers in political forums, in Athenaeums, assemblies, their professions, university Chairs, and publications: freethinkers *intellectually* and socially, but fervent Catholics in the bosom of their family: men made *two*] (60).[74] It is this splitting of the male liberal intellectual, progressive in public and conservative in private, with which Acuña takes umbrage through Ramón. Seen in a wider context, such a split is also symptomatic of what feminist scholars have identified as the dichotomy between the public and domestic realms in liberal thought.

In *El Padre Juan* Ramón demonstrates how even the most progressive thinkers can be subject to prejudice in terms of gender and blind to incongruities in their own behavior. Hence, while in theory Ramón defends female equality, a central premise in liberal thought, he also sees women as inferior due to their supposedly emotional nature, which overwhelms reason, as apparent in his remarks about his mother: "No razona sino con el sentimiento que se desborda en ella, anegándolo todo" [She does not think rationally but is overwhelmed by floods of sentiment that drown out all else] (Acuña 1989c, 215) and "Naturalezas de mujer, llenas de amor y faltas de raciocinio" [Woman's nature, replete in love but lacking in reason] (225). Such a stance defines reason as the province of men. Women's reason is calibrated as essentially derived from, and inferior to, theirs, as is reiterated in Ramón's following comment to Isabel, which presents him as her intellectual begetter: "¡Isabel, alma de mis amores! . . . ¿No has nutrido tu corazón y tu inteligencia, con las palpitaciones de mi inteligencia y de mi corazón?" [Isabel, my dearest soul! . . . Haven't you nourished your heart and intelligence with the beatings of mine?] (213). In essence, although Ramón has enabled Isabel's intellectual development through books, he still perceives her in terms of the Romantic "Angel in the House" paradigm, calling her "¡Ángel de mi vida!" [Angel of my life!] (216).[75] Thus Ramón's attitude toward Isabel's education reflects that of many late nineteenth-century Spanish intellectuals, both men and women, who saw the strengthening of women's education as fitting them to be agreeable wives and effective mothers of future citizens, but never to enter fully the public sphere.[76]

For Acuña, women are not born into subjection but are socially inducted into their subordination to men. The greatest obstacle to the liberal project, she maintains, is the masculine construction of Woman through her unequal education, denounced in "Valiosísima adhesión."[77] There Acuña identifies women's ignorance, the cause of her excessive sensitivity or emotion, as inimical to the liberal ideals of knowledge and freedom: "¡Ah! los campeones del libre-pensamiento en España! ¿No habeis pensado con amargura que la mujer os espera en vuestros hogares con las gracias de su cuerpo, con las astucias de su ignorancia y las sutilezas de su sensibilidad, ocultando entre los encajes, ó el percal de su vestido, al enemigo de la sabiduría y de la libertad?" [Oh! Champions of free thinking in Spain! Haven't you ever thought bitterly that your wife waits for you in your home with all her physical graces, the cunning of her ignorance and the subtleties of her sensitivity, concealing in her lace, or the fabric of her dress, the enemy of knowledge and freedom?]. The stumbling block to freedom and progress, Acuña maintains in the following meditation, is the liberal construction of the domestic sphere, identified with Woman:

> "¡Qué lucha—me decía—han entablado estos hombres en pró de lo *bueno*, de lo *justo* y de lo *bello*! –¿Vencerán?"—Un velo se extendió ante mis ojos, y al disiparse, como telon de comedia de magia, se me apareció el hogar del hombre, es decir, *la mujer*, que en nuestras actuales sociedades sintetiza el hogar. . . . "Hé aquí el escollo—me dije—hé aquí el abismo profundo y erizado de abruptas aristas donde podrá caer despedazada la libertad." (1992e, 56–57)
>
> ["What a battle—I thought—these men have entered into in the name of all that is *good, just* and *beautiful*! –Will they win?" —A veil spread over my eyes, and on melting away, like the curtain in a magic show, there appeared before me man's home, or rather, *Woman*, who, in our contemporary societies embodies the home. . . . "Here is the obstacle—I thought—here is the deep abyss, bristling with jagged edges, where freedom can be shattered into tiny pieces."]

Acuña then proceeds to contextualize this engendering of ignorance by placing it alongside an analysis pertaining to social class, so as to draw an implicit comparison between the situation of women and that of the working classes, similarly disadvantaged through policies of inadequate education: "Y . . . ¿qué no se podrá decir de esas grandes masas perdidas en los abismos de la ignorancia, rebajadas por tantos siglos de tiranías, por tantos miles de años de miseria? ¡Qué no se podrá decir de esos hijos del pueblo. . . !" [And . . . what cannot be said about those great masses lost in the abysses of ignorance, downtrodden by so many centuries of tyranny, so many thousands of years of poverty? What cannot be said about those children of the nation!] (1992e, 61–62).[78]

However, fault for such neglect of women and the lower classes, Acuña stresses, also lies with women themselves, who form future generations according to religious superstition rather than the natural and social sciences: "¡Ella no puede vivir sin fé. Desconociendo la fé de la Naturaleza, de la ciencia y de la Humanidad, se aferra á la que la enseñaron en su niñez, y . . . se convierte en ariete que socaba [*sic*] el edificio del progreso y el templo de la libertad! ... " [She is incapable of living without faith. Ignorant of the faith of Nature, science and Humanity, she clings to what she was taught in her childhood, and . . . becomes the battering ram that undermines the edifice of progress and the temple of liberty!] (63). Consequently Acuña criticizes women's lack of agency, enjoining educated upper-class women like herself to educate their ignorant sisters: "¿No hay mujeres en mi pátria? ¿No hay mujeres que piensen lo que pienso y sienten [*sic*] lo que siento? ¿No hay una pléyade femenina que trabaja heroicamente para el bien de sus hermanas, para la redención de las víctimas?" [Aren't there women in my nation? Aren't there women who think what I think and feel how I feel? Isn't there a group of brilliant women who work heroically for the good of their sisters, for the redemption of victims?]. These so-called victims are also lambasted for refusing to acknowledge and take responsibility for their shortcomings: "Y esas mismas víctimas, ¿no llegarán á saber, por muy encerradas que estén en los geniceos modernos, . . . que se pelea por salvarlas, . . . y, poniendo en juego el poder de su debilidad, nos ayudarán desde aquellos rincones para la realización de la gran obra?" [And those same victims, won't they ever realize, however encloistered they may be in their modern gynaeceums, . . . that others fight to save them, . . . and, putting at risk the power derived from their weakness, won't they help us, from those isolated corners, to carry out the great work?] (64).

Furthermore if freethinking is to be regenerated from within, Acuña states that women will need to have the courage to withstand attack from those men who perceive themselves as the exclusive guardians of reason and the nation: "¿Pero acometer la obra de regeneración del libre-pensamiento no será arrostrar el sarcasmo, la sátira, la desestimación de los *prudentes*, de los *sensatos*, . . . personajes respetabilísimos en el mundo del oropel, y los cuales . . . tienen grandes influencias en mi pátria? Sí. No hay duda" [But won't undertaking the regenerative work of freethinking mean confronting sarcasm, satire and loss of esteem from the *prudent* and the *sensible*, . . . highly respectable figures in the world of pomp and ceremony, and who . . . are very influential in my nation? Yes. Undoubtedly] (64). Finally Acuña does not frame such a process within a paradigm of linear progress, in keeping with the master narrative of liberalism. On the contrary, she emphasizes the always provisional nature of the struggle against ignorance and religious superstition (67–68). It is to this struggle that men and women must equally commit, because true humanity can only be achieved by serving truth and reason: "[N]o venceremos, pero habremos servido á la razón y ceñiremos en nuestra frente la corona de humanos" [We will not win, but we will have served reason and will wear on our forehead the crown of humanity] (69). Consequently Acuña underlines that the liberal enterprise, grounded on the essential rationality of the human being, cannot succeed while it remains flawed at its very heart. Liberalism cannot see the female sex in terms of negative difference nor perpetuate the split between the domestic and public spheres, as such constructions undermine the basis of a liberal constitution and nation, premised on equal access to the public good and opportunities for all citizens.[79]

Liberal philosophy is important for obtaining greater rights for women, especially in the areas of education and law reform, given that its claim that one is human because one is rational challenges the patriarchal belief, exemplified by Ramón above, that women, due to their alleged emotional nature, cannot be fully rational beings and hence, full members of human civilization. Acuña challenges the type of reductive thinking displayed by Ramón by having both him and Isabel exhibit traits of reason and emotion. Ramón is cast as a highly Romantic, charismatic character, whose reason is often clouded by excessive passion and Romantic topoi, as exemplified in his following exclamation: "¡Destino cruel! . . . ¡Oh, madre Naturaleza! ¡Préstame fuerzas! ¡Vive en mí, según te plugo hacerme! ... Loco o héroe, que sea fiel hasta morir a la órbita que me trazaste" [Cruel fate! . . . Oh, Mother Nature! Give me strength! Live in me, as it pleased you to create me! ... Whether madman or hero, may I be faithful until death to the path that you've marked out for me] (Acuña 1989c, 216–17).[80] The dangers of allowing Romantic desire to outweigh reason are stressed to Ramón by Luis: "[M]e apena mucho verte obcecado en tus ideas, un tanto románticas y fuera del medio en que vivimos" [It really distresses me to see you so blinded by your ideas, which are somewhat Romantic and removed from the context in which we are living] (184). Moreover, despite his altruistic intentions, Ramón's behavior is ultimately selfish, with Acuña noting that "Ramón no ama a nadie más que a su obra de redención" [Ramón only loves his work of redemption] (235). Ramón thus highlights an inherent problem in liberal philosophy with its stress on the individual. His depiction as "el héroe de todos los tipos" [the epitome of the hero] (179) enables Acuña to take issue with what Michael Freeden has described as "the nineteenth-century liberal individualist iconography in which heroic entrepreneurs . . . were seen to propel society forwards" (Freeden 2005, 15). By presenting Ramón as ultimately irrational and as embodying an ethos grounded on force rather than mutual consent between social subjects, Acuña clearly implies that this model of liberalism is inappropriate for forging a democratic Spain. Indeed, to a large extent, Ramón exemplifies what Pateman terms the self-isolating "contractarian individual, [who] . . . can and must see the world and other individuals only . . . from the perspective of his self-interest" (1988, 55).

In contrast, although Isabel, too, manifests traits typical of Romantic desire, as in her search for personal freedom through love, she rejects the masculine Romantic ideals regarding Woman's contained virtue and submission. She therefore refuses the label of "Angel in the House" implicit in María's description of her as an angel (Acuña 1989c, 164), and defies her father, a symbol of "natural" authority, by initially declaring her intention to wed Ramón in a civil ceremony (200), outside the jurisdiction of the Catholic Church. The fact that civil marriage is the foundation of Ramón's and Isabel's plans to transform village society points to Acuña's vindication of the inseparability of the domestic from the public sphere. The role of emotion and love in producing social good and regenerating a "pueblo" or nation is underscored through the ideal, potentially embodied by Ramón and Isabel, of the companionate marriage and consensual love.

The significance of these models for liberal thought and its pursuit of equality has been signaled by Jones. While companionate marriage challenged the older aristocratic model of marriage for economic interests, consensual love, formalized through the marriage contract, implied "a 'contractual subjectivity' for women . . . ultimately incompatible with women's subjection. If men and women entered marriage voluntarily out of mutual regard, this implied that a woman . . . was presumably capable of other important choices and of taking responsibility for her life" (Jones 2005, 5). Such premises appear to be reflected in Acuña's Isabel, who sees her approaching civil union with Ramón, a social contract between theoretically free and equal individuals, as an alliance of passion and reason, with the power to create new worlds: "[C]uando el corazón y la inteligencia se unen, la muerte es una separación momentánea. ¡Los mundos nuevos debe crearlos el amor de dos almas semejantes! ... " [When the heart and intelligence meet, death is but a fleeting separation. New worlds must be created by the love of two kindred spirits!] (Acuña 1989c, 165).[81]

Ultimately it is Isabel who incarnates the more viable option for Acuña. Not only does she survive Ramón, but it is her emotional intelligence that makes her far more pragmatic and reasonable. Consequently her social skills prevent a fight breaking out between Ramón and other villagers at the *romería* (190) and she again calms troubled waters when she calls on female relations to remember family ties and abandon violence: "Sois de nuestra propia sangre; en nombre de tan sagrado lazo, olvidemos este suceso" [You are our blood relations; in the name of such a sacred tie, let us forget what has happened] (194). When Isabel proposes to Ramón that he postpone his plans (212), seconded by María, Luis describes the women's suggestions as prudent and reasonable: "[L]o que te van a pedir es sólo prudencia" [What they are going to ask of you is mere prudence] and "es de razón lo que piden" [what they are asking is reasonable] (219).

While Ramón can only see life in terms of Romantic extremes—"¡Heroísmos y demencias! ¡He aquí los polos de nuestra vida humana!" [Heroic deeds and mad acts! These are the extremes of our earthly lives!] (220)—Isabel stresses the importance of both emotion and reason, in keeping with a differential model of female rationality that fuses both: "Mi cariño y mi inteligencia sabrán convencer a mi padre" [My affection and intelligence will succeed in convincing my father] (219). Whereas Ramón's reason remains anchored to an obsessive ideal—"aferrado a su ideal"—(167), for Acuña Isabel embodies a more adaptable reason, "emancipada de todo dogma, de toda doctrina" [free of all dogmas and doctrines], which would constitute the distillation of the heroic achievements of past women and the intellectual contributions of contemporary illustrated women: "[P]roducto acumulado de todas las herencias de nuestras heroicas *antepasadas* y de nuestras ilustradas *presentes*" [The culmination of all the legacies of our heroic female *ancestors* and of our enlightened women *nowadays*] (Acuña 1989a, 233). Above all, what Isabel emphasizes are the relationships of mutual recognition, cooperation, and interdependency necessary for human survival and collective happiness.

These representations of Isabel and Ramón emphasize that, just as women pondered the ideal of the New Woman, they were also concerned with whether, as Elaine Showalter puts it, "the age [was] producing a New Man, the companion who would share their lives and who would evolve by their side" (1990, 49). The hesitancy that Acuña reveals regarding this possibility is intimated in Ramón's untimely disappearance from the script. Furthermore, while Isabel welcomes the prospect of a life wedded to Ramón, the play provides ample proof of her beloved's misogyny, to question whether an equal union of souls, as within the companionate framework, is truly feasible.[82] It is thus significant that the dramatic dénouement leaves Isabel single and alone, with her future as shrouded in darkness as the theater stage. Such open endings, typical of Acuña's plays, suggest both the desire to depart from known sociocultural and political plots and also the inability to see the way clear to the future.

Paramount in *El Padre Juan* is the liberal debate over how needed changes are to be effected. One option, that of a well-meaning, but ultimately patronizing, revolution from "on high," appears discarded, as suggested by Ramón's death. Another possibility, revolution by the masses, is associated with uncontrolled violence and disorder, and hence perceived as damaging to the sought-after unity of the nation. A third option, which premises national transformation on the slower process of sociocultural education, is the route preferred by the Institución and defended by Acuña's Isabel.

Conclusion

Acuña's work examines and opens up for scrutiny the diverse positionings within Moderate and Progressive liberalisms in the late nineteenth century. The desired unity of the Spanish nation aspired to by more conservative liberals is harnessed to the Progressive ideal, defended by Acuña, of federal republicanism. This decentralized political model grants greater voice and independence to the different regions that compose the nation, at the same time that it privileges their mutual cooperation and interdependence. Such a paradigm, which approximates what Iris Marion Young terms "*differentiated* citizenship" (1998, 402), affirms the need for all regions and their citizens to contract into the liberal nation while recognizing their differences and autonomy. Furthermore, within Acuña's context federal republicanism heralded important changes for women, legally and culturally second-class citizens within the public sphere, as well as for the working classes, deprived of full citizenship rights due to their lack of education and property.

It is through Acuña's female protagonists that the incongruities of a liberalism that grants only theoretical equality and natural rights to its diverse constituencies are rendered especially patent. Hence in *Tribunales de venganza* Andrea's marginalization within the plot is symbolic of a more general discrimination against women effected through the modern fraternal contract, which pays lip service to women's participation in the civic realm. Conversely, in *Amor á la patria,* Acuña emphasizes the ability of women to underwrite the sociopolitical contract through Inés and María, who demonstrate devotion to the defense of national unity over and above emotional interests. As for Isabel in *El Padre Juan,* she embodies the ideal of a nation governed by reason yet tempered by emotion or compassion, thus restoring balance to dichotomies that privilege masculine over feminine and public over domestic spheres. Nevertheless it is significant that, with the exception of Andrea, Acuña's female protagonists are women who are either widowed, as in the case of Inés, or still to be married, as exemplified by María and Isabel. Acuña therefore manages to skirt the difficulties for married women inherent in a social contract premised both on women's natural subjection to men and also on their freedom and equality.

Another noteworthy factor in Acuña's work is her stress on the economic independence of all her protagonists, male and female. This aspect has major implications for the real equality of classes and genders, given that economic independence was a fundamental requirement for citizenship. However, also consistently critiqued by Acuña is the liberal premise of individualism taken to an extreme and manifest in the social economy through unregulated capitalism, seen to intensify rather than mitigate class divisions. Hence Acuña foregrounds embracing a life in greater consonance with nature, emblematic of the liberal state of nature on which equality is premised, so as foster relationships of cooperation, not competition, among social classes. She posits that nature and civil society are not antithetical states but necessarily contingent.

Despite their aspirations for social and gender equality, however, Acuña's works prove unable to integrate convincingly the lower classes, other "races" and women into the Progressive liberal project for Spain's transformation. Traditional prejudices, the nation's calamitous lack of scientific education and cultural capital, and the inability of elite social groups to find common ground from which to address satisfactorily the needs of the socially disadvantaged, present Spain with an impasse beyond which, like Acuña's Isabel, liberal intellectuals cannot easily move.

Whereas Acuña revindicates the ideals associated with Spain's first attempt at republicanism, the poetic work of Ángela Figuera, the subject of Part 2, constitutes an elegy for the spirit of the Second Republic, brought to an untimely end by the victory of Franco's Nationalist forces in 1939. The fears held by late nineteenth-century liberal intellectuals like Acuña with regard to the negative impact of the Catholic Church on Spanish politics, culture, and society are shown to be justified in the right-wing brand of national identity generated by the National Catholicism of the Franco dictatorship. As I will develop, it is to a relentless undermining of the gendered, exclusionary principles of the Franco regime and to the narration of dissident histories that Figuera's poetry is dedicated.

Part 2
The Spanish Civil War and Franco Dictatorship: History as Trauma and Wound in Ángela Figuera's Poetic Work

> Mujer de carne y verso me declaro,
> pozo de amor y boca dolorida,
> pero he de hacer un trueno de mi herida
> que suene aquí y ahora, fuerte y claro.
>
> "Aunque la mies más alta dure un día,"
>
> —Figuera 1986, 284

> [Woman of flesh and verse I declare myself,
> a well of love and suffering mouth,
> but I must fashion a thunderclap from my wound
> that may resonate here and now, loud and clear.]

Narratives of Trauma

In 1940, the year following the victory of Nationalists over Republicans in the Spanish Civil War, the Exhibition for the Reconstruction of Spain was held in Madrid. On display there was the Fresco of Destruction, depicting the Nationalist vision of the sociopolitical fragmentation of Spain allegedly arising from the Second Republic and the Civil War, and its claim to eliminate it.[1] In this Fresco, the map of Spain, placed centerstage, is partitioned into white and red areas. The colors of the medieval crusade, here they symbolize the Nationalist and Republican causes respectively: a holy crusade waged by Catholic Christianity against red communism. On the side of "White" Spain stands the figure of the Virgin Mary, in an attitude reminiscent of prayer, holding Christ's amputated right (and writing) hand. On the side of "Red" Spain kneels the disciple John, about to stand and cross the intervening space bearing the crucified Christ, symbolic of the imagined destruction wrought by communism.

This act of restoring Christ to his Mother, the Fresco suggests, is one with the Nationalist resurrection and reunification of Spain, a sacred site and Holy Family separated unnaturally by Republican politics. As intimated by the apocalyptic figures in the upper half of the Fresco and by John, author of the book of Revelation that foretells the Apocalypse, the Franco regime represents itself as inaugurating a postapocalyptic age that denies further historical change,[2] and reduces competing national identities to what Amartya Sen terms "singular affiliation" (2006, 20). The destruction that informs the title and content of the Fresco, and that is equated with the devastation allegedly caused by the defeated Republicans, is to be superseded by its opposite of reconstruction, synonymous with the Nationalist victory.[3]

At the same time, the split at the center of national space and time in the Fresco encapsulates the historical trauma produced by the Civil War and its aftermath. Concepts of split, rupture, and fissure are common to the description of trauma, with Shoshana Felman, for instance, explaining that trauma is "a shock that creates a psychological split or rupture" (2002, 171). Moreover images of fragmentation powerfully illustrate the processes suffered by the trauma survivor, who, as Susan Brison declares, "experiences a figurative dismemberment—a shattering of assumptions, a severing of past, present, and future, a disruption of memory" (1999, 48).

The tension present in the Fresco between fissure and unification, openness and closure, enacts the concept of trauma as a wound to the physical and psychic self. As Cathy Caruth puts it, trauma "is always the story of a wound that cries out, that addresses us in the attempt to tell us of a reality or truth that is not otherwise available. This truth, in its delayed appearance and its belated address, cannot be linked only to what is known, but also to what remains unknown in our very actions and our language" (1996, 4). The gap or void at the center of the Fresco unwittingly reveals the breakdown of coherent meaning that characterizes traumatic memory. The historical event that produces trauma is experienced after a temporal delay, in belated fashion. Unable to be located in any definite space or time, the trauma constitutes what Caruth calls a "symptom of history," in that those traumatized carry inside them "an impossible history . . . that they cannot entirely possess" (1995, 5). Their history, therefore, is one that they cannot completely open nor close.

Traumatic memory of the Civil War from the perspective of a defeated Spain in the 1950s and 1960s under the Franco dictatorship is the theme to which the poetry of dissident Basque writer, Ángela Figuera, constantly returns. During the Second Republic Figuera identified with its policies of social, cultural, and political reform and became a secondary school teacher. Throughout the Civil War, she supported the Republican cause and her husband fought for its fragile democracy. However, on the victory of the Nationalists in 1939, Figuera was stripped of her teaching position for life, in accordance with the repressive policies leveled by the dictatorship at its political opponents. For the duration of the regime, then, Figuera joined the ranks of those dissidents classified officially as Anti-Spain. Figuera's forced retirement to the home for political motives was also colored by issues pertaining to gender. The regressive ideals of Spanish womanhood promulgated by the regime returned women to a social, cultural, and legal situation regulated by the 1889 Civil Code of Napoleonic origin (Scanlon 1986, 320–28). The model to be emulated was that of the Virgin Mary, who embodied the traits of abnegation and purity paraded by the dictatorship as essential not only for Spanish women but also for its nation-state. Positioned by reason of politics and gender both within and outside the Spanish nation, it is from the limits of Francoist politics and thought that Figuera will argue for a different vision of Spanish identity.

Despite the restrictions placed on her gender and the inevitable censorship that coerced literary production, Figuera's first volume of poetry was published in 1948.[4] For the next decade, her work was well-received by the literary establishment, given that her early publications center on maternal themes that apparently concur with the regime's exaltation of the chaste mother.[5] Nevertheless, as Roberta Quance has incisively indicated, Figuera's work deploys a "maternal politics" that constitutes "a discourse contesting hunger, poverty, violence, oppression, war" (1986, 14). This evaluation is shared by Jo Evans (1996), who develops in depth the feminist implications of Figuera's stance.[6] It is on the readings of such scholars that my own analysis of Figuera's work will build.

Figuera's semantic warfare against the symbolic capital of the regime becomes more pronounced in her poetry from 1958 onward, the year in which her collection, *Belleza cruel* [Cruel Beauty], was published in Mexico, due to Spanish censorship. Around the same time, Figuera also began to work as a translator, which supplemented the income earned as a part-time librarian at the National Library in Madrid. Subsequent to the 1962 publication of her collection entitled *Toco la tierra: Letanías* [I Touch the Earth: Litanies], Figuera practically ceased writing, except for short pieces for children.[7]

With the experiences of the defeated Spain denied public expression, Figuera's compositions work against an imposed historical amnesia. Her poetry inflects differently the figures and themes present in the Nationalist Fresco of Destruction—Christ and Mary, the Apocalypse, and Day of Judgment—as well as key moments in their histories: the Annunciation, Christmas, the Crucifixion, and the Resurrection. Standing for what is held sacred by distinct sociocultural and political groups, these representations enact the narratives of triumph and trauma that conform the fractured but contingent identities of two Spains: that of the victorious and that of the conquered.

Figuera's recourse to those same symbols and images that formed the cornerstone of Francoist National Catholicism could well be considered ineffective for conveying counterhistories. By drawing on Catholic symbols, however, Figuera taps into a powerful affective reservoir of Spanish national and cultural identity. Her reconfigurations of these symbols not only remind us that memory depends on the availability of forms and narratives peculiar to a given culture.[8] Her representations also allow her to voice dissident memories censored by official historiography, while framing them within sanctioned parameters. Although disempowered politically and socially, Figuera employs religious themes and figures to bestow on her poetic personae the moral authority to reveal disallowed historical truths.

Furthermore, in a right-wing political climate that deployed Catholic belief as an indispensable condition for membership of the Spanish nation, Figuera's use of Catholic symbolism challenges the Francoist relegation of Republicans, labeled atheists because of their socialist beliefs, to the category of stateless persons, the enemy occupants of an imaginary Anti-Spain. Santos Juliá sums up this situation as follows: "If the State defined itself as national, for that same reason it had to identify itself as Catholic, since not to be Catholic was not to be national, to be the anti-Spain or anti-*patria*" (2004, 310). These simplistic Francoist correspondences overlooked the multiple and often contradictory interleavings of layers of identity, which made it perfectly possible for Republicans to be devout Catholics and lovers of their nation.[9]

Undeniably Figuera's utilization of a symbolic system dominant in Francoist representations of history and nation can be read in terms of disidentification, defined by Shannon Bell as a perversion and displacement of hegemonic discourses, through giving their elements new meanings (Bell 1994, 14). Such a transformation depends on a process of semantic shadowing, which permits the original texts being displaced to remain visible despite the insertion of differences into them. At the same time, and of equal importance, Figuera's employment of hegemonic Catholic imagery and symbols serves to encourage emotional identification with the subject matter by a much wider social group than the immediate victims of trauma. As Jeffrey C. Alexander has stipulated, "[o]nly if the victims are represented in terms of valued qualities shared by the larger collective identity will the audience be able to symbolically participate in the experience of the originating trauma" (2004b, 14). Figuera's poetry heralds such a possibility, inviting contemporary readers to confront and reevaluate experiences of trauma, radicated in the Civil War and Franco regime, that affected, albeit to differing degrees, much of the Spanish population.

In the discussion that follows, I propose to explore how the Franco regime founded its national narrative on a particular deployment of Catholic paradigms that functioned to close off the histories, memories, spaces, and figurative bodies associated with Republican Spain. In contrast, Figuera's poetry reinflects these paradigms, to recount the repressed history of the liberal Spain defeated in the Civil War. Hence the early sections of my analysis will focus on contested visions of national time and space. Subsequently I develop how Figuera reworks those representations of Christ and Mary favored by the regime, in order to confuse the exclusive identities essential to the dictatorship's social and political composition. I will argue that in Figuera's poetry Mary's transition from Virgin to Mother of Compassion and the poet's increasing emphasis on a female Christ, crucified or in exile, testify to the suffering and marginalization inflicted by the regime on its feminized dissidents. Figuera's Mary and Christ become symbols, I will stress, of a hybrid discourse that challenges monologic and monolithic sociopolitical systems, opening them up for examination and judgment.

Reconfiguring Francoist Time

National histories frequently construct collective identity by taking their bearings from what Alexander describes as "injuries that cry out for revenge" (2004b, 8). Both Nationalist and Republican histories were fashioned according to contrasting models of trauma. For the Nationalists, their trauma resided in the secularization of society, the alleged fragmentation of national unity, and the perceived attack on traditional class privileges by the Second Republic. For the Republicans, their trauma can be said to derive from the assault, through the Nationalist coup d'état, on the principles of popular sovereignty and legal consensus that underpinned their fledgling democracy. In both cases, significant damage was inflicted on sociocultural and political premises held as sacred for the identities of their particular constituencies.

One of the ways in which Republican and Nationalist paradigms of national identity procured their moral authority was by casting their respective legends in terms of two different moments in the Passion of Christ: namely, his Crucifixion and Resurrection. For both Nationalists and Republicans, Christ's crucified body became the symbol of a nation torn by political conflict, while his resurrection was synonymous with the hoped-for dawning of a new era. Nevertheless the historical narratives owned by these respective groups manifest diverging temporal frames. According to the Republican narrative, the Civil War initiated the suffering of Christ's Passion, which would not end until after the Franco dictatorship itself. This legend coexisted with that of the Fall, whereby Republican Spain was cast out of its Eden of democratic government by the Nationalist uprising (Labanyi 1989, 45). The recovery of such an Eden would not depend, as for the Nationalists, on the nostalgic return to and reinstating of an idealized past. Rather, as in the narrative of the Apocalypse and in Figuera's poetry, it would rely on transforming a troubled historical present into a better future, in a metaphorical transcendence of Eden.[10]

For the Nationalists, in contrast, the Republican years constituted Spain/Christ's betrayal, Calvary, and death. Consequently it was the Nationalist uprising or *Alzamiento,* identified with Christ's Resurrection and Spain's Liberation, that signaled the first step toward reunifying a Spain seen as threatened by imminent destruction, due to Basque and Catalan demands for secession. Fear of Spain's political dismemberment and the need for reunification featured prominently in Falangist writings throughout the early 1930s. Emblematic of this stance is Ernesto Giménez Caballero, who, in *Genio de España* (1932), accuses the Second Republic of causing Spain's "última desvertebración" or ultimate collapse. There Giménez Caballero underlines the need to reshape a feminized, lax body politic that has exceeded ideal proportions—"to encorset . . . these broken, loose limbs"—indicating that the means to unification is fascism, described as "Catholicism" (quoted by Rodríguez Puértolas 1987, 64).

Thus, throughout the Civil War, the Nationalists represented themselves as performing a work of redemption, enabling Basques and Catalans to overcome their separatist leanings and once again become Spaniards: "It is necessary to bring Bilbao and Barcelona loftier realities than those that Basques and Catalans might achieve through their separatist aims. . . . Then Spain will be Great and Free by being One, and Basques and Catalans will—once again—be proud to call themselves Spaniards."[11] Equivalences drawn between the resurrection of the nation and that of Christ are patent in the speech delivered by the Francoist ideologue, José María Pemán, to celebrate the Nationalist victory over the Republican cause in Seville in July 1936: "The severe Lent of our Homeland has finally passed. Today the purple veil that was thrown over its true face has been torn away. Today is the Easter of Spain's resurrection."[12] Although it is the religious implications of the color purple that Pemán exploits, it also possesses unmistakable political overtones. One of the three colors in the Republican red, yellow, and purple flag, purple had long been associated with the liberalism of the Comuneros and the First Republic (Álvarez Junco 2004, 554).

For the Nationalists, Spain's figurative crucifixion and resurrection became embodied in two fundamental political figures. One was the Falangist leader, José Antonio Primo de Rivera, whose execution in the Republican-held prison of Alicante in 1936 served both to signal the waning of the Falange's power and also to enshrine its founder as Christ-like martyr (Labanyi 1989, 36). Hence, according to Dionisio Ridruejo, the sacrifice of José Antonio, a "word able to bring together all parts of Spain," made possible Spain's redemption, since he came, like Christ to earth, "to die on the cross."[13] Such a representation is but one of many on a similar theme, whereby Spain "has forever bound herself to Christ."[14] The other key figure was the victorious Franco, cast as a resurrected Christ arising from José Antonio's grave as the "saviour of Spain and Maker of her future History."[15]

The temporal stages symbolized by José Antonio and Franco were continued in the distinction established between an "Evangelical Era" under José Antonio and a "Triumphant Era" under General Franco.[16] Such rhetoric allowed Francoist Spain to represent itself as originating a new historical epoch, to establish what Benedict Anderson has referred to as "a profound rupture with the existing world" (1991, 193). Hence Nationalist time was measured from the date of the uprising to parallel directly the recording of Christian history from the year of Christ's birth.[17] In turn, the Nationalist victory was represented as the culmination of an ascensional history that completed the imperial, Catholic destiny of Spain.

The effects of these processes on historical memory have been amply documented by Rafael R. Tranche and Vicente Sánchez-Biosca in their analysis of time and memory in the Francoist propaganda newsreels known as No-Do, produced from 1943 to 1981. Due to the Nationalist collapsing of an imperial past into the present, time became synchronic and mythical, defined by key words devoid of precise historical references, such as *Cruzada, Alzamiento, Imperio,* and *Caudillo* [Crusade, Uprising, Empire, Leader]. Such an absence of dates and hence of precisely locating occurrences in time and space, worked against any contextual representation of dissident political acts, such as strikes, student revolts, terrorist attacks, and political assassinations (Tranche and Sánchez-Biosca 2002, 113, 240). By portraying events as reiterations of past glories, history as change was denied and reduced to an endless, seamless cycle of the same. Consequently, as Herzberger has affirmed with regard to Francoist historiography, "time (history) is perceived not as a progression or a becoming, but rather as a static entity anchored in all that is permanent and eternal" (1995, 33).

Conversely, for the dissident memory given voice in Figuera's work, the Nationalist victory and ensuing Franco régime constitute a "ground zero" that registers the physical and symbolic erasure of the

Second Republic and all associated with it. Thus time is now measured by concepts such as exile, alienation, absence, and death. Although also drawing on a paradigm of resurrection similar to that in Nationalist rhetoric, Figuera's poems, as I will elucidate, resist bringing history to closure, stressing instead its always incomplete, dynamic nature.

One of the principal means by which the Franco dictatorship measured historical time, as documented by Tranche and Sánchez-Biosca, was through its religious festivals, especially those of Christmas and Easter, which mark the birth and Passion of Christ. Representations of the "Christmas cycle" of Christmas Eve, Christmas Day, and Epiphany permitted the regime to emphasize two primary concepts. One turned on the ideal warmth and unity of the family, envisaged as a microcosm of Francoist Spain. The other stressed the innocence of the child, which symbolized the imagined purity of the Spanish people but also unwittingly connoted their political infantilization. While the rural scenarios of Christmas foregrounded a rhetoric of charity that did little to alter social inequities, representations of Epiphany, set in urban contexts, highlighted the nation's supposed economic recovery, denying the hardship of the 1940s and 1950s. Not coincidentally, Christmas Day was also the moment when Franco virtually entered Spanish homes, through radio broadcasts and later, television, to deliver his annual speech as *Caudillo* or *Jefe del Estado* [Head of State]. This event recalled, in idealized fashion, the year just past and looked forward to an equally homogeneous future. Above all, its discourse of peace and goodwill belied ongoing ideological divisions (Tranche and Sánchez-Biosca 2002, 539–49). In a sense, it can be argued, the birth of Christ signified the moment when the regime yet again gave birth to itself, in a constant reiteration of unchanging values. Such mythical repetitions served to close history off from open interrogation and proved, as Michael Richards points out, "deeply reassuring in the maintenance of traditions, of the possession of history, for particular groups" (1998, 7).

The temporal spaces of Christmas and Epiphany occupy a privileged position in many of Figuera's poems. There, however, the semantic patterns deployed by the regime are undone to expose the lack of charity, peace and goodwill in Spain. The birth of the Christ-child no longer stands for the continuation of an immovilist history in a static present. Instead Figuera's representations insert differences into this history, and with them, contingency and change. Consequently "Niño con rosas" [Child with Roses] from *Belleza cruel* (1958), relates how a child is born with roses for eyes. Through the association of roses with the wounds of the crucified Christ,[18] the implied Nativity scene of the birth of Christ is collapsed into the Passion of his death, overturning the Francoist historical paradigm of national rebirth. Except for the mother, all the middle-class family members view such a miraculous occurrence with horror and reject the child. The family, representative of the Francoist state, is shown to adhere to principles of excessive social order, stressed through the satirical reiteration of meaning in practically synonymous adjectives such as "decente," "comedida," "honesta," "respetable," and "discreta" in the opening stanza [decent, circumspect, honest, respectable, discreet]. This rigid sociopolitical body is challenged by the child's tears, which cannot be contained, suggesting a perspective of compassion with pain and suffering: "El seguía llorando por sus rosas. Seguía / dulcemente llorando" [He continued crying for his roses. He continued / sweetly crying] (Figuera 1986, 209).[19]

In similar fashion, Figuera's reworking of the temporal space of Epiphany questions the regime's discourses of socioeconomic recovery and foregrounds the class war that underpins the dictatorship. In "Carta abierta" [Open Letter], also from *Belleza cruel,* the context of the traditional letter written by children to the three Wise Men serves to expose the material want in Francoist Spain. Stressed in the title, "Carta abierta," is the implication that its author, one Segundo López, is petitioning on behalf of others in his situation, and that their common history of social injustice awaits response and redress. Significantly Segundo is a carpenter who, because of his trade, identifies with Jesus as Carpenter, a common figurehead for trade unionism during the French Second Republic.[20] As a result, Segundo's missive is not addressed to one of the Wise Men, figures of authority and social privilege, nor to Christ as the Nationalist "Cristo-Rey" [Christ the King], but to Jesus of Nazareth, the son of God. The fact that both Christ and Segundo are workers or "obreros" invites the poem to be placed within the context of socialism, represented by the outlawed Partido Socialista Obrero Español (PSOE, Spanish Socialist Workers' Party) and symbolized by the rose. Denouncing the hardships still widespread in Spain in the late 1950s,[21] Segundo urges Jesus to share in and witness the existential conditions of his class:

No sé cómo andaría en aquel tiempo
lo de vivir del tajo y ser un pobre,
pero lo que es ahora es un milagro
mayor que el de los panes y los peces
poner algo en la mesa y repartirlo
para que llegue a todos. Haz la prueba.
(Figuera 1986, 226)

[I don't know how it might have been in those times / to live from hand to mouth and be poor, / but what nowadays is a miracle / greater than that of the loaves and the fishes / is to put something on the table and eke it out / so that it might go around everyone. Just try it.]

In such an environment of social exploitation, religious hypocrisy and political censorship, it would be impossible, Segundo intimates, for Christ to effect miracles, given that circumstances under Franco are harsher than those experienced by Christ in his own times:

. . . Y sal por los caminos
y ponte a predicar como solías
contra los fariseos . . .
. . . .
y echa a los mercaderes de la iglesia,
y a ver qué pasa. . . .
. . . .
Si no te crucifican como entonces
es porque ahora, apenas se abre el pico
te hacen callar. Bonita está la cosa.
(226)

[And go out on the road / and begin preaching like you used to / against the Pharisees . . . / . . . / and throw the traders out of the temple, / and see what happens. / . . . / If they don't crucify you like before / it's because now, as soon as you open your trap / they make you shut it. What a pretty pass.]

Through a series of colloquial sayings that capture the voice of an uneducated people, such as "se abre el pico" [you open your trap] and "Bonita está la cosa" [What a pretty pass], the poem attests to social protest that is violently squashed: "[T]e hacen callar" [they make you shut up]. Nevertheless, while the poem suggests that effective retaliation is, for the moment, futile, given the daily struggle for survival experienced by the dispossessed,[22] it also foregrounds a coded dissidence that fuels revolution: "Pero es ya mucho machacar el hierro. / Luego se pone al rojo y se arma una" [But enough striking of the iron. / Then it becomes red-hot and feeds revolution] (227).

These descriptions of the fraught circumstances obtaining in Francoist Spain can be seen to function in Figuera's poem in analogous fashion to similar depictions in the postwar novels of social realism. As Herzberger maintains, social realist novels reveal a historical present of dire experiences and a past from which writers and characters feel excluded (1995, 41). As with Figuera's poetry, these narratives, Herzberger continues, are "placed in the service of the unforgettable (i.e., countermyths of poverty, isolation, alienation, and the like), which the State plainly set out both to annul and to forget. . . . Hence the present, rather than emerge as the inevitable or final outcome of a completed history shaped by postapocalyptic order and truth (as the State would have it), becomes . . . the inaugural force of a history that implies a past of divergence and a future of dissent" (1995, 45).

In Figuera's poem, the final emphasis on the act of petitioning and signing places the letter within a legal framework that restores visibility to the victims of sociopolitical crimes and grants them a narrative space from which to articulate a history founded on premises of equality: "De obrero a obrero te lo pido y firmo" [From one worker to another I request this and sign] (Figuera 1986, 227). Hence the signature of "Segundo López" with which the poem ends must be understood in the sense explained by Elizabeth Grosz, for whom "[t]he trace of the signature . . . is an effect of the text's mode of materiality, . . . an effect of a labor, a work on and with signs, a collaborative (even if hostile) labor of writing and reading" (1995, 20). Segundo's letter constitutes such a material process, situated within specific modes of social, economic, and political production. As suggested by his first name, these modes emphasize a second or different history. As intimated by his common surname, López, they refer to experiences known to all the defeated.

The theme of Epiphany is also prominent in another of Figuera's poems, "A Baltasar Lobo después de haber visto su 'Maternidad'" [To Baltasar Lobo after Having Seen His "Maternity"]. Here the word-play inherent in the first name of the exiled Spanish artist, Baltasar Lobo, connotes one of the three Wise Men. Lobo's sculpture of the Virgin and Child, entitled "Maternidad," becomes a gift of hope and new life to a Spain in inner exile, making him a "Rey Mago prodigioso cargado de presentes" [marvelous Wise Man, laden with presents] (Figuera 1986, 330). Returning to Spain on a visit from Paris at Epiphany in 1959, Lobo, figuratively cast as a Virgin wreathed in smiles and tenderness, brings with him the twenty-year-old memory of Republican Spain, incarnate in his Christ-child:

> Llegaste, Baltasar en la fecha precisa;
> . . . .
> . . . estabas a veinte años,
> a veinte odios, a veinte dolores de distancia.
> Y nos llegaste intacto, vestido de sonrisas,
> caliente de ternuras. Y nos trajiste al Niño.
> (330)

[You arrived, Baltasar, on that very date; / . . . / . . . you were twenty years away, / twenty hatreds, twenty sorrows. / And you came to us intact, wreathed in smiles, / warm with tenderness. And you brought us the Child.]

Lobo's rendition of the Christ-child symbolizes the turning of a fresh page in Spain's history, imagined as free from the imprint and memories of the recent past: "Y en su menudo rostro, sin rasgos ni recuerdos / soñamos y leemos la nueva faz de España" [And in his tiny countenance, free of defining features and memories / we dream of and read the new face of Spain] (331). That the child represents a love that might erase the hatred among Spaniards is reinforced through Figuera's epigraph from Miguel de Unamuno's novel, *Abel Sánchez*: "Por qué he vivido odiándome; / por qué aquí todos vivimos / odiándonos. / Pero ... traed al niño" [Because I've lived hating myself; / because here we all live / hating one another. / But ... bring forth the child] (330).

The thematics of rebirth and the use of dates as sites of memory are especially evident in two memorialistic, commemorative poems by Figuera, centered on the date of 1962. Underlying this temporal choice can be glimpsed the writer's contestation of the celebration, scheduled by the regime for 1964, of the twenty-five years of peace allegedly brought to Spain as a result of the Nationalist victory.[23] This uneasy conflation between peace and legitimized military action had already been signaled in 1961, when the regime had also celebrated twenty-five years since the outbreak of war. One year later, in June 1962, this "peace" campaign, the greatest exercise in propaganda in the entire dictatorship (Aguilar 2002, 112), became a focus for dissent with the so-called Munich conspiracy, when members of the opposition within and without Spain revindicated a reconciliation between the two Spains (Tranche and Sánchez-Biosca 2002, 423–24).[24] Contradicting, however, the official rhetoric of peace were the summary sentences passed in the early 1960s on enemies of the state,[25] the miners' strikes of 1962, and, Rafael Abella states, a police presence so intense that it suggested a country under occupation (1984, 261). Given the ambiguity surrounding the celebrations of 1961 and 1964, it should hardly be surprising that it was during the three intervening years, as Paloma Aguilar notes, that No-Do dedicated most space to consolidating the official memory of the Civil War (2002, 54).

The repeated presence in Figuera's poems of the date of 1962, whether implied or voiced, arguably functions as a site of dissident memory, driving a wedge into a time occupied by the regime and opening up space for the emergence of counterhistories. To the temporal borders of homogeneous tradition, such a narrative counterposes the contested performance of the nation's present, in the sense specified by Homi Bhabha (1990a, 300, 306). One such site of memory can be observed in Figuera's "Romance de Puebloespaña" [Romance of the Spanish People], significantly subtitled "(1962)" and dedicated to the "huelguistas de mayo" [May strikers] (Figuera 1986, 323).

The poem opens by portraying the destruction of the Civil War and the repression by the ensuing dictatorship in mythical terms:

Después del plomo y el rayo,
la cárcel y la mordaza.
Después de la vida en juego,
túneles de suerte amarga.
(323)

[After the lead and lightning, / the prison and gag. / After life on the line, / tunnels of bitter fate.]

Here Figuera uses myth as the preparatory setting for another legendary moment, the Day of Judgment, that will mark the end of history as humankind knows it. This framework of promised justice is, at the same time, set within precise historical coordinates: namely, 1962, when strikes and civil disturbances in the mining areas of Asturias and the Basque country led to the regime declaring a state of emergency for three months in Álava, Vizcaya, and Guipúzcoa (Abella 1984, 241).[26] Protesting against the repression of the striking Asturian miners was Figuera, who in 1961 and 1962 was among the one hundred and one writers and intellectuals who signed two letters addressed to Manuel Fraga Iribarne, then minister of information (Bengoa 2002, 121).

This was not the first time that the mines, traditional centers for radical revolution, had been singled out for Francoist repression. Immediately after the Civil War, as Richards indicates, the mines were systematically purged by the imprisonment and execution of thousands of miners, acts to which Figuera alludes as follows: "Si todos vimos su sangre / correr por calles y plazas, / llorar por los paredones" [But we all saw their blood / stream through streets and squares, / shed before the firing squads] (Figuera 1986, 323). Subsequently prisons were constructed next to coal mines, so that political prisoners could "redeem" themselves through forced labor (Richards 1998, 81–83).

Within the poem, the date of 1962 interrupts this cycle of repression, transforming the miners' historical death into resurrection, and their enforced silence into articulated demands for justice:

Mayo de mil novecientos
sesenta y dos: algo pasa:
aquellos fieles difuntos
del gran funeral de España
se han puesto de pronto en pie
con un grito en la garganta
que, en Asturias y en Vasconia,
alza en vilo las montañas.
Son mil, veinte mil, cien mil ...
Uno a uno se levantan
y, juntos, echan a andar,
pisan recio, exigen, mandan.
(Figuera 1986, 323)

[May 1962: / something is happening: / those faithful dead / of Spain's great funeral / have suddenly stood up / with a cry in their

> throats / that, in Asturias and the Basque country, / places the mountains on alert. / There are one thousand, twenty thousand, a hundred thousand ... / One by one they rise up / and, together, begin walking, / their step firm, they demand, they command.][27]

In contrast to the destruction of the Civil War—"Si se trizaron sus huesos, / si se les negó hasta el alma" [But they minced up their bones, / even denied them their soul] (323)—this is envisaged as a revolution effected without bloodshed, with the miners' hands symbolizing the inextinguishable hopes held by the working classes:

> Manos desnudas, vacías
> de cuchillos y de balas.
> Manos de hierro y carbón
> ardiendo con esperanza.
> (324)

> [Unarmed hands, empty / of knives and guns. / Hands of iron and coal / burning with hope.]

The revindication of justice by the disadvantaged is reinforced by the poem's emphasis on the month of May. May not only connotes May 1 or Labor Day, the feast when all workers traditionally reaffirm their rights and which regularly served as a ritualistic focus for dissident resistance during the Franco regime (Richards 1998, 157).[28] May also recalls another moment in Spanish history when the lower classes rose up against the foreign invader: the allegedly founding moment of modern Spanish nationalism, May 1808, commemorated by Goya's paintings *The Second of May 1808* and *The Third of May 1808*. Given that Francoist rhetoric drew on these events to depict the Civil War in terms of a "new War of Independence, a new Reconquest, a new expulsion of Moors,"[29] Figuera's work again challenges an official historiography by modifying the key elements on which it depends.

By recording the miners' strikes in 1962, Figuera also implicitly commemorates another moment in history when miners' strikes were severely repressed, albeit then under the Republican government: the Asturian strikes of October 1934. Through this subtext the poet moves away from a Manichean view of history that would equate the Franco regime with evil and the Republican dissidents with good. Rather history is represented as a battleground between those with the sociopolitical and economic power to defend their interests and those who cannot. The poem thus points to the contradictions inherent in hegemonic orders that claim to represent the underprivileged while simultaneously silencing them. At the same time, however, it is significant that it was Franco who was informally placed in charge of quelling the 1934 miners' revolt, to be labeled thereafter by the left the "butcher of Asturias" (Preston 1993, 103–5, 123). In this sense, the policies of systematic violence characteristic of the Nationalist Crusade during the Civil War are presented in Figuera's poem as beginning well before 1936.[30]

Silence, however, is not only the product of fear and censorship, but also of resistance and secret meanings. According to Figuera's poetic voice, the dead miners of 1934 live on in those of 1962 to become ghosts or revenants that, unacknowledged, continue to haunt Spanish history:

> Aquellos muertos de ayer
> —polvo de historia enterrada—
> son éstos mismos de hoy:
> el pueblo que sufre y calla;
> que duerme pero no muere;
> nuestro pueblo, PUEBLOESPAÑA.
> (Figuera 1986, 324)

> [Those dead yesterday / —dust of buried history— / are these same ones today: / the people that suffers in silence; / that sleeps but does not die; / our people, THE PEOPLE OF SPAIN.][31]

Silence is not death but slumber, from which a Spain that defends the causes of its working classes will awake. Hence the coded theme of Judgment Day refers to a future time when, as Felman remarks, "the past [will] come into full possession of its meaning: a meaning in which even the expressionless of history (the silence of the victims, the muteness of the traumatized) will come into historical expression" (2002, 14–15).

The date of 1962 again serves as a site of memory in "Carta de cumpleaños a Rafael Alberti" [Birthday Letter to Rafael Alberti], written on the occasion of the poet's sixtieth birthday. The private celebration of birth among friends, in itself a commemorative ritual, becomes a means of recording a history of united dissidence against the regime. At the same time that Figuera congratulates an Alberti in exile on turning sixty, each year of his life becomes representative of a continued defiance of death and, by inference, the dictatorship, connoted by the symbol of the axe: "[S]esenta años son sesenta triunfos / del corazón que aguanta reciamente / sesenta golpes de hacha y sigue andando" [sixty years are sixty triumphs / of the heart that resists staunchly / sixty blows from the axe and continues beating] (Figuera 1986, 321).[32]

As in "Romance de Puebloespaña," the poem fashions a narrative of sustained opposition in the face of threatened annihilation and privileges dissident presence despite its enforced absence. It thus contrasts the construct of a singular state nationhood ("España" or Spain), here denied by the collective poetic voice, with the absence of a nation as experienced by the poetic persona: "Ya ves, aquí seguimos, día a día / capeando temporales sucesivos, / viviendo en la noespaña que es España" [As you can see, we here continue, day by day / to weather storm after storm, / living in the non-Spain that is Spain] (321). Remembering those absent from an official history and culture, Figuera's verses cast exile and death as mutual losses that affect both those who go and those who remain:

> [N]osotros y vosotros; de este lado
> del mar y al otro lado; y bajo tierra
> (Miguel, Jesús, Antonio, Blas, Gabino,
> Ángel, Gabriel, José Agustín ...)
> (322)

[We and you; on this side / of the sea and the other; and dead and buried / (Miguel, Jesús, Antonio, Blas, Gabino, / Ángel, Gabriel, José Agustín)]

Through this roll-call of poets' names, Figuera honors those disappeared in action, whether physically or metaphorically, in their struggle against a Nationalist and Francoist Spain.[33]

In Figuera's poem, it is the beginning of the Franco régime that causes the poets' collective death and simultaneous rebirth. Although Alberti, in chronological terms, turned sixty in 1962, in terms of dissident memories and histories his age is the same as that of his fellow poets, twenty-three years: that time elapsed since the end of the Civil War. In this respect, the poem displaces set notions of historical time while preserving the contingencies of cause and effect. It both records how time has been detained and distorted through the regime's imposition of its history, as well as how a subversive sociopolitical history of difference has survived. Recalling Gabriel Celaya's notion of poetry as weapon,[34] the following verses articulate this counterhistory of opposition, unsuccessfully suppressed by the Francoist alliance of military state and religious power, and the exploitative indifference of Western nations:

> [Y] todos
> tenemos una edad: veintitrés años
> trepados con tesón, a puro empeño;
> lanzando los poemas como balas
> contra la espdada [*sic*], el látigo y la mitra;
> contra la fuerza en dólares o en plomo;
> mordiendo los talones del tirano
> aunque la espuela rasgue nuestras bocas.
> (322)

[And we all / are the same age: twenty-three years / tenaciously scaled, through sheer will; / firing poems like bullets / against the sword, the whip and the miter; / against the power wielded by dollars or weapons; / biting at the heels of the tyrant / even though the spur may wound our mouths.]

Figuera's imagined communion of hearts on the occasion of Alberti's birthday is cast in terms of the commemorative ritual of Holy Communion, whereby the past, embodied in the crucified Christ, is made present in the living. The wine glasses raised to toast Alberti connote a chalice that contains the intellectual life-blood of Republican Spain, which will enable its rebirth: "[S]esenta manos con sesenta copas / —amor y vino de la España *nuestra*—" [sixty hands with sixty glasses / —love and wine of *our* Spain—] (322). Just as Christ's body and blood spiritually renew those who receive it, here the sixty years of Alberti's life are incorporated into the one body of the sixty poets, both alive and dead, present and absent, who make up this imaginary national community. Such a transformation is aided by the reiteration of the number sixty throughout the poem, which, similar to the symbolic repetition of numbers in the book of Revelation, acts as an incantation with the power to transform death into life. The community represented by Alberti and the celebrants confirms that, although trauma can divide a community, it can also create one, with Kai Erikson noting that "the shared experience becomes almost like a common culture, a source of kinship" (1995, 186). The experience of historical rift or estrangement produced by the Civil War here serves as a common point of union between those who went into exile and those who remained in figurative confinement.

Redefining Francoist Space

As developed by Tranche and Sánchez-Biosca, Nationalist Spain remembered its dead through a politics of presence, reliant on the erection of grandiose memorials and monuments such as the Valley of the Fallen, dominated by the Cross.[35] On many occasions, ruins were also used as sites for the construction of buildings, effectively mausoleums for the dead who fell there. Such a memorialistic purpose was served by the reconstruction of the devastated University City on the northern fringe of Madrid, the scene of intense fighting in the last days of the war. Its buildings, Tranche and Sánchez-Biosca indicate, "rise up, like flags, and are equally symbolic of the Victory" (2002, 231). Where ruins were left by the regime, these also served as ongoing reminders of Nationalist victory and Republican loss.

In contrast, many of Figuera's poems constitute memorials to an absent Spain and the landscapes depicted often refer to a nation rendered one giant mass grave. Now ruins are not buildings but fragmented corpses in unmarked graves, human remains that testify to "the will of totalitarian domination to have its victims disappear without a trace" (Miller and Tougaw 2002, 8).[36] They also allude to the impossibility for survivors to take proper leave of their dead and put behind them the event that felled their loved ones. As Felman has remarked with regard to mass victims of war, "[i]t is because the bodies cannot be properly buried that the corpse of youth becomes a ghost that never will find peace. The grave, symbolically, cannot be closed. The event cannot be laid to rest" (2002, 44).

In Figuera's poem, "Toco la tierra" [I Touch the Earth], from her 1962 volume of the same title, the poetic subject figuratively uncovers such a gravesite in search of a historical genealogy that has been enchained and buried:

Toco la tierra. Toco
la tierra: palpo, siento
su centro visceral; busco el origen
el núcleo; la raíz de la cadena.
(Figuera 1986, 254)

[I touch the earth. I touch / the earth: I gently touch, feel / her visceral center; I seek the origin / the core; the root of the chain.]

Unlike Francoist rhetoric, redolent with the grandiloquence of martyrdom, Figuera's work stresses dismembered bodies deprived of identity and voice:

Toco la tierra. Miro: cuerpos, rostros,
frentes de piedra, corazones
como carbones encendidos.
. . . .
ojos de niño desgranados.
. . . vientres
robados de las madres
(255)

[I touch the earth. I see: bodies, faces, / foreheads of stone, hearts / like live coals. / . . . / children's eyes ripped out. / . . . wombs / stolen from mothers]

The poem thus testifies to what Elaine Scarry describes as "the sentient memorialization in the damaged bodies and the continuously experienceable memorialization in the land" (1985, 114). Contrary to the regime's official history, which in 1962 was proclaiming its burial of the war and that past in the name of peace, the struggle that Figuera literally embodies in the limbs lives on in the present: "Manos abiertas como rayos; / puños cerrados como balas" [Hands open like lightning bolts; / fists clenched like bullets] (1986, 255). It is the poetic subject who recovers this history of defiance and dissidence through a process of touch or compassion, to open up a psychological space in which secret stories can be heard: "Toco la tierra. Escucho: son labios, son gargantas, / son lenguas; oigo voces, / palabras, besos, gritos, antiguas contraseñas" [I touch the earth. I listen: there are lips, throats, / tongues; I hear voices, / words, kisses, screams, ancient passwords] (255).

Similarly, in "Ahora me dirijo a un muchacho" [Now I Address a Young Boy] from the same volume, a younger generation is invited to consider the land with reverence, as it is the guardian of a history that, although mutilated, cannot be totally silenced:

> Toca la tierra, hijo; con cuidado,
> que tocas una ruina de alma o nido
> . . . .
> Toca esta tierra que, de lado a lado,
> es un muñón tascando su alarido,
> una prisión de muertos sin olvido . . .
> (261)

[Touch the earth, son; with care, / since you are touching the remains of a soul or nest / . . . / Touch this earth that, from one extreme to the other, / is a stump consuming its scream, / a prison for the unforgettable dead]

The body parts represent an incomplete articulation of history, an "alarido" or scream denied a language but defying oblivion. What is here related is a history of ellipsis, in which fragments of lives must be reassembled by the viewer or reader into a whole, so as to reconstruct disappeared historical subjects. Their remains constitute traces in the sense explained by Paul Ricoeur: as "vestiges of the past" or silent "unwritten testimonies" (2004, 170), traces partake of both presence and absence, rendering visible an unspoken, prescribed past.[37]

Figuera's poetry thus represents what Nora has called a "memorial nation," in which "[s]tones and walls come to life, sites begin to stir, landscapes are revitalized" (1998, 636). In that configurations of space are produced through human activity and agency, her representations of Spain as a graveyard both recall the Civil War that produced it and denounce the effects of that event in the present. The graveyard, as Felman declares, "stands for space in culture and in history: a grave materializes the survival of a name in the deterioration of the corpse. Symbolically . . . casualties of war remain outside the map of history" (2002, 45). Despite the attempts by a totalitarian power to eliminate all trace of its others, Figuera's unofficial cemeteries recount a history that has survived in memory and demands inclusion in the national narrative.

Mass graves are but one manifestation of the wounds or "record[s] of war" etched into the minds, bodies, buildings and topography of a nation (Scarry 1985, 113). Within postwar Spain the wound symbolized an ongoing climate of war reliant on divisions between inside and outside, "us" and "them," purity and corruption. Although war officially ended on April 1, 1939, there was to be no quarter given to the enemies of the Nationalist state, as Franco's words, delivered the following day on national radio, made patently clear: "Spain continues at war against all enemies, both within and without" (quoted by Abella 1984, 16). After the Civil War the alleged degeneration of the dissident national body was to be cured, Richards points out, by a violent "ascetic mortification of the flesh" (1998, 49–50).

Such a sacrificial atonement and painful castigation of a recalcitrant national body are themes developed in Figuera's "La frontera" [The Frontier], also from *Toco la tierra.* Here the topos of the frontier as the dividing line between civilization and barbarity, self and other, life and death, becomes the focal point for the poetic voice's critique of Francoist Spain, whose proclaimed unity is, in effect, founded on enforced divisions and suffering. Figuera's title recalls Franco's description of the Civil War as a "'frontier war,' where the objective was the permanent suppression of the enemy and not simply its surrender" (Richards 1998, 34–35). Malcolm Anderson also stresses the military origins of the word "frontier," indicating that it signifies "the zone in which one faced the enemy." Furthermore "frontier" carries with it legal connotations, because it denotes "the precise line at which jurisdictions meet" (1996, 9). These legal implications are reiterated in Figuera's use of verbs such as "se repartieron," "se adjudicaron," "se escindieron," "hicieron apartijos," "formaron lotes," and "se disputaron" [they distributed, awarded, split apart, made into lots, disputed] (Figuera 1986, 269), to describe how a contested partitioning of territory is rendered legitimate by manipulating the discourse of law.[38]

In the poem, the men who arrive to divide up the land are portrayed in militaristic terms as wearing the "botas despiadadas" [pitiless boots] of fascism and as bearing maps (269). In that maps, as J. B. Harley puts it, "foster the notion of socially empty space" (1988, 284), the land is represented as open to colonization and occupation. Moreover, the scientific gridding of space through maps aims, as Henri Lefebvre specifies, to remove human contradictions and "reduce reality in the interests of power" (1993, 367). At stake in the violent requisitioning of natural wealth and communal space, denoted by the poetic allusions to "[l]a nieve, el pájaro, la brisa, / la mina, el mar, el sol, la calle" [the snow, bird, breeze, / mine, sea, sun, street] (Figuera 1986, 269), is the creation of a new sociopolitical economy, that of a totalitarian state. Such a state arguably takes to an extreme the violence that, for Lefebvre, is at the root of all states: "[E]very state is born of violence . . . This violence originated in nature, as much with respect to the sources mobilized as with respect to the stakes—namely, wealth and land. At the same time, it aggressed all of nature, imposing laws upon it and carving it up administratively according to criteria quite alien to the initial characteristics of either the land or its inhabitants" (1993, 280). Similarly, with regard to the creation of the Francoist state, it was violence, Richards stresses, that marked out "the economic and social boundaries of the territories of 'Spain' and 'Anti-Spain'" (1998, 27).

In Figuera's "La frontera," the violence required for this remodelling of the Spanish state is represented as a matricide, whereby the heart of a sacred mother is cut into pieces: "A filo de ansia y de cuchillo / iban abriendo y troceando / el pecho santo de la Madre" [On the edge of anguish and the knife / they gradually opened and cut up / the sacred breast of the Mother] (Figuera 1986, 269). Such an analogy not only suggests the murder of the mother at the very foundations of patriarchy (Irigaray 1993, 36), and thus the unnatural death of a loved motherland. The savage extirpation of Spain's heart by the knife of fascism also has strong connotations of cannibalism, an act symbolic of civil war. The impersonal agents who effect the butchery are portrayed as nonhuman, wolf-like creatures with "largos dientes, largas uñas" [long teeth, long claws] (Figuera 1986, 269).[39] The opposite of the ritual of Holy Communion, premised on voluntary sacrifice and the gifting of the self to others, cannibalism represents the violent appropriation and consumption of others without their consent or symbolic contract.

Echoing what Richards describes as the Nationalist "ordering of recaptured physical space" (1998, 68), Figuera's text emphasizes, both typographically and semantically, that the division of a nation requires the forceful rearrangement of natural boundaries such as rivers, lakes, and mountain ranges:

> Los ríos vieron sus orillas
> a la distanca real del odio.

Los lagos fueron divididos
como se saja un ojo abierto.

Las cordilleras se escindieron.
(Figuera 1986, 269)

[The rivers saw their banks / at the real distance of hatred. / The lakes were divided up / like ripping out an open eye. / The mountain ranges were split apart.][40]

Together with this mutilation and partitioning of a former space represented as natural, its inhabitants are also divided into "castas diferentes" [different castes] (270), social categories from a feudal world. The frontier, a marker of this confrontation of self with other, becomes a wound deliberately kept open, a border painfully demarcated with boundary stones: "Al borde mismo de la herida / se colocaban los mojones" [At the very edge of the wound / marker stones were placed] and "Así quedó trazada la frontera" [In this way the frontier was fixed] (269–70).

With all possibility of healing thus impeded, these verses foreground the reluctance of the Franco regime to allow wounds to heal and forgive the defeated (Richards 1998, 27). Reconciliation was anathema to the dictatorship, given that much of its legitimacy was founded on the notion of a necessary moral victory over its enemies (Aguilar 2002, 109). Consequently the fragmentation of a former unity by a totalitarian state, as described by Figuera, is not paradoxical. On the contrary, it illustrates the premises elaborated by Lefebvre as follows: "Power aspires to control space in its entirety, so it maintains it in a 'disjointed unity,' as at once fragmentary and homogeneous: it divides and rules" (1993, 388).

Figuera's "La frontera" foregrounds the importance played by not only physical but also conceptual borders in delimiting nation-states and their communities. The final image of the vultures that guard both sides of the border constitutes a virtual description of autarky, the sociopolitical system under which Spain, in the immediate post-Civil War years, closed her borders against both external and internal enemies:

Así quedó trazada la frontera.
Y llegaron los buitres.
Y posáronse a un lado y a otro lado.

Y se pusieron a esperar.
(Figuera 1986, 270)

> [In this way the frontier was fixed. / And the vultures arrived. / And they took up position on one side and the other. / And they began to wait.][41]

Nevertheless that very positioning of the vultures alludes to the difficulty in maintaining boundaries. The adversary of Francoism does not so much lie on the other side of the frontier as between and within, in the transitional zone between inside and outside where symbolic space is forever contested. Such a borderland, as Héctor Calderón and José David Saldívar affirm, constitutes "a vague and undetermined place created by the emotional residue of an unnatural boundary. It is in a constant state of transition" (1991, 3). It is with the transformative possibilities of a border or dissident culture in postwar Spain, as it is constantly negotiated by the defeated Spain, that my discussion will now engage.

The Wounds of War

When Ángela Figuera likens writing poetry to being an "herida sin bordes" [a borderless wound] ("Silencio" [Silence], 1986, 185), she is doing more than affirming solidarity and commitment to voicing the suffering of others. Her analogy not only expresses the yearning for a space of articulation unconstrained by limits and potentially infinite. It is also steeped in the symbolic systems current in Nationalist Spain and the Franco dictatorship, based on rigid demarcations and artificial separations, as just explored. The fact that Figuera gives voice to such sentiments in a volume published in 1952 should come as no surprise, given the continuing climate of repression in Spain for years after the war. Trench warfare might well have finished, but Franco's systematic campaign of ideological purification throughout the 1940s did nothing to close psychic wounds and heal emotional trauma. Indeed even in 1964 Figuera alluded to the ongoing trauma as follows: "La poesía española del 39 hasta hoy . . . [e]s una poesía, en cierto modo, clandestina y de guerra, la continuación de la guerra, sorda y sangrante" [Spanish poetry, from 1939 until today . . . is, to a certain degree, a clandestine war poetry, the continuation of the war, muffled and bloody] (Lechner 1975, 143).

Figuera's image of a borderless wound, however, is clearly a paradox. While it contains difference, predicated on the distinction established by the wound between the inside and outside of a given body, its lack of closed borders undermines that difference at the same time. The tension inherent in this image, then, is suggestive of a constant negotiation of the limits and possibilities of identity. Such encounters between the self and other may engender a space of hybridity produced by both, or what Nikos Papastergiadis, drawing on Bhabha, refers to as a "'unity' [that] is not found in the sum of its parts, but emerges from the process of opening . . . a third space within which other elements encounter and transform each other" (1997, 258). It was this third space that seemed unthinkable within the ethos of Francoist Spain, as Juliá notes: "In the Civil War of the twentieth century there was a conqueror who exterminated the defeated and who did not leave any room for a third party that might have negotiated peace or served as arbitrator between the two sides" (Juliá 2004, 287–88).[42]

Figuera's poetry seeks to elaborate such third hybrid spaces through moving the boundaries of exclusive identities culturally assigned to physical and figurative bodies. As I will now discuss, Mary and Christ, embodiments of a sacred space, came to symbolize for the Francoist state political, cultural, and economic autarky. The closure of history and memory that these figures represented, and the politics of self-sufficiency and collusion with which they were associated, are countered by the premises of hybridization expressed in Figuera's poetry. Hybridization, Peter Stallybrass and Allon White note, "produces new combinations and strange instabilities in a given semiotic system. It therefore generates the possibility of shifting the very terms of the system itself . . . by erasing and interrogating the relations which constitute it" (1986, 58). Central to this process is Figuera's progressive fusion of a suffering Mary and Christ, symbolic of the qualities of compassion and communion—feeling and sharing with the other—as well as the growing importance in her work of a feminized Christ.

Figuera's poetry testifies to the bleak conditions endured by fellow Spaniards in the postwar years far beyond the 1940s. The following verses from "Posguerra" [Postwar], published in 1952 in *El grito inútil* [The Useless Cry], call on a community that has survived, against all odds, summary execution and death: "Alegraos, hermanos, porque es bueno quedarse / como espiga escapada a la hoz y a la muela. / Como res condenada que evadió la cuchilla" [Be happy, comrades, because it is good to survive / like wheat that has escaped the scythe and grindstone. / Like condemned cattle that have evaded the butcher's knife] (Figuera 1986, 174). Even so, those who remain are but shadows of former selves, with lives subjected to tyrannical restrictions: "[S]oy un resto, una fuga, / una angustia cercada de horizontes difíciles, / un pulmón oprimido por tiránicos puños" [I am a remnant, a flight, / an anguish surrounded by difficult horizons, / a lung oppressed by tyrannical fists] (175).[43] In the face of such existential difficulties, the very purpose of aesthetic production is placed in doubt by dissident poets. Figuera is no exception, exclaiming in "Silencio": "Ser poeta es inútil en un mundo acosado. / . . . / Mejor fuera callarse. Licenciar la metáfora" [To be a poet is useless in a persecuted world. / . . . / Better to be silent. To send the metaphor on leave] (185–86). The dilemma of a creativity that pursues beauty amidst misery is articulated through the symbol of the rose in "La rosa incómoda" [The Uncomfortable Rose]. As an aesthetic object born involuntarily from the poet—"Me nació" [It was born to me]—the rose stands for the lost innocence of poetic creation, before the exile from paradise caused by civil war and the complacent poetic topoi that dominated in the immediate postwar years: "[T]an tierna e inocente como antes de la culpa, / como antes de esta paz y aquella guerra, / como antes de tan lindos sonetos a la rosa" [as tender and innocent as before original sin, / as before this peace and that war, / as before such pretty sonnets to the rose] (215).[44]

The historical awareness acquired through the war also makes the rose or poem an element that inflicts pain on the poet in the very act of producing or writing it: "A esto nada menos hemos llegado, amigos, / a que una fresca rosa nos lastime la mano" [It has come to nothing less than this, friends, / to a fresh rose hurting our hands] (215). Poems, the following verses affirm, should dare to bring out into the open hurtful historical truths, engraved on the poetic body like bloody wounds: ". . . Bastante me he arriesgado / publicando mis años sin quitar una fecha / y mis largos poemas con la sangre en los bordes" [I've already risked enough / publishing my years without omitting dates / and my long poems with blood on their edges] (215).[45] In Francoist Spain, the poetic voice maintains, pure beauty is out of place in a world where shame and fear have reduced social exchange to empty formulaic expressions: "Sí, me gusta mirarla. Pero siento vergüenza. / Pero temo encontrarme con cualquier conocido. / ¿Cómo estás? Muy bien, gracias. ¿Y esa rosa? ¿Esa rosa?" [Yes, I like to look at it. But I feel ashamed. / But I fear running into casual acquaintances. / How are you? Very well, thanks. And that rose of yours? That rose?] (216). As pure beauty, the poetic rose risks being contaminated by the triumphal discourse of the public sphere:

> Oh, demasiado bella y delicada
> para llevarla en triunfo por la calle,
> para ponerla al lado de un periódico
> para alternar con tanto futbolista
> (215)

[Oh, too beautiful and delicate / to carry in triumph down the street, / to place next to a newspaper / to socialize with so many soccer fans]

The "uncomfortable" rose, then, is emblematic of the discomfiture of the poet, caught between the beauty of her art, the pain of her world, and her inadequacy at expressing either.

Armored Bodies, Totalitarian Systems

Typical of fascist and totalitarian regimes is the perception of the body as armored, and hence as closed and invulnerable. For Klaus Theweleit, the representation of the fascist body as armored protects its sociopolitical system, engendered as masculine, against feminized internal and external others (1987, 434). Drawing on Theweleit, Hal Foster argues that this configuration is also applicable to survivors of traumatic events, whose damaged subjectivity becomes encased in an autistic alienation, symbolized by an armored body (1995, 221). Armor, then, becomes a metaphor for a state of liminality, referring to both the cause and also the effect of the trauma: to fascism and to the alienation resulting from it.

Such concepts can be traced in the following verses from Figuera's composition, "Belleza cruel," from the 1958 volume of the same title, where the poetic subject desires to be encased in a figurative armor in order not to see nor feel:

> Dadme un espeso corazón de barro,
> dadme unos ojos de diamante enjuto,
> boca de amianto, congeladas venas . . .
> . . . .
> Quiero dormir a gusto cada noche.
> (Figuera 1986, 207)

> [Give me a thick heart of clay, / give me eyes of icy diamond, / a mouth of asbestos, frozen veins . . . / . . . / I want to sleep well at night.]

Indeed, in Figuera's poems from the early 1950s, the image of the body as armored is a recurrent one. In "Ésta que soy" [This That I Am], for example, the poetic voice exclaims: "Cerrada voy. Armada de corteza. / Ceñida en un acero sin fisura. / Inmensamente separada y sola" [I go through life enclosed. Encased in armor. / Tightly girded in seamless steel. / Infinitely separate and alone] (152). The state of separation described in this quotation produces what Foster alludes to as "the third-person signature of an alienated subject" (1995, 221), whose self-recognition, as evidenced in Figuera's following verses, is impossible in the sanctioned mirrors or discourses that frame what constitutes legitimate identity under the regime: "Ni me conozco ni me aprendo. / Por todos los espejos me he buscado / y sé que no soy yo la que me mira" [I neither recognize nor can know myself. / I've searched for myself in every mirror / and I know that I'm not she who looks back at me] (Figuera 1986, 152).

In Figuera's case, her sociopolitical body is a marginalized, feminized one that endeavors to protect itself against the harm inflicted by the masculine totalitarian body of the Francoist state and discourse. At the same time, however, through duplicating the closed invulnerability of this masculine body in order to reject it, the subject risks becoming complicit with the very system that she would disown. Fusi has described how closing off the self from surrounding circumstances is the hallmark of a process of accommodation or adaptation to what would otherwise be unbearable sociohistorical circumstances:

> Accommodation means adapting to a given situation for the sake of convenience, rather than emotionally identifying with it. And that is what . . . happened in Franco's Spain: a society that did not identify with the official Francoist ideology . . . adapted to it, not only nor mainly because of the repression effected by the regime . . . but be-

> cause Franco knew how to appeal to certain traditional values of Spanish society: its Catholic way of thinking . . . ; its traditional concept of the family, its sense of order and authority. (Quoted by Tranche and Sánchez-Biosca 2002, 181)[46]

The armored composition of a totalitarian system becomes evident in Nationalist depictions of Mary as Virgin during the Civil War. In keeping with the traditional wedding between military states and Marianism in Catholic theocratic contexts, as discussed by Nicholas Perry and Loreto Echeverría, Mary was first and foremost the "Virgin Captain" who protected Spain throughout a conflict represented by the Nationalists as a Holy Crusade. Hence, as these scholars observe, "the Immaculate Conception, patroness of the infantry, and the Virgin of the Pillar, patroness of the Guardia Civil and Spanish Legion, Grand Captain of the Spanish Armies and symbol of Mary's convenant with Spain, constituted the alpha and omega of the fascist forces" (Perry and Echeverría 1988, 223, 215).[47]

The identification of not only Mary but also Christ with a militaristic sociopolitical body is patent in the Nationalist construction of Spain as sacred space. Superimposed on maps of Spain were the countenances of these holy figures, thus merging political and religious spheres. Likewise posters that promoted the Nationalist cause showed soldiers wearing on their breast the sacred hearts of Christ and Mary, or bearing prayers in their name.[48] Cities were similarly identified with these figures, as evident in the Nationalist association of Zaragoza with the Virgin of the Pillar or the description of the castigation of Republican-held Malaga by General Queipo de Llano's troops as Christ's "Calvary" (Richards 41). Nationalist visual representations of Mary and Christ invariably presented them as pure, closed, monumental figures that illustrate perfectly the concept of the masculine classical body as developed by Mikhail Bakhtin, whereby "the opaque surface . . . acquire[s] an essential meaning as the border of a closed individuality that does not merge with other bodies and with the world. All attributes of the unfinished world are carefully removed" (1984, 320). In comparison, Republican depictions of these same figures usually associate them with a crucifixion or Pietà scene, or portray them with women, children, and feminized others.[49] In this sense, they constitute examples of what Bakhtin calls the "grotesque" body, which, in contrast to the classical, is open to the world, an incomplete "double body" that irreverently transgresses normative boundaries in a constant process of becoming (1984, 317–18).

Subsequent to the war, the Virgin's historical identification with the imperial Spain emulated by the dictatorship was palpable when Franco confirmed her alleged protection of the Nationalist war effort as follows: "Her fiestas are the fiestas of the Empire. Without her we could not have won the laurels of triumph, nor could we have liberated the Fatherland."[50] Throughout the 1940s and the early 1950s, Mary as Virgin guaranteed the alleged incorruptibility and self-sufficiency of Francoist Spain, and validated the purity of its cause. Her closed, inviolate body thus represented the Francoist policies of autarky, "an imposed quarantine or silencing [that] signified the continuation of the war as a work of cultural destruction" (Richards 1998, 2).

Indeed, as Perry and Echeverría trace, the Franco regime was founded on an intense process of Marianization; Mary supplied a key component of nationalism, in that her immaculateness became inextricably linked to the imperial ideal of purity of blood, by which moral superiority depended on having untainted Christian roots. A complete ideological conflation was produced between the Virgin and the Francoist cause, which functioned to belie the marked militaristic and patriarchal characteristics of the latter. Thus Giménez Caballero was able to state that "Franco's smile has something of the Virgin's mantle held over sinners" (quoted by Perry and Echeverría 1988, 217). Due to pressure from Spain, in 1950 the Vatican recognized the doctrine of the Assumption and in 1954 Franco consecrated Spain to the Heart of Mary (Perry and Echeverría 1988, 246).

From Warrior to Witness, Virgin Mary to Mother: Conceiving Compassion

With regard to Figuera's work, Mary becomes a mediating vehicle that permits the poetic subject not only to articulate her autism and unwitting collusion with the regime, but also to develop a stance of sociopolitical commitment.[51] Such a process is conveyed in two contiguous compositions entitled "Egoísmo" [Egoism] and "Vencida por el ángel" [Conquered by the Angel] from Figuera's third collection of poetry, *Vencida por el ángel* (1950).[52] Drawing on the figure of Mary as Virgin, "Egoísmo" portrays the poetic subject's attempt to isolate her self from the nightmare engendered by the Franco regime. While the title highlights the importance of individuality and autonomy for the poetic voice, the anaphora of the key words "contra" [against] and "fuera" [outside] in stanzas 1 to 7 foregrounds concepts of resistance and rejection, as exemplified in the following quotations: "Contra el sucio oleaje de las cosas / yo apretaba la puerta" [Against the flood of filth / I held fast my door] and "Fuera, el naufragio; fuera, el caos; fuera / ese pavor, abierto como un pozo" [Outside, the shipwreck; outside, the chaos; outside / that fear, gaping like a pit] (Figuera 1986, 111). The trauma resulting from extreme fear constitutes a "pozo" or pit where meaning founders.

The attempt by the poetic voice to take refuge in a private domain that might not be invaded by the apocalyptic terror outside is further stressed by the first-person pronoun "yo" [I] and the noun "puerta" [door]. These words frame the initial and concluding stanzas: "[Y]o apretaba la puerta. Mis dos manos, / resueltas, obstinadas, indomables, / la mantenían firme desde dentro" [I held fast my door. My two hands, / resolute, obstinate, indomitable, / kept it tightly shut from within] (111) and

> Yo, dentro. Yo: Insensible, acorazada
> en risa, en sangre, en goce, en poderío.
> Maciza, erguida; manteniendo firme,
> contra el alud del llanto y de la angustia,
> mi puerta bien cerrada.
>
> (112)

[I, inside. I: Unfeeling, armored / with laughter, blood, pleasure, power. / Solid, upright; holding firm, / against the avalanche of sorrow and anguish, / my door tightly shut.]

Given that "puerta" connotes the Marian *porta clausa* or closed gate, symbolic of the pure invulnerability of the Virgin's body, here the door held fast similarly guards a fortress-like space. From there the poetic voice colludes with the regime by endeavoring to deny trauma and loss, and closing herself off from what is occurring in Francoist Spain. Nevertheless such a withdrawal into the private sphere also served as a strategy of survival for a defeated people

(Richards 1998, 24). The "sucio oleaje" [flood of filth] and the "alud del llanto" [avalanche of sorrow] to which Figuera's poetic subject alludes speak of a world that threatens to overwhelm the fragile boundaries of the self unless it dons armor to become "acorazada" [armored]. Thus the constant dialectic established between seeing and not seeing, between opening and shutting the eyes—doors to the body/mind—expresses both recognition of the devastation caused by the war and dictatorship, and disavowal of the same. This kind of partial blindness has been perceived by Richards as symptomatic of a political regime's attempt to control memory (1998, 10).

The inability and refusal to see are the themes that open the following poem, "Vencida por el ángel": "Yo cerraba los ojos" [I closed my eyes] (Figuera 1986, 113). This composition narrates the struggle between an angel and a Marian-like poetic subject, desirous of maintaining her armored impregnability: "[Y]o apretaba los puños; / yo blindaba mi pecho con metales helados" [I clenched my fists; / I armored my breast with icy metals] (113). The identification of the subject with the Virgin is strengthened by the many textual references to attributes of hers: the flowers of spring, synonymous in the Northern Hemisphere with the month of May and symbolic of the incorruptibility of Mary (Warner 1985, 99–100); the presence of clouds, invariably reproduced in iconography of the Virgin; the allusion to stars, evocative of the crown of twelve stars or *stellarium,* and the prayers to the Virgin in the form of "canciones":

> . . . He reído
> sobre todas las flores de los mayos ingenuos;
> cabalgando las nubes; fabricándome estrellas;
> derramando canciones.
>
> (Figuera 1986, 113)

[I have laughed / above all the flowers of innocent Mays; / riding the clouds; fashioning stars for myself; / overflowing with songs.]

Such a figure, however, is also reminiscent of the winged Virgin of the Apocalypse, often conflated with the doctrine of the Immaculate Conception (Stratton 1994, 58–60). Also known as the Empress of Hell, this Virgin descends to Hell to see the fate of the damned and redeem them (Warner 1985, 321, 327). Signifying a revelation or disclosure of past or future events, the suggested theme of the

Apocalypse functions in Figuera's poem as a paradigm of liminality to prophesy the death of a former self and the birth of another. The subject's progression from a state of icy virginity to an acknowledgment of collective sorrow is evident in the contrast established by the following series of quotations. On the one hand, the poetic voice reiterates her determination to preserve invulnerability and dissociation, as implied by the highlighted adjectives: "Me he proclamado *limpia* contra el asco y la ruina. / Me he declarado *libre* contra el tedio y la duda. / Me he creído excluída, separada, *intocable*" [I have declared myself *unsullied* against the horror and ruin. / I have declared myself *free* against tedium and doubt. / I have believed myself to be excluded, separate, *untouchable*] (Figuera 1986, 113; my emphasis). On the other hand, in what is a reinscription of the scene of the Annunciation, the subtext of the angel's foretelling of Christ's birth to Mary is rewritten as the conceiving of a stance of sociopolitical commitment in the poetic subject:

> Pero el Angel llegaba. A pesar de mis puños,
> de mis ojos cerrados, de mis labios tenaces,
> con su vuelo impasible, con su copa colmada,
> me ha tocado; me ha roto la coraza soberbia;
> me ha deshecho los muros; me ha cortado la huída.
>
> Sin espada, sin ruido, me ha vencido. En la entraña
> me ha dejado clavada la raíz de la angustia
> y ya siento en mi alma el dolor de los mundos.
>
> (113)

> [But the Angel kept on coming. Despite my fists, / my closed eyes, my tenacious lips, / with his impassive flight, his chalice brimming, / he has touched me; he has broken through my proud armor; / he has brought down the walls; cut off my flight. / Without sword or sound, he has conquered me. In my womb / he has nailed the root of all anguish / and I now feel in my soul the sorrow of worlds.][53]

The subject's rebirth is due to the angel proffering her a chalice, "una ancha copa de licores amargos" [a generous chalice of bitter content] (113). The incorporation of its contents, an act reminiscent of Holy Communion, engenders awareness of the death and devastation created by the Franco regime, and with it, solidarity with those who suffer.[54]

Figuera's account reveals remarkable similarities with the experience related by the Spanish mystic writer, Teresa de Ávila, referring to her experiencing God's love: "I saw an angel next to me on my left, in bodily form, something that I do not usually see unless by a miracle. . . . He was not tall, but small and very beautiful . . . I saw in his hands a long, golden arrow and at the end of its iron tip there seemed to be fire. He seemed to plunge it into my heart several times, and it reached my innermost being. When it was withdrawn, it seemed to take me with it, leaving me completely consumed by God's great love" (1989, 173). In both narratives the wounding of the writing subject produces her compassion: a love so intense that it opens up a matrix of feeling and thought formerly closed. Mary as Virgin has been transformed into Mary as *Mater Dolorosa* or Mother of Compassion, who, as grieving witness beside Jesus's cross, was pierced by a spiritual sword that "caused the fount of her mercy to flow" (Warner 1985, 216). The poetic subject's identification with a crucified Christ/Spain is strengthened by the emphasis on nailing in Figuera's following verses: "En la entraña / me ha dejado clavada la raíz de la angustia / y ya siento en mi alma el dolor de los mundos" [In my womb / he has nailed the root of all anguish / and I now feel in my soul the sorrow of worlds] (1986, 113).

The figure of Mary grieving for a crucified Christ is again foregrounded in Figuera's poem "Piedad," from *Víspera de la vida* [Eve of Life] (1953). Here the play on the double meaning of "piedad"—both compassion and Pietà—depicts the death of poet José Alfonso de Gabriel and the sorrow of his mother in terms of the Holy Mother and Child. The death of the son is cast as an amputation for the mother, whose very structure or skeleton is broken without possibility of healing, making her breast an open wound:

> Y tú, madre, amputada sin remedio
> en carne tuya propia; . . .
> . . . .
> . . . rota sin sutura
> la intimidad más dulce de tus huesos,
> . . . .
> tu pecho en pura llaga . . .
>
> (164)

[And you, mother, incurably amputated / from your own flesh; . . . / . . . / . . . broken without suture / the sweetest intimacy of your bones, / . . . / your breast, pure wound]

The equation of these figures with those of the Pietà is made explicit in the following verses:

> ¿Qué fuerza de calvario consentido
> te tuvo firme con el hijo en brazos
> en trance largo de Descendimiento,
> muda Piedad tallada en mármol vivo?
> (164)

[What power of a consented Calvary / kept you steadfast with your son in your arms / in a never-ending moment of Descent from the Cross, / a mute Pietà sculptured in living marble?]

The never-ending moment of Christ's taking down from the cross—"en trance largo de Descendimiento"—and the censorship implied in the muteness of the figures function as an allegory for the poet's Spain, a mother whose child or future is perceived as dead and without hope of resurrection.

Feminizing Christ, Placing Spain on Trial

During the Civil War and ensuing Franco dictatorship the figure of Christ, like that of Mary, became embedded in sociopolitical struggles of legitimation and deauthorization, of inclusion and exclusion. For those who constituted the defeated Spain, Christ was the son of God, the innocent babe and the dispossessed sower of seed, whose Crucifixion represented their suffering. For the victorious Spain, Christ as King and all-powerful Maker underwrote the alleged reconstruction of the New Spain, symbolized by the Resurrection.

Figuera's deployment of the symbol of Christ as a means of critiquing the Franco dictatorship intensifies from 1958. This was the year in which *Belleza cruel* appeared in Mexico, due to censorship that impeded its publication in Spain until 1978 (Wright 1986, 155). The tone is set by the prologue penned by León Felipe. His comparison of Spain with a "father's house," from which "the Spaniards in exile and mourning" are expelled, establishes an implicit comparison with the house of God/Franco from which Christ/dissidents have been exiled, "thrown out of the orchard . . . through the farthest gate" (Figuera 1986, 205). The exile experienced by the regime's opponents, cast out into the desert of Spain but at the same time imprisoned in the "old enclosed estate" (206), is clearly an inner exile, and their poetry becomes a "psalm of the desert" (205), epitomized for León Felipe by Figuera's collection. Figuera's critique of the regime is baldly stated in her opening poem, "Belleza cruel." There the reality of the dictatorship is cast as totally contrary to grandiose tales of heroic deeds, revealing "todo el revés atroz de la medalla" [all the atrocity behind the military medals] (207). Implicit in the description of Spain's suffering humanity, "con el miedo al hombro" [bearing fear on their shoulders] and "el hambre a cuestas" [burdened with hunger], is the figure of Christ shouldering his cross to Calvary.

It is also in *Belleza cruel* that the poet, representing Spain as both Mary and feminized Christ, definitively challenges the masculine identities that the dictatorship ascribed to the figures of Christ and Mary.[55] In "Canto rabioso de amor a España en su belleza" [Angry Song of Love to Spain in her Beauty], the multiple meanings that Spain assumes rework the relationship between Holy Mother and Son on which the Francoist state modeled itself, to stress a mother/daughter relationship, in a series of fluid exchanges of categories and identities. First, Spain is the poetic subject's mother: ". . . me vienes, madre" [you come to me, mother] (235) and "Tú me has parido y hecho . . . " [You have given birth to me and made me] (236). Secondly s/he is an ambiguous lover who transforms the subject into a symbolic mother of poetry, as evident in the following verses: "Me viene tu belleza tierna y dura, / tu corazón rodando enamorado / hasta embestirme, hasta llenarme toda" [Your tender, hard beauty comes to me, / your heart roaming enamored / until you charge me, to fill me completely] (235). Thirdly Spain is the dying feminine object of love: "Porque eres bella, España, y te me mueres / porque eres mía, España . . ." [Because you are beautiful, Spain, and you are dying / because you are mine, Spain] (236). Representations such as these cannot help but recall the various positions occupied by Mary vis-à-vis Christ, as noted by Julia Kristeva: "*[M]other* of her son and his *daughter* as well, Mary is also, and besides, his *wife*" (1986, 169). The poetic body is the jubilant but suffering host for Spain/Christ, just as, for mystic writers, Christ was their source of happiness and pain:

> Tú me has parido y hecho y traspasado
> de dicha y de dolor hasta los huesos

con tu belleza que se clava y ciñe
como un cilicio rojo en mi cintura.
(Figuera 1986, 236)

[You have given birth to me and made me and pierced me / with joy and suffering to the marrow / with your beauty that pierces and tightly clasps / my waist like a burning hairshirt.]

In verses that evoke the prayer of "Hail Mary," Figuera's poetic voice initiates a laudatory review of Spanish history: "Belleza sobre ti y en tus entrañas / de miel y de granito, y en tu cielo" [Beauty to you and your flesh / of honey and granite, and in your heaven] (235). The periods surveyed include those ruled by the Iberians and Moors, as well as more recent times. The historical panorama described is one of material well-being, gradually elaborated over centuries:

De siglo en siglo en olas y torrentes
de barro ibero, en sucesivas olas
de tierras y metales agregados,
de frutos madurados poco a poco.
(235)

[From century to century in waves and floods / of Iberian clay, in successive waves / of soils and metals combined, / of fruits ripened little by little.]

Spain's formation, the poetic persona intimates, is based on a cultural diversity represented as natural to it and symbolized in its "sierras nevadas, florecidos valles, / pardas llanuras, parameras ásperas, / cierzos helados, delicadas brisas" [snowy mountain ranges, valleys in bloom, / brown plains, harsh plateaus, / icy north winds, delicate breezes] (236).

In contrast, the present historical moment is depicted as one of utter poverty and decadence, a far cry from the glorious culmination of history proclaimed by the regime. The nation is described in terms of a female Christ wandering in the Calvary of the desert left by the Civil War and condemned to be crucified: "Porque te veo andando entre zarzales / por todos los caminos rezagada / con una cruz al cuello y otra al hombro" [Because I see you wandering among thorn bushes / straggling along every path / with one cross around your neck and another on your shoulder] (236). In a powerful allusion to a nation consumed by indigence and internal divisions, this Christ is a cannibal forced to devor her own meager sacramental body to survive: "Porque te veo escuálida y desnuda, / comiendo el pan moreno de tu vientre, / bebiéndote el gazpacho de tu sangre" [Because I see you squalid and naked, / consuming the dark bread of your belly, / drinking the gazpacho of your blood] (236). Moreover, just as Christ was sold out by one of his own disciples, Figuera's Christ is forced to beg from the principal supporter of National Catholicism, the Vatican: "[P]or todos malcomprada y malvendida, / pordioseando impúdica en la puerta / de la opulenta Catedral del Mundo" [by all bought and sold under value, / begging shamelessly at the door / of the opulent Cathedral of the World] (236). Verses such as these reproduce a topos common among Republican poets: that of a betrayed, impoverished motherland, yet another version of the nineteenth-century symbol for the nation, the *Mater Dolorosa*.[56]

In her representations of an alternative history of Spain through the personae of Christ and Mary, Figuera transforms them from the abstract myths of the regime into embodied beings. Through their inherent authority, she authorizes the right of Spain as victim to speak and be heard. Therefore it is not surprising that "Canto rabioso" is couched in terms of a legal document that places Spain on trial, in an imagined Day of Judgment or *dies irae* connoted by the pervasive theme of anger rendered explicit in the poem's title.[57] The poetic subject's recourse to a legal order in her pursuit of justice is indicated by the prevalence of formulaic legal expressions, such as "canto y firmo" [I sing and sign] (235), "a mil años y un día condenada" [to a thousand years and one day condemned] (236), and "y no te absuelvo / del mal de España" [and I don't absolve you / of Spain's suffering] (237). The fluidity of the positions assigned to the nation, however, undermines any categorical attribution of guilt or innocence: Spain is both murderer and murdered—"viuda, asesina y mártir de tus hijos" [widow, murderer and martyr of your children] (236); both gaoler—"con tu belleza que se clava y ciñe / como un cilicio rojo en mi cintura" [with your beauty that pierces and tightly clasps / my waist like a burning hairshirt] (236)—and prisoner: "[Y] en tus encadenadas cordilleras / y en tus encadenados hombres, canto" [and on your enchained mountain ranges / and among your enchained humanity, I sing] (235). Here avoiding a paradigm of perpetrators and victims, the poetic voice judges the entire nation unworthy of absolution, in an assumption of collective guilt.

Especially important are the acts of witnessing and signing emphasized in the initial and final stanzas. As before, in "Carta abierta," these acts grant legal presence to the poetic subject, affirm her identity despite censorship, and allow her to insert herself within an authoritative discourse:

> [Y] fecho y firmo a corazón parado,
> boca cerrada y a apretados puños,
> clavándome la lengua con los dientes,
> porque no quiero blasfemar tu nombre.
> (237)

> [and I date and sign with stopped heart, / my mouth shut and with clenched fists, / nailing fast my tongue with my teeth, / because I don't want to defile your name.]

While references to the subject's stopped heart suggest terror and imminent death, the insistence on the act of dating through the verb "fecho" restarts historical time. Similarly the clenched fists or "apretados puños" not only recall the writer, pen in hand. They also convey the contained anger and resistance of a repressed socialism, connoted through its symbolic gesture of solidarity.

Consequently the framework observed in Figuera's poem confirms Felman's thesis that the structure of the trial grants traumatized victims "semantic authority over themselves and over others" (Felman 2002, 127). Elaborating further, Felman declares that

> the victims/witnesses are not simply expressing their suffering: they are reclaiming legal subjecthood and autobiographical personhood. . . . Through this recovery of speech and this recovery of history, they reinvent an innovative logos that is no longer simply victims' logos but constitutes a new kind of legal language. In the act of claiming their humanity, their history, their story, and their voice before the law and before the world, they are actively (and sovereignly) reborn from a kind of social death into a new life. (2002, 226–27n.58)

Through Figuera's recourse to the intertwined figures of Christ and Mary, victims and witnesses of historical injustice and violence become one, transforming individual trauma into a collective history that invites universal identification. Rather than constituting omniscient narrators, Christ and Mary perform the function of outsider witnesses, who may, as Dori Laub puts it, "step outside of the coercively totalitarian and dehumanizing frame of reference in which the event was taking place, and provide an independent frame of reference through which the event could be observed" (Felman and Laub 1992, 81).

Within Figuera's work, her fusion of Christ and Mary represents a process vital for restoring a damaged national community. Although within the contexts of the Civil War and ensuing Franco regime the figure of Christ was deployed symbolically by both perpetrators and victims, within Figuera's poetic corpus s/he becomes the mediating term par excellence between opposing visions, and the ultimate symbol of innocent atonement that might potentially permit the Spanish nation to acknowledge atrocities and reconcile differences.[58]

Commemorative Liturgies for a Defeated Spain

Equivalences drawn between a crucified motherland and a female Christ come to the fore in Figuera's 1962 volume, *Toco la tierra: Letanías,* permeated in its entirety by themes of the Crucifixion and Resurrection. Although the poet saw this collection as harping on issues considered outdated in the climate of economic expansion and poetic innovation during the 1960s, such an evaluation belied the pertinence of her message.[59] As noted above, 1962 was a year of significant political agitation on the part of dissident sectors and of fierce retaliation from the authorities. Especially relevant for the political resonances of Figuera's religious symbolism was the galvanization of members of the clergy, whose growing opposition to the regime revealed that they were no longer willing to condone systematic repression through their silence. Within an environment that identified Franco's Spain with God's chosen nation and Christ's church (Abella 1984, 231–32), the fissures within the Catholic Church were noticeable.

With the publication of the encyclicals *Mater et Magistra* and *Pacem in terris* in July 1962 and April 1963, respectively, the Catholic Church underwent convulsive changes and renovation (Gómez Pérez 1986, 102–3). Increasingly the younger clergy shared the conditions of poverty endured by the working classes, laboring with them side by side. Even conservative Catholic organizations such as the Hermandades Obreras de Acción Católica [Workers' Brotherhoods of Catholic Action] began to favor the working classes whenever labor disputes arose. In 1962 three hundred and thirty-nine members of the Basque clergy denounced, in a letter to their bishops, the lack of freedom and continued use of torture against enemies of the state. Also in 1962, with regard to the miners' strikes mentioned previously, the May publication of *Ecclesia*, the voice of Acción Católica, supported the right of the workers to strike, against the government newspapers of *Arriba* and *Pueblo* (Abella 1984, 240–41).

In *Toco la tierra: Letanías*, the consistent deployment of the structure of the litany effectively serves as a harrowing protest against the regime. First the litany signifies a catalogue or account, the itemization of a historical record. Secondly this particular form of supplicatory prayer is especially associated with the Reproaches of Good Friday, whereby the crucified Christ cries out hourly against the cruelty of humankind (Warner 1985, 307). The repetition at stake thematically and formally not only reproduces the structure of prayers to form an integral part of meditation. Reiteration also suggests the difficulty of making oneself heard in an environment of censorship, conventionally symbolized by a cross.[60]

Scholars concur that the articulation of traumatic memory is fundamental for overcoming trauma and integrating it into lived experience. Thus Brison stresses the importance of "speech acts of memory" in the reconstruction of a damaged self. She argues that all memory of trauma caused by fellow human beings is cultural memory, in that traumatic events take place within given sociocultural contexts and are represented by a privileging of specific images over the exclusion of others. Moreover, Brison continues, because traumatic events are culturally produced by processes of interpretation and contextualization, how they are represented over time will also depend on the response, or lack of response, of others to their articulation (1999, 39–42). In this sense, the reiterative nature of Figuera's poetry partially attests to the deafness of a wider sociopolitical body to her message. Yet its repetition also points to an attempt at mastering trauma itself, in that, as Brison affirms, it is only when one repeats a story and attempts to control its narrative that traumatic memories can eventually become meaningfully reintegrated into life histories (46–47).

Made up of a series of petitions to be answered by the congregation, the litany demands a response (Jo Evans 1996, 143–44). This factor is implicit in *Toco la tierra* through the dialogic structure of Figuera's untitled opening poem, where the poetic subject addresses the people of Spain as sons and daughters: "Hijos, ya veis: no tengo otras palabras" [Children, as you can see: I have no other words] (1986, 253). The anonymity of the poem, implicit in its lack of title, opens up the traditionally private utterance of prayer to all. Likewise the emphasis on sight in the phrase, "ya veis" [as you can see], highlights the process of reading, through which others might participate in an individual vision, thus rupturing boundaries between author and reader. The poetic act therefore constitutes a figurative transubstantiation, by which experiential pain is literally poured into verse, a semantic vessel that, if taken into oneself by reading, enables compassion, a sharing of pain through love: "[I]nsisto, insisto, insisto: verso a verso, / repito y enumero lo evidente, / lo que en los ojos se me clava a diario" [I insist, insist, insist: verse by verse, / I repeat and enumerate what is evident, / what pierces my eyes every day] (253).[61] The silenced devastation of Spain crucifies the poet—"se me clava" [pierces me]—but must also be brought out into the open through alternative historical accounts: "Y lo que está escondido bajo el lodo, / para que surja y brille, lo enumero" [And of what is hidden under the slime, / so that it may come forth and shine, I render account] (253).

The elements that provoke the poetic persona's cry result in a syntax broken by the context of symbolic war and real violence within Spain:

> Golpe tras golpe, digo lo que duele,
> mi larga letanía: tierra, tierra,
> dolor, dolor, dolor; España, España;
> el hombre, el hombre, el hombre, el hombre, el hombre,
> repito y clamo con el llanto al cuello.
>
> (253)

> [Blow after blow, I tell of what hurts, / my long litany: earth, earth, / pain, pain, pain; Spain, Spain; / humanity, humanity, humanity, humanity, humanity, / I repeat and shout out, choking on tears.]

Almost immediately, however, this unremitting meditation on Spain's pain creates solidarity with a suffering humanity in general, similar to how the turning inward that prayer encourages can be the first step in expanding a personal universe:

> Repito, vuelvo, sigo, en letanía:
> la tierra, el mundo, España, el hombre, el hombre;
> temor (y esclavitud); trabajo (y hambre);
> codicia (y guerra); vida (y exterminio)
> y amor, amor, amor que me calcina.
>
> (253)

[I repeat, return, continue with my litany: / earth, world, Spain, humanity, humanity; / fear (and slavery); work (and hunger); / greed (and war); life (and extermination) / and love, love, love that burns me to the bone.]

The casting in this first long stanza of the poetic persona as a Christ-like figure, bearing a metaphorical cross of tears—"con el llanto al cuello" [choking on tears]—intensifies in the third. Here the image of Christ in the garden of Gethsemene, unheard by his sleeping disciples, prevails: "No sé, no sé si ya querréis oirme [*sic*], / decir amén, seguirme, acompañarme" [I don't know, don't know if you still want to hear me, / say amen, follow me, accompany me]. It is not until nearing the end of the poem that Christ's gender is revealed as feminine, forcing a readjustment of the traditional paternal-filial frame hitherto constructed by writer and reader: "Hijos, ya veis: soy vieja y me repito" [Children, as you can see: I'm an old woman and I repeat myself] (253). Such a realignment also creates an implicit equation between this female Christ and Spain, described earlier as "sola y mártir" [alone and martyred] (253).

Imitation of Christ's suffering assumes greater prominence in "Seguir" [To Continue]. Here the poetic voice addresses a loved land and depicts the ideological differences that provoked Spain's Civil War through contrasting visions of Christ. The first, as established in the opening stanza, represents Spaniards using Christ, connoted by the heart and soldier's spear, to embrace a sacrificial culture of war and death:

> Muchos por ti mataron, tierra mía.
> Hicieron de sus huesos plomo airado
> y mataron por ti.
> Convirtieron

su dulce corazón en fiera lanza
y mataron por ti.
(256)

[Many killed for you, my land. / They fashioned from their bones air-borne lead / and they killed for you. / They transformed / their tender hearts into fierce spears / and they killed for you.]

The act of war, the poetic voice suggests, requires the dehumanization of the sociopolitical body, transformed from "natural" subjects into alienated objects, as indicated by the references to bones that become bullets and hearts, spears.

As stanza 3 continues to underscore, the Civil War was not, as the Francoist historical narrative of the 1960s would portray it, an inevitable "natural" disaster or "oscura galerna" [stormy northwest gale] for which no blame could be attributed.[62] On the contrary, it was the result of ideological constructs that cast dying in battle as a voluntary self-sacrifice necessary to save the nation:

Se ofrecieron
desnudos e impasibles
a la oscura galerna
y murieron por ti.
(256)

[They offered themselves up / naked and impassive / to the stormy northwest gale / and died for you.][63]

Through the biblical images of the sterile seed, and the forgotten wheat and grapevine, symbolic of Christ's body and blood, the poem critiques a militaristic ethos that has rendered Spain barren:

Muchos murieron derramados
sobre tus campos pobres
como simiente sin futuro.
Se olvidaron
del beso y de la cuna,
de la vid y del trigo.
(256)

[Many died strewn / over your barren fields / like seed without a future. / They forgot about / the kiss and the cradle, / the vine and the wheat.]

In contrast, acting as a mediating bridge between stanzas 1 and 3, stanza 2 offers an alternative representation of Christ that charts a history of transplantation, transfusion, and ultimate restoration of life. Identified with this Christ, the feminine poetic subject fashions from her bones a revolutionary cross or Tree of Life,[64] and extracts from her heart, a figurative grapevine, new blood to revive a nation extenuated by inquisitorial-like persecutions, as suggested by the "árbol quemado":

De mis huesos
hice yo un árbol nuevo y atrevido
y lo planté en tu pecho
junto al árbol quemado.
Prensé mi corazón
y procuré una copa
de sangre nueva y pura
a tus mermadas venas;
(256)

[From my bones / I made a new, daring tree / and I planted it in your breast / next to the burnt tree. / I pressed my heart / and obtained a chalice / of new, pure blood / for your depleted veins;]

In this process a language imagined as free from the residues of a tragic past is created: "[Y] añadí / un nombre sin pasado / a los sagrados nombres de tus hijos" [and I added / a name without a past / to your children's sacred names] (256).

The oscillation between states of death and life that informs the poem's entire structure traces an inconclusive process of transition between this world and the next, present and future, Crucifixion and hoped-for Resurrection, Francoism and desired democracy. In particular, this kind of transformation for the poetic subject and Spain is contingent on the healing or purification of wounds, suggested by references to "vinagre" and "vino," the vinegar and sacramental wine or blood of Christ's crucifixion and resurrected body, respectively:

Trasegando
tu vinagre y tu vino,
tu sudor y tu llanto,
he seguido viviendo.
(257)

[Decanting / your vinegar and wine, / your sweat and tears, / I've continued living.]

As in "Hijos," such a process requires a decantation denoted by the gerund "trasegando": the transferring of given contents from one vessel to another without carrying over their sediment or past. This action can be read as metaphorically displacing dichotomized systems of meaning; clear-cut divisions are presented as elided through the poetic subject cutting across—"trasegando"—both vinegar and wine, bitterness and fertility, hate and love.

In the final stanza Figuera's rewriting of the Crucifixion scene acquires even greater impact through the repetition of the words of the Catholic Mass, delivered to bless Christ's Eucharistic body and blood: "En ti, por ti, contigo" [In You, for You, with You] (257). Here, once again, there is a reiteration of themes related to Christ's/Spain's crucifixion, such as censorship ("amordazada" or gagged), the nailing down of an infinite body of meaning ("clavada"), the inability to move on and forward ("paralítica" or paralyzed), and betrayal by others ("vendida" or sold out). However, the sacrament of communion transforms death into life through the act of remembrance performed as the celebrants ingest the symbolic body and blood of Christ. Just as the priest's role in the Mass is to serve as intermediary between humanity and God, so, too, does the poetic voice, identified with a Christ of life, represent herself as bridging oppositions within Spain, transforming suffering into redemption and death into love: "[S]ufriéndote, perdiéndote, ganándote; / muriéndome, muriéndote, adorándote" [suffering you, losing you, winning you; / dying, dying for you, adoring you] (257). Surviving the horrors of a past still perceptible in the present is implicit in the present perfect and gerund of the verse "he seguido viviendo" [I've continued living], reiterated throughout the preceding stanza 4 and now repeated in the concluding section:

yo he seguido,
he seguido,
he seguido,
viviendo.
(257)

[I've continued, / continued, / continued, / living.]

It is in these lines especially that Figuera's poetic persona exemplifies the situation experienced by trauma survivors, who, Laub explains, "live not with memories of the past, but with an event that . . . has no ending, attained no closure, and therefore . . . continues into the present and is current in every respect." The process of recuperation for trauma victims, Laub continues, depends on the "re-externalization of an event [that] can occur and take effect only when one can articulate and *transmit* the story, literally transfer it to another outside oneself and then take it back again, inside" (Felman and Laub 1992, 69). Christ as persona offers Figuera the means of projecting her trauma; Christ as Eucharistic blood and host enables the reincorporation of this same trauma, in a process of reconciliation and absolution essential for the healing of psychological scars.

Laying the Past to Rest: Toward a Future of Hope

Figuera's equation of an exiled, feminized Christ with a dissident Spain is a constant motif in her later work. Frequently, as discussed, this analogy is strengthened through the many references to the symbols of wheat, bread, and wine, allusive to Christ's body and blood.[65] Particular relevance is granted to the plough, which opens up a closed land to light and air, in preparation for a symbolic harvest. Although such metaphors form part of semantic fields common to both Republican and Nationalist writing,[66] Figuera's stress on wheat and bread takes on wider implications when set against Francoist slogans such as "Ni un hogar sin lumbre ni un español sin pan" [Not one home without light, not one Spaniard without bread] and "Por la patria, el pan y la justicia" [For the fatherland, bread and justice]. It is also significant that the Nationalists' victory was termed by Franco "the victory of wheat," due to their securing the food-producing areas of Spain in the interests of the landed elites (Richards 1998, 40). Indeed wheat for Figuera and other dissident writers arguably comes to symbolize the regrowth of liberalism and the redistribution of political and economic power within a Francoist heartland, identified with Castile's granary (Carr 1982, 740).

Poems such as Figuera's "Canción del pan robado" [Song of the Stolen Bread] from 1958, therefore, may be seen in a different light when read against the class monopolization of wheat during the 1940s, which saw the production and trade of wheat regulated ideologically according to principles of autarky and as a means of castigating the defeated (Richards 1998, 132–33). Figuera's denouncing of such a situation is evident in the following verses, which question laboring comrades or "brothers" about the bread that they made and has been stolen from them:

> Hermano de la hoz y de la trilla,
> Hermano del molino atareado,
> . . . .
> ¿dónde está el pan que hiciste con fatiga?
> . . . .
> pero, del trigo hasta la boca,
> ¡cuántos ladrones acechando!
> (Figuera 1986, 244)

> [Brother with the scythe and thresher, / brother laboring at the mill, / . . . / where is the bread that you wearily made? / . . . / indeed, from the wheat to your mouth, / what a lot of thieves lying in wait!] [67]

Wheat and bread also become synonymous with the difficult task of growing collectively a future of peace, as can be seen in "El trigo" [Wheat]: "Es tan difícil ver crecer el trigo / (el trigo casi pan, casi futuro, / casi alegría, casi paz granada)" [It is so difficult to see the wheat grow / (wheat almost bread, almost future, / almost happiness, almost ripe peace)] (275).[68] Such an undertaking is, in turn, equated with fashioning a symbolic sacramental wafer with the power to redeem humankind: ". . . amasamos / una redonda forma venerada / cuando miramos el perfil del trigo" [we knead / a round, revered form / when we contemplate the form of wheat] (275).

Just as the wound connotes the liminality of a body poised between injury and recovery, death and life, so, too, do the poems in *Toco la tierra* point to the tenuousness of Spain's future, viewed from 1962. The uncertainty of its figurative harvest is summed up by Figuera in the sonnet "Aunque la mies más alta dure un día" [Although the Highest Corn May Live Only a Day]. Here, in apocalyptic tones, the subject describes herself, like Christ, as a word or "verso" made flesh: "Mujer de carne y verso me declaro" [Woman of flesh and verse I declare myself] (284).[69] The poetic expression of her reality is represented as not only a fountain of love but also the abyss of psychic trauma: "[P]ozo de amor y boca dolorida" [a well of love and suffering mouth]. Nevertheless such a deep wound, it is suggested, can be transformed into a trumpet-like funnel with the power to project the poet's word into the world and give birth to a future Day of Judgment: "[P]ero he de hacer un trueno de mi herida / que suene aquí y ahora, fuerte y claro" [but I must fashion a thunderclap from my wound / that may resonate here and now, loud and clear] (284).

Rewriting a Francoist rhetoric of sacrificial suffering, loss, and death, in "Donde veas" [Wherever You See] Figuera replaces the soldier's spear that pierces Christ's side with a transitive verb of sharp contestation, a language of negativity envisaged as symbolically saving the world:

> Donde veas
> . . . .
> que los fusiles amenazan muerte,
> acércate y, a pecho descubierto,
> lanza un tremendo NO que salve al mundo.
> (268)

> [Wherever you see / . . . / that guns threaten death, / draw near and, with bared breast, / send forth a tremendous NO that might save the world.]

Negation in this sense has been explained by Kristeva as "the act of a judging subject" and negativity, as "the mediation . . . the liquefying and dissolving agent that does not destroy but rather reactivates new organizations and, in that sense, affirms" (1984, 28, 109).

Negativity as affirmation and as mediation between contesting discourses is implicit also in Bhabha's discussion of how cultural identity, founded on difference, is "constituted through the locus of the Other . . . in a process of substitution, displacement or projection" (1990a, 312–13). For Bhabha, cultural identity constructed through a positive recognition of differences does not emerge from disregarding or eliminating others but by drawing close to them (314). Recalling Figuera's emphasis on repetition, Bhabha characterizes such a process as "the repetition that will not return as the same, . . . where adding-*to* does not add-up but serves to disturb the calculation of power and knowledge, producing other spaces of subaltern signification" (312). Such premises of supplementation of, or approximation and contribution to, the one by the other are also intimated in Figuera's poem, "Donde veas," through the constant reiteration of the command of approximation, "acércate" [draw near], and the privileging of the notion of adding to, not assimilating, the other, as suggested in the following verses: "[A]cércate y añade tu simiente" [draw near and add your seed] and "acércate . . . y deja un trozo / del propio corazón junto a sus labios" [draw near . . . and leave a piece / of your heart next to their lips] (Figuera 1986, 268). In the sense that supplementation always comes after the "original" event or structure, it also permits the latter to be challenged and modified (Bhabha 1990a, 305). It is the very belatedness of supplementation that allows for a revisiting and judging of history, in what constitutes a second coming. Such a second coming is performed in Figuera's poetry through her reworking Nationalist/Francoist representations of Christ in her contemporary context.

The quest for a language that might articulate pain, heal psychic wounds, and engender a new historical consciousness comes to the fore in Figuera's "Hombre naciente" [Nascent Humanity], from *Belleza cruel.* Here her epigraph, "Pido la paz y la palabra" [I ask for peace and the word] (Figuera 1986, 249), reproduces the title from Blas de Otero's 1955 volume of poetry (Otero 1992, 99), to present a prayer for peace and the right to speak out. By linking peace and voice, the verse alludes to the hope for the end of a figurative war and the advent of democracy.[70] Stressing the theme of rebirth, an embryonic poetic subject exhorts her motherland to prepare a cradle for her future coming:

> Prepárame una cuna de madera inocente
> y pon bandera blanca sobre su cabecera.
>
> Voy a nacer. Y, desde ti, mi madre,
> pido la paz y pido la palabra.
>
> (249)

[Prepare my cradle of innocent wood / and place a white flag at its head. / I am about to be born. And, from within you, my mother, / I ask for peace and the right to speak.]

At the same time, the birth will also signify a death or laying to rest, as intimated by the white flag, a burial shroud draped over the ambiguous cradle/coffin. Thus the poetic voice envisions a myth of nationhood that affirms the imminent demise of the Francoist past and envisages the birth of a viable future. In contrast to the red and white banner of the Nationalist Crusade that figures in the Fresco of Destruction, the poetic voice's plea is for a flag washed free of blood and for a healed land in which to sow a fresh history: ". . . Saneada tierra / para sembrar a pulso la simiente / que tengo entre mis dedos apretada" [A healed earth / in which to sow with bare hands the seed / held tight between my fingers] (249). The theme of reconciliation central to the poem is underlined in the subject's request for a nation without war, ruins, and frontiers, where wounds will not longer exist: "Pido una tierra sin metralla . . . / . . . / libre de escombros" [I ask for a land without shrapnel . . . / . . . / free of ruins] and "un mapa sin fronteras, / una argamasa de sudor caliente / sobre las cicatrices y fisuras" [a map without borders, / a poultice of warm sweat / on scars and wounds] (249). By asking for the right to speak out, the subject embodies a process of public debate and eventual reconciliation of divisive differences, as intimated by the warm poultice or "argamasa," intended to soothe and heal a loved body.[71]

Figuera's poetic subject couches her message in terms of a figurative call to arms in the name of peace, not war. The following verses exhort all humankind to participate in an apocalyptic baptism in the mythical river of creation, so as to inaugurate a world from which death, decay, and greed have been definitively banished:

> Que se levanten al rayar el día
> y vayan al más próximo arroyuelo.
> Laven allí sus manos y su boca,
> se quiten los gusanos de las uñas,
> saquen su corazón que le dé el aire,
> expurguen sus cabellos de serpientes
> y apaguen la codicia de sus ojos.
>
> Después, que vengan a nacer conmigo.
> Haremos entre todos cuenta nueva.
>
> (249)

[Let them arise at daybreak / and go to the nearest stream. / Let them there wash their hands and mouths, / clean out the worms from under their nails, / put their hearts out to air, / expunge the serpents from their hair / and extinguish the greed in their eyes. /

> Then, let them come to be born with me. / Among us all we will render a new account.][72]

Privileged in this account of future resurrection is the theme of rebuilding a damaged community. Within this new social economy, a democracy constructed by all, peace and life are represented as due by right and guaranteed by law, as suggested by the play on "derecho": "Quiero vivir. Lo exijo por derecho" [I want to live. I demand it by lawful right]. The delivery of future peace, however, can only be ensured through hope and trust in such a personal and collective rebirth: "Pido la paz y entrego la esperanza" [I ask for peace and deliver hope] (249).

Conclusion

The incessant return of a history that refuses closure is the dominant theme in Figuera's poetry, haunted by the events and consequences of the Civil War. Whereas the Franco dictatorship buried the progressive ethos of the Second Republic under the weight of reactionary tradition, Figuera's poetic corpus is dedicated to reviving the Republican spirit and a repressed liberal community. For much of the dictatorship, history was figuratively integrated into a mythical time based on events in the lives of the Holy Family, representative of the sacred space of an ideally monolithic and monologic nation-state. Hence the emphasis at Christmas, Epiphany and Easter on birth, charity and resurrection served to underscore the regime's alleged reconstruction of a New Spain and the nation's supposed economic recovery.

In contrast, Figuera's rewriting of such paradigms depends on reinserting historical struggle into a detained time and opening up mythologized bodies to contemporary injustices, so as to transform representations of the victorious into incarnations of the defeated. Themes particularly highlighted are Christ's exile in the desert and Crucifixion, which cogently depict a historical space and time marked by continued loss, and psychic and material devastation. Similarly Mary as *Mater Dolorosa* and compassionate witness to the Crucifixion testifies to the inhumanity and suffering caused by the dictatorship. Figuera's oppositional history, therefore, gives voice to the exiles of Francoist history, ghosts or revenants that, as Labanyi notes, "refuse to have their presence erased but insist on returning to demand that their name be honored" (2000, 66). Her poetry rewrites Christianity as a religion of the people that defies exclusive memberships based on political power and is reminiscent of liberation theology.

Figuera's insistence on anchoring her contemporary context to the causes and effects of the Civil War gathered momentum from 1958 to 1962, at precisely the point at which the restructuring of the Spanish economy appeared to promise a similar opening up of hardened political policies. In this sense, it can be seen as part of the ground swell of the increasing radicalization of culture from the late fifties onward (Fusi 2001a, 773–76). Yet the poet's silence after 1962 suggests that her voice remained unheard by the general Spanish population, who were eager to acquire material stability and move on from a troublesome past.

Conversely the recovery of the work of vanguardist writer Rosa Chacel after Franco's death can be seen to participate in the reclaiming by the governments in power from 1976 to 1984 of chapters of liberal cultural history officially disregarded by the Franco regime. From the years of the so-called Transition to democracy (1975–82) and the subsequent socialist government of 1982–86, Chacel's *Barrio de Maravillas* (1976) and *Acrópolis* (1984) remember the dynamic first three decades of twentieth-century Spanish culture. At the same time, significant aspects of her work promote the modern, Europeanist image that Spain, from Franco's demise onward, is eager to cultivate. Chacel's texts then, look back to the nation's past but also capture the post-Franco present and look forward to Spain's future.

PART 3
Recovering Cultural History in Post-Franco Spain: Rosa Chacel's Novels of Memory

Ahora se pinta en la mente de todos el paso de la Historia.
—Chacel 1984, 358

[Now on the minds of all the passage of History is painted.]

INTRODUCTION

IN 1976, AT THE AGE OF SEVENTY-EIGHT, ROSA CHACEL PUBLISHED THE first text in a novelistic trilogy that evokes in dazzling fashion the intellectual, cultural, and sociopolitical histories of early twentieth-century Spain. Comprising *Barrio de Maravillas* (1976), *Acrópolis* (1984), and *Ciencias naturales* (1988), the trilogy spans practically a century of Spanish life, from the last decades of the nineteenth century to the 1980s. Melding biography and autobiography, history and philosophy, these works preserve the memory of the Madrid-based avant-garde to which Chacel herself belonged and that forms part of the so-called Generation of 1927 or Generation of the Republic, bringing their world back to life.[1]

Described by Chacel as the "biografía de mi tiempo" [biography of my time], the trilogy substantiates her claim that she is the "cronista único—en el terreno novelístico—de aquella pompa [de la vanguardia]" [only chronicler—in the field of the novel—of that (avant-garde) bubble] (Chacel 1993p, 380). Countering the ongoing perception of the avant-garde as a social minority of intellectual quality, Chacel considers that her literary and cultural generation was "la oleada más vital que haya agitado a España desde sus raíces" [the most vibrant current that has ever shaken Spain to its core]. The entire trilogy, Chacel states, is an attempt to elucidate its truths (1993z, 291).[2]

The cultural and sociohistorical contexts foregrounded in Chacel's trilogy are also those present in her own life. With early training in painting, she studied sculpture at the Madrid School of Fine Arts between 1914 and 1918, and grants a privileged position to both these artistic forms in *Barrio de Maravillas* and *Acrópolis.* From 1922 to 1927, years spent in Rome with her painter husband, Timoteo Pérez Rubio, Chacel immersed herself in the works of Joyce and Freud, and the avant-garde intellectual currents disseminated by Ortega's *Revista de Occidente.* Subsequently entering the Madrid cultural world on her return to Spain, she contributed to prominent literary journals and published her avant-garde novel, *Estación: Ida y vuelta* [Station: Round Trip], in 1930. Chacel's support for the Second Republic was evident in her signing in July 1936 the Founding Manifesto of the Alliance of Antifascist Intellectuals, as well as protests against the arrest and ill-treatment of the poet, Miguel Hernández, and against repression in Puerto Rico, in January and March that same year. When the Civil War broke out, Chacel worked for a short time as a nurse in the Red Cross, and published in the Republican journals *El Mono Azul* and *Hora de España.*[3]

From 1937, Chacel spent the Civil War in Greece and Paris, and in 1939 emigrated to Río de Janeiro and Buenos Aires. Her years in exile in these latter cities, well-documented in her diaries, *Alcancía (Ida)* [Money Box (Departure)] and *Alcancía (Vuelta)* [Money Box (Return)], were plagued by financial difficulties and low self-esteem, with Chacel alternating her own writing with translation work. The recipient of a Guggenheim Foundation grant to New York from 1959 to 1960, she also visited Spain in 1961, 1971, and 1972. A grant from the Juan March Foundation in 1974 to assist in her completion of *Barrio de Maravillas* made possible Chacel's permanent return to Spain that year, just prior to Franco's death.[4]

It was only subsequent to the dictatorship that Chacel began to garner the critical acclaim and accolades denied her previously.[5] Her prior marginalization as a significant literary figure can be attributed to various factors. First, as in Acuña's case earlier, Chacel had to contend with contemporary intellectual prejudices regarding women as cultural producers in the 1920s and 1930s.[6] Second, during the Franco dictatorship and her long years of exile, she was ignored by a conservative literary establishment, for whom many avant-garde writers of the pre–Civil War period were suspect, due to their contravening bourgeois aesthetic norms and their support of the Republican cause. Third, avant-garde writing, precisely because of its quest for constant innovation and originality, is often perceived as divorced from sociopolitical issues. In this sense, the formal complexity of many avant-garde works may well have contributed to their falling out of favor also with some dissident writers during the dictatorship, who saw social realism as better fulfilling the imperative of denouncing the sociopolitical context of Francoist Spain.[7]

Chacel's successful reentry onto the Spanish literary scene in the mid-1970s was undoubtedly influenced, I argue, by the aesthetic and sociopolitical contexts peculiar to Spain at that time. Since 1962 texts such as Luis Martín Santos's *Tiempo de silencio* were heralding new ventures in aesthetic form, spurred on by the Latin American boom novels and the *Nouveau Roman.* This aesthetic experimentation, José B. Monleón has declared, was part and parcel of the beginning of Spain's ideological transition to Europeanization and democracy (1995b, 11, 14). Nor is it coincidental that Chacel was rediscovered by members of a younger avant-garde generation known as the *Novísimos,*[8] who in the 1960s were rejecting a social realism in crisis and proclaiming the autonomy of language in the name of a "democratic pluralism" (Rodríguez Puértolas 1995, 267–68). Almost exclusively from conservative upper- and middle-class families, they formed part of a dissident body that used the economic advantages of their class to critique it (Jordan 1990, 31). Chacel's relationship with Novísimos Ana María Moix and Pere Gimferrer in particular led her to believe that what the Generation of 1927 had represented could be revived in Spain through these younger writers (Chacel 1993w, 250).

Chacel represents a position that disputes any demarcation between sociopolitical concerns and aesthetic innovation. Undeniably, right until the end of her life, Chacel situated herself at the vanguard of literature. Seeing herself as having anticipated the Nouveau Roman of the 1950s and early 1960s, she also avowed her unswerving adherence to principles proposed by Ortega regarding the "new novel."[9] In keeping with Ortega's stance, Chacel always aligned herself with intellectual currents that perceived culture as playing a vital role in effecting the necessary social, cultural, and political reforms to place Spain on a par with a modern northern Europe. This inseparability of cultural and sociopolitical matters for Chacel is clear in her 1977 essay, "Sendas perdidas de la generación del 27" [Lost Paths of the 1927 Generation]. There, quoting T. S. Eliot, she insists: "Nunca se puede trazar el límite entre la crítica estética y la crítica moral y social: . . . se empieza con la crítica literaria y, por más severo esteta que uno sea, tarde o temprano habrá cruzado la frontera, entrando en otra cosa" [Aesthetic critique can never be separated from moral and social criticism: . . . you begin with literary criticism and, irrespectively of how strictly you may adhere to aesthetics, sooner or later you will have crossed that boundary, entering the other sphere] (1993w, 254).

Such a stance is representative of the kind of committed modernism referred to by Williams as "modernist in both theory and practice," due to its deployment of "forms which engage with history and with specific social formations" (1989, 77). That attitude is crucial, moreover, to the European avant-garde project of the first three decades of the twentieth century, which upheld, as Andreas Huyssen has remarked, "the reintegration of art and life as its major project" (1986, 163). Huyssen's argument that the recuperation of the historical European avant-garde by North American postmodernism in the 1970s corresponded to common attitudes to formal experimentation and to the undermining of bourgeois art traditions (168) can be extrapolated to the cultural situation in Spain at that same time. Emerging from the Franco dictatorship and the sociopolitical protests of the 1960s and early 1970s, Spain, like the Western industrialized nations cited by Huyssen (1986, 171), was also facing its own identity crisis, albeit for different reasons, on cultural and political fronts. Part of the solution was to turn to a contestatory aesthetic tradition and alternative history buried by the Franco regime, and partially embodied by the avant-garde of the 1920s and early 1930s.

Thus intrinsic to any consideration of the Spanish historical avant-garde is the desire by contemporary actors to understand their own present, as underlined by Jaime Brihuega: "Any immersion in the phenomenon is, inevitably, a way of connecting with the present. When the concept and the creative works of the avant-garde are debated and researched, even those of the historical vanguards, what appear, ghost-like, are phenomena intrinsic to the most contemporary creative production" (1981, 38). Such a dialogue between past and present is at the heart of Chacel's trilogy, as the following quotation from her essay, "Volviendo al punto de partida" [Returning to the Point of Departure], reveals: "[P]uede un tiempo profundamente atesorado volcarse sobre un presente vivo y activarlo, en cuyo caso actúan tanto el uno como el otro: *se responden, dialogando* hasta entenderse del todo, hasta comprenderse, y una vez fundidos siguen adelante, como si nunca hubiera habido silencio entre ellos" [It can happen that the carefully accumulated riches of an era are upturned onto a present moment and stimulate it, with each era exerting equal influence: they *respond to one another, conversing* until they completely understand and include each other, and once one, they go forward as if there had never been silence between them] (1993z, 275–76). The trilogy constitutes, Chacel insists, that dialogue reinitiated after a long silence (277) and made possible through the conjunction of favorable sociopolitical circumstances.[10]

In her trilogy, Chacel obsessively returns to the past to reconstruct a cultural home that she considers would have provided necessary shelter to the nation, had it been allowed to flourish. However, the Civil War and subsequent dictatorship, she affirms, resulted in the destruction of this intellectual edifice and the eviction of its inhabitants by a conservative postwar Spanish literary establishment: "Estas generaciones, imbricadas, podían haber cubierto y cobijado muy cumplidamente el área de nuestro pueblo, pero . . . la techumbre se derrumbó . . . componíamos . . . la avanzada que los críticos posteriormente desahuciaron" [These overlapping generations, a symbolic home, could have provided excellent shelter and refuge for our people, but . . . the roof collapsed . . . we were . . . the vanguard that the critics later evicted] (1993g, 313–14).[11] It was only after Franco's death, Chacel states, that she and her generation could fully reenter the cultural, and indeed national, home whose foundations she had contributed to laying: "Nosotros éramos un primer fenómeno, un esbozo que fue tachado por cincuenta años de repudio y descrédito, pero que ahora ingresa naturalmente en el edificio cuyos cimientos, cuyos sótanos y cisternas cavé con instrumentos primarios" [We were a first sign, an experiment erased by fifty years of rejection and disrepute, but who now naturally enter the edifice where I dug out the foundations, cellars, and reservoirs with pioneering instruments] (1993w, 254).

Chacel, then, declares her generation to be the indisputable foundation of Spain's cultural and political renaissance after Franco. The recovery of their history is one with reconstructing a liberal past expropriated, denied, and denigrated by the Franco regime, and subsequently misinterpreted by literary criticism.[12] Chacel's literary project constitutes an attempt to recompose, from memory and from later historical moments, the sociocultural consciousness of her generation, and those generations with whom they coexisted. In so doing, her work not only interrogates established versions of cultural history but also attests to the continued currency of the avant-garde vision for the nation's present and future, in what she describes as the "continuación del ayer por el hoy" [the continuation of yesterday by today] (Chacel 1993x, 270). As her character Antonia from *Barrio de Maravillas* notes, memory constitutes a necessity or even an imposition, centered on the continued presence of something that has never become past (Chacel 1981, 142).[13]

The ensuing analysis will focus on *Barrio de Maravillas* and *Acrópolis*, given that it is these first two texts in the trilogy that recall the modernist period so central to Chacel's reclaiming and revalorization of her cultural history. *Ciencias naturales*, which deals with the exile suffered by characters from these first novels in Argentina during the Franco dictatorship, will therefore not be examined. *Barrio de Maravillas* and *Acrópolis* not only present characteristics of the philosophical novel so prevalent in Spain during the early twentieth century.[14] They also fall within the genre of the *bildungsroman* or novel of development, portraying the cultural formation of Chacel's coprotagonists, Elena and Isabel. Through these dense, polyphonic works Chacel conveys the intensity, dynamism, and diversity of the cultural and sociopolitical scene lived by different generations of liberal intellectuals, whose common aspiration, as presented in her fictionalized accounts, was for a democratic Spain. Elena's and Isabel's passage to maturity, then, becomes representative of the journey, with all its challenges and setbacks, undertaken by liberal Spain in the early twentieth century toward the goal of egalitarian nationhood.

Barrio de Maravillas charts the sociocultural history of Spain from the last third of the nineteenth century up until 1914, marked by the beginning of World War I. The middle-class Elena, born, like Chacel, in 1898, comes from a background rich in cultural awareness: her grandfather was an opera composer and her mother, a former opera singer married to an librettist turned civil servant. In contrast, Isabel, born in 1900, is the illegitimate daughter of a seamstress, Antonia, seduced by a member of the aristocracy. Both Elena and Isabel attend a school for young women in their Madrid apartment block, a microcosm of Spain at that time in terms of the different social classes that inhabit it. Their teacher, doña Laura, the guardian of her orphaned sister, Piedita, comes from a family of liberal educators and freethinkers. It is through her that the friends come into contact with her philosopher brother, Manuel, a university professor, and his disciple Máximo Montero, representative of ultimately diverging generational positions, as will be discussed below. Equally instrumental in Elena's and Isabel's development are relationships established with friends, such as with Tina Smith, the Catalan art patron, whose brother marries Piedita, and with families such as the Olmedos, who avidly pursue cultural knowledge.

Acrópolis opens with the sociopolitical difficulties present in Spain toward the end of World War I, symptomatic of which is the Spanish flu. In this novel, Elena and Isabel initiate their studies, in sculpture and painting, respectively, at the Madrid Academy of San Fernando, at the same time as they become increasingly exposed to cultural and political debates raging in Spain between 1918 and the early 1930s. Just as crucial as Elena's and Isabel's intellectual trajectory in this novel is that of characters like Manuel, who becomes an important mouthpiece for Chacel's retrospective judgments on the period from her authorial context of post-Franco Spain.

In the first section of my discussion, I posit the construct of generation as a *lieu de mémoire* or place of memory, in the sense developed by Pierre Nora.[15] Generational consciousness, Nora argues, is a retrospective construction arising from the interplay of memory with history. Moreover the emergence of generational consciousness depends on relationships with other social groups and their symbolic investments in sociocultural and political discourses and practices. I will here evaluate these notions with regard to Chacel's avant-garde generation and the relationships that it established with other modernist generations—specifically, the so-called Generations of 1898 and 1914—placing particular emphasis on their shared commitment to the concept of "school" in national transformation.

Chacel's renegotiation of masculine modernist configurations of the spaces of home and city are the subject of a second section. Like Acuña's, Chacel's texts challenge the patriarchal separation of the domestic and public spheres, and by extension, of a feminized nature from an allegedly masculine culture, to revindicate the home as an important space for cultural practice. Likewise the modernist city, conceived according to exclusionary class and gender premises, is rewritten to critique sociocultural discrimination.

Such a reinscription of the house and city, symbols for the nation, depends on displacing hegemonic paradigms of vision. In keeping with this need, in a third section I will suggest that Chacel consistently presents, through Elena and Isabel, cultural practice as an always embodied and open process of inquiry, which interrogates the past in order to illuminate the present and inform the future. My fourth and final section will address a debate paramount for the avant-garde and its cultural contemporaries, and of considerable relevance for post-Franco Spain: the role of culture vis-à-vis society and politics.

Recovering Forgotten Paths: Generations as "*Lieux de mémoire*"

In her essay, "Sendas recobradas de la generación del 27" [Recovered Paths of the 1927 Generation], Chacel refers to her trilogy as the "School of Plato" (1993x, 270–71). In so doing, she draws an implicit parallel between the cultural generations depicted therein and the foremost thinkers and scientists of classical antiquity immortalized by the Renaissance painter, Raphael, in his fresco *The School of Athens* (1509–10), discussed in *Acrópolis* (Chacel 1984, 7, 48–49). Hanging in the Apostolic Palace of the Vatican City, Raphael's work honors the great minds of his own day through earlier intellectual giants: Plato, centered with Aristotle, is given Leonardo da Vinci's features, for example; Heraclites is Michelangelo and Raphael himself is included. Among other thinkers represented are Socrates, Diogenes, and Pythagoras. The entire scene is the epitome of feverish intellectual engagement, either through solitary pursuit of interests or, as in most cases, through earnest dialogue among different generations.

Chacel's indirect alignment of the School of Athens with the generations with which the avant-garde coexisted, the so-called Generations of 1898 and 1914, intimates that the Spanish modernist groups of the first three decades of the twentieth century are worthy inheritors of that Golden Age of classical intellectual endeavor.[16] Indeed,

Chacel's own Generation of 1927, to which she refers as the "School of Ortega" (1993u, 370), due to the influence of the philosopher on many of its members during the 1920s and early 1930s, was seen as inaugurating a Silver Age of cultural renaissance.[17] Connections between Plato, Socrates, and Ortega are suggested in Chacel's following observation regarding the ability of a name to conjure up entire physical and epistemological landscapes: "[B]asta el nombre de Platón o de Sócrates para que *veamos* el azul de un cielo y *sintamos* una vida henchida de pensamiento. . . . Si nombramos a Ortega, seguramente hay quien *vea* la luz implacable de Madrid y *sienta* el perfume de alguna flor serrana . . ." [The name of Plato or Socrates is all that is needed for us to *see* the blueness of a sky and *feel* a life bursting with intellectual thought. . . . If we name Ortega, there will surely be those who *see* the relentless Madrid light and *smell* the fragrance of mountain flowers] (Chacel 1993u, 384).[18]

When considering the overlapping modernist groups that created in Spain in the first third of the twentieth century the concept of generation, although polemical, still proves useful. I share Michael Ugarte's view that "the very formation of any literary tradition or history assumes the presence of a historical continuum, a dialogue between and among specific historical moments in all their political, economic, social and technological complexity, and the term generation can be a useful tool (pedagogically as well as critically) in the understanding of the dialogue" (1994, 262).[19] As far as the avant-garde is concerned, it constitutes a minority culture that distances itself from a mainstream considered to pander to traditional aesthetic tastes.[20] Nevertheless its identity is derived from the dialogic positions that it assumes with regard to other contemporary cultural groups, as the production of physical and figurative spaces depends on the interrelationships among the components that delimit them (Lefebvre 1993,124).

The relationships that configure the cultural identity of the Madrid avant-garde and Chacel's literary project are those established with the Generations of 1898 and 1914.[21] All three generations inform the complex, multifaceted composition of Spanish modernisms, as noted by Mary Lee Bretz (2001). In a general context, such a heterogeneous grouping of cultural producers is also defended by Williams, who emphasizes that the avant-garde is composed of "successive formations which challenged not only the art institutions but the institution of Art, or Literature, itself, typically in a broad programme which included, though in diverse forms, the overthrow and remaking of existing society" (1989, 67).

In contemporary Spanish literary history, assigning generational consciousness to a given group has usually taken place retrospectively around significant historical events. Thus it was not until 1913 that Azorín definitively baptized his literary contemporaries as the "Generation of 98" (Dobón 1996, 59n.2), due to their quest to identify reasons and find solutions for Spain's "Disaster" and decline as a nation. Similarly the subsequent modernist generation that coalesces around the figure of Ortega becomes known as the "Generation of 1914," the year when World War I begins. In the case of Chacel's cultural generation, the coordinates of its identity are marked by World War I, the homage in 1927 commemorating three hundred years since the death of the Baroque poet, Luis de Góngora,[22] the Second Republic and the cataclysmic events of the Civil War. Generational consciousness, therefore, is produced through remembering, through retrospective evaluations of a given generation's interactions with specific sociohistorical and cultural circumstances.

This interdependence of the creation of a generation with remembering is underlined by Nora, who argues that "the self-affirmation of a generation" cannot be divorced from "[t]he construction of a memory." As Nora continues, "[t]he emergence of a 'generation' in its pure, intransitive state revealed the sovereignty of the notion's retrospective explanatory power, thereby constituting it, from its inception and in a primary, purely temporal sense, as a *lieu de mémoire*. . . . A generation is not something that emerges spontaneously from the heat of action: it is an observation, a summing up, a self-examination for the purpose of giving a firsthand historical account" (1996b, 500, 522).[23] Moreover Nora stresses that the birth of generational consciousness is closely connected with the avant-garde and is fashioned by history: "The advent of generational consciousness presupposes an idea of history. . . . This deep immersion in history is absolutely inseparable from the emergence of an active generational consciousness" (521, 515).

Nora's theories hold for the three modernist generations depicted in Chacel's trilogy, where modalities of generational consciousness are forged through concrete relationships with historical events and their challenges. It is these relationships, Chacel declares in 1977 in "Sendas perdidas," that make living at a particular historical time analogous to inhabiting and belonging to a nation: "[E]s indiscutible que el ser de nuestro tiempo significa una consanguinidad circunstancial inesquivable—trato, pues, de suscitar en las mentes de hoy la idea del *tiempo* como *patria*, con todo el esplendor y la fuerza adhesiva que tiene esta palabra" [It is indisputable that living in our times brings with it unavoidably close ties with context—I therefore endeavor to evoke in contemporary minds the idea of *time* as *nation*, with all the splendor and binding force inherent in this word] (1993w, 249).[24] The emphasis by both Nora and Chacel on generational consciousness being founded on relationships forged within specific sociohistorical times and places recalls Halbwachs's theories, for whom memory is never a matter of individual, subjective psychology. Rather it is contingent on "cadres sociaux" or social groups to whom one relates, and who provide the symbolic capital on which an individual draws (Kritzman 1996, xi).[25]

The physical and figurative sites where Nora considers that generational consciousness finds most cogent expression and that foster a sense of belonging and community among those who frequent them are those sites also foregrounded by Chacel throughout *Barrio* and *Acrópolis*: centers of collective intellectual participation, such as art exhibitions, museums, colloquia, newspapers, and literary cafés (Nora 1996b, 526). Furthermore Chacel's trilogy, with its elliptic allusions, mix of narrative persons, and use of key words with generationally contextualized connotations, exemplifies all the characteristics of Nora's *lieux de mémoire* or mnemonic sites, "charged with unfathomable powers of symbolic evocation, passwords and mutual recognition signals, all endlessly revivified by narrative, documents, firsthand accounts" (526). It is the generation, Nora asserts, that fashions such sites, since these "form the fabric of their provisional identities and stake out the boundaries of their generational memories. . . . The exploration of a generational memory begins with an inventory of these sites" (526).

Among the key words that stand out in Chacel's *Barrio* and *Acrópolis* are *instalación*, *clima*, *clan*, *esteta*, and *decadente* [installation, climate, clan, aesthete, decadent], all of which constitute subtle generational markers. In the case of *instalación*, the term was used by Ortega to refer to the need for history to position itself as a dynamic, creative process: "History, when it is what it should be, consists of an elaboration of *films*. History is not content with merely installing itself within each date and seeing the moral landscape glimpsed from there . . . but substitutes that series of static images . . . with the image of a movement" (1981e, 139).[26] In keeping with such a concept, in *Acrópolis* one of Chacel's narrators of Ortegan inclinations, the philosopher Manuel, alludes to his self as a house in which he is historically installed: "Es hora de volver uno hacia su casa, hacia sí mismo, y no hay prisa en volver porque está uno tan bien instalado en sí mismo" [It is time to turn back toward home, toward your self, but you're in no hurry to return, because you're installed in yourself so well] (Chacel 1984, 96).[27] As for *clima*, employed by Ortega to signify the ethical and historical spirit of a given nation,[28] it is adopted by Chacel's coprotagonist, Elena, to designate a sociohistorical moment that creates an environment propitious to dialogue and intellectual exchange: "Lo que prima, en resumen, es que estoy instalada. Todas esas cosas tremebundas, si las miramos como tú y yo podemos mirarlas, conservan sus dimensiones sirviéndonos, sin embargo, de refugio, de dulce hogar . . . si no consigo meterte en el clima no hay confidencia y no hay diálogo . . ." [In short, what most matters is that I'm installed. All those dreadful events, if viewed as you and I can view them, retain their dimensions, serving, however, as our refuge, as home sweet home . . . if I can't situate you in that climate, confidences and dialogue don't take place] (Chacel 1984, 290, 292). Regarding *clan*, this term appears repeatedly in *Barrio* and *Acrópolis* to denote a group of intellectuals with common ideals, and recalls Nora's point that generational memory is also contingent on the internalization of networks of loyalty, within which "'I' is simultaneously 'we'" (1996b, 526).[29] With respect to *esteta* and *decadente*, these words denote specific debates in modernist aesthetics examined in Chacel's *Barrio*, as will be taken up later in my analysis.

Nora's emphasis on a generation coming into existence through relationships founded on shared interests, freedom of association, and open debate, rather than through "assigned social membership and defined existential limits," leads to his premise that a generation is underpinned by horizontal relationships representative of a "democratic individualism" (1996b, 507, 499). Hence he elaborates, "[p]ure generational solidarity, which is the whole essence of the phenomenon, is freedom, insofar as the horizontality that it assumes is in a sense the ideal and idealized image of egalitarian democracy. A generation embodies and epitomizes the principle of equality out of which it was born" (507–8). Nora's equation of generation with an imagined egalitarian democracy is pertinent to the context of Chacel's *Barrio* and *Acrópolis*, works which critique the gender and class discrimination that impede effective national advancement.

The significance that modernist generations attributed to culture in the anticipated transformation of Spain is highlighted in Chacel's *Barrio* and *Acrópolis* by the value granted there to the plastic and literary arts,[30] especially through her young coprotagonists, Elena and Isabel. Chacel's own creative trajectory is mirrored in Elena, who initially dedicates herself to sculpture to embrace later writing, while Isabel becomes a painter. They embody the ideals of the "gente novísima" [those at the cutting edge] of modern Spain, the avant-garde generation mentored by the Generations of 1898 and 1914.[31] Among characters corresponding to the Generation of 1898 are Elena's father, the philosopher Manuel and his sister school-teacher, Laura, while the Generation of 1914 is represented in the figures of Máximo Montero and the art critic Martín. As for Chacel's portrayal of the Madrid avant-garde, its values are incarnated not only in Elena and Isabel but also in their friends, Ramón, Luis, and Octavio. Nevertheless, while Chacel signals that the novelists of the 1898 Generation were indeed the maestros of her literary group, she also asserts that there were great differences between these two generations, due to their distinct historical contexts: "[H]abía entre ellos y nosotros grandes abismos, . . . sus mundos personales no eran continuables en el tiempo que se ofrecía a nuestro mundo" [There were deep chasms between us, . . . their private worlds could not be continued in the times that presented themselves to our world] (1993w, 240).

The process of rigorous mentoring of a younger intellectual group by more established ones, in order to prepare the former to effect its mission, is explained by Chacel in her essay, "Volviendo al punto de partida." There she identifies such preparation with the concept of "school" present in the generic title bestowed on her trilogy and foregrounded in Raphael's painting: "[S]abíamos que para entrar en ella [la escuela] teníamos que ejercitarnos en un concienzudo preparatorio y pasar por un examen de ingreso: esto es, de conciencia" [We knew that to enter it (the school) we had to undergo conscientious preparation and pass an entrance exam: that is, an examination of conscience] (1993z, 283–84). Similar connotations of "school" were already paramount in the writings of one of

Chacel's principal mentors, Ortega,[32] for whom the expression "tener escuela" encapsulated the intellectual preparation and scientific education considered vital for Spain to qualify truly as a democratic nation or *pueblo*: "What is needed is a technology of invention, to 'have a profession,' a school, intellectual preparation. Otherwise, only elementary, crude solutions will be proposed, typical of café-talk" (Ortega 1981b, 137). According to Ortega, whose words recall Acuña's critique, Spain still occupied the category of tiny village or "aldea," trapped in cyclical tasks tied to nature's seasons (109). He maintained that the way to build a modern nation was through a class of intellectuals, who, independent of political and religious beliefs, would constitute an elite minority charged with the mission of guiding the state and the ethical development of a largely uneducated population (Llera 1991, 42). Although initially this was to be a revolution, like that of Acuña's Ramón, directed from "on high," Ortega maintained that it was synonymous with an open democracy continually in the making, with the disinterested intellectual as the conscience of society.[33]

Affective relationships among "teachers" and "students," allusive to those pertaining to the Generations of 1898, 1914, and 1927, abound in *Barrio* and *Acrópolis*.[34] Figuring prominently are characters from the school and art academy attended by Elena and Isabel, together with others who perform the role of educators and mentors: the maestro, the art-teacher, the patron of the arts, the art collector, Elena's father, and Elena herself, who is instrumental in the cultural education of Isabel. It is only through the formation of a strong "school" of educators that the nation, described in *Acrópolis* by the school-teacher, Laura, in terms highly reminiscent of Giner's, as "la casa sin barrer" [the house that needs sweeping out],[35] can be made habitable and healthy: "Pero ¿es que son las grandes personalidades las que tienen que barrer la casa? . . . Los que tienen el poder no son los que manufacturan los productos cocinables, son otros ... somos nosotros, los de las dosis homeopáticas, los del granum salis ... " [But is it the responsibility of great personages to sweep out the house? . . . Those who have the ability to do so are not those who manufacture the cooking ingredients but others ... those of us who administer homeopathic doses, the grain of salt] (Chacel 1984, 175).

It is this shared concept of "school," I suggest, that best summarizes the historical consciousness of the modernist generations depicted in Chacel's trilogy and born with Giner's Institución, described by Chacel as the institution that taught Spaniards European ways (Chacel 1993h, 105).[36] Continued by the Generations of 1898 and 1914, the project of Spain's education reached its pre–Civil War culmination in the cultural pedagogy undertaken by the Second Republic, supported by many of the avant-garde. As Sandie Holguín notes in *Creating Spaniards*, the aim of the Second Republic was to nourish the spirit and "shape a national identity that was held together by the glue of culture" (2002, 47–48). In this vein Chacel's avant-garde generation, states a character from *Acrópolis*, exploded into Spanish cultural life promising to further national formation through its own brand of school, only to be truncated by the Civil War:

> Se organizó aquello que parecía una eclosión, . . . que iba a difundir su personalísima escuela ... eso sobre todo, iba a ser una escuela . . . que absorbería el ímpetu de las mentes jóvenes, que proyectaría ese resplandor que fascina . . . Eso es lo que habría sido, si al darla por terminada no hubiera quedado todo ello disipado entre lo que vino después ... . (Chacel 1984, 171–72)

> [There took place what was akin to an explosion, . . . which would spread its particular brand of school ... above all, it was to be a school . . . that would capture the energy of young minds, that would project the kind of brilliance that captivates . . . That is what would have happened if, on considering that goal accomplished, it had not all been swept away by what came next.][37]

Here the words uttered by Chacel's fictional persona corroborate Nora's thesis that generational memory is not so much derived from what its members experienced in common as from "what they have not experienced. . . . a painful, never-ending fantasy that holds them together far more than what stands in front of and divides them" (1996b, 525). It was the failure of the avant-garde project to realize its full potential in harnessing culture to democracy, due to the Civil War and Franco regime, that no doubt constitutes a major catalyst for Chacel's retrospective recreation of its world.

In Chacel's *Barrio* and *Acrópolis*, the growing of a nation through culture and the creation of appropriate offerings to whet the appetite of cultural consumers and educate their taste are prominent themes,[38] conveyed through an abundance of agricultural and culinary metaphors. The notion of a planned evolution of society and culture, whereby a democratic *polis* is purposefully "grown" through (agri)culture, is paramount in the following meditation from *Acrópolis* by Elena's father, representative of the 1898 Generation, which is replete with agricultural tropes: "Los surcos, los pechos o mentes están húmedos de vida, labrados y abonados para recibirlas [las notas] y allí también es íntimo y propio lo que se arma: allí germinan con las sustancias del terreno" [The furrows, hearts or minds are moist with life, worked and fertilized to receive them (the musical notes) and what is created there is also something intimate and personal: there they germinate thanks to what is in the soil] (Chacel 1984, 168).[39] The very title of *Acrópolis* captures the vision of a cultured Spain based on the secular principles of a republic. Chacel's positioning of her fictional Acropolis, on a rise overlooking the Madrid racecourse, implicitly identifies it with the Residencia de Estudiantes [Students' Residence], similarly situated, where so many of the Generation of 1927 were formed. Its purpose as a figurative oven for creating an intellectual republic is suggested in Manuel's following words: "Esta colina de los Altos del Hipódromo es la ACRÓPOLIS . . . como si el tiempo fuese un horno fortísimo que cociese las grandes construcciones—secularmente cocidos . . . Con estos ladrillos rosados se podría tal vez esbozar una república platónica ... " [This hill above the racecourse is the ACROPOLIS . . . it is as if time were a very hot oven that cooks great constructions—cooked in the world over the centuries . . . With these pinkish bricks, perhaps the beginnings of a platonic Republic might be set in place] (222).

The metaphorical oven of time evident in Manuel's statement reappears in Laura's reference to how different "hornadas" or generations are "cooked" by variable historical contexts: "[L]as semejanzas y las diferencias se esconden, se acumulan en el último rincón donde no llega el humo de las especias, . . . de lo permanentemente cambiante en cada olla, en cada hornada ... " [Similarities and differences hide and accumulate in the most remote nook, untouched by the scent of spices, . . . of what is continually changing in each cooking pot, in each generational batch] (175). In turn, Ramón, one of the characters identified with the avant-garde, underlines the importance of innovative cultural offerings in fashioning a sociopolitical future different to the present and past: "[L]o que hace falta es oler lo que no se guisa, lo que hay que guisar, lo que uno, cada uno, tiene . . . que hacer que se guise" [What is necessary is to smell what is not being cooked, what needs to be cooked, what each and every single person must . . . ensure is cooked] (242).[40]

Chacel's use of agricultural and cooking metaphors, therefore, clearly pertains to contemporary debates concerning the cultural foods that the Spanish nation requires in order to develop a robust political constitution. Such tropes pertain to a paradigm of nation formation whereby, as Ernest Gellner remarks, "cultivated" cultures are "sustained by literacy and by specialized personnel" (1983, 50). At the same time, by representing the production of culture through metaphors of cooking, associated with a domestic sphere traditionally assigned to women, Chacel, like Acuña, also implicitly argues for the full participation of women in elaborating Spanish culture and history.

Emblematic of the role to be played by women in Spain's cultural enterprise are characters like Laura, who, as an atheist from a family tradition of freethinkers (Chacel 1981, 74, 109),[41] permits Chacel to revindicate a scientific liberalism. Likewise it is through Tina Smith, the Catalan art patron, whose worldliness gives her the air of a foreigner, that Chacel presents travel as necessary for acquiring the intellectual and cultural capital with which to develop Spain: "Tina era como una extranjera: no es que era de otro barrio, sino de otro país: el país del dinero—no de una Jauja nebulosa, sino de regiones industriales pujantes . . . ¡Viajar! ... era necesario viajar para saber, para saber como saben otros, siendo nosotros ... sin dejar de ser nosotros" [Tina was like a foreigner: it wasn't that she was from another part of town, but from another country: the land of wealth—not from a nebulous land of plenty but from powerful industrial regions . . . Travel! ... it was necessary to travel to know, to know what others know, while being ourselves... without ceasing to be ourselves] (1984, 65).

Consequently characters such as Laura and Tina embody the mobility across intellectual and physical frontiers that defined the metropolitan and cosmopolitan distinctiveness of the modernist generations (Williams 1989, 59). Indeed one of the principal characteristics of modernism, Williams explains, was its literal and figurative strangeness or foreignness: "It is a very striking feature of many Modernist and avant-garde movements that they were not only located in the great metropolitan centres but that so many of their members were immigrants into these centres, where in some new ways all were strangers" (77). In this sense, the many northern European immigrant characters in *Acrópolis*, like Bertha and Tob, Ira Lago, who is a refugee from the Russian Revolution, and Señor Waksman, all of whom are connected with the artistic world, bear witness to the Europeanist, socially committed stance that Ortega's and Chacel's generations considered vital for the regeneration of Spain.[42] Hence, in "Volviendo al punto de partida," Chacel underscores the desirability of Spain's Europeanization, explicitly associating that project with the avant-garde: "La europeización de España era, pues, la empresa de mi generación. . . . Pensada desde Europa, la vida de España no era más que pobreza. . . . lo más urgente y necesario era estudiar las causas de esa pobreza—material ante todo—y combatirla . . ." [Spain's Europeanization was, then, my generation's undertaking. . . . Considered from Europe's perspective, Spanish life was pure poverty . . . what was most urgent and necessary was to study the causes of that poverty—primarily material poverty—and fight it] (Chacel 1993z, 282–83). A similar enterprise of Europeanization was crucial to Spain's reinvention of itself as a modern democracy after the Franco dictatorship: a recreation to which Chacel's novels of memory contribute.

From Exclusion toward Integration: Rewriting Domestic and Public Space

Memory and places go hand in hand. As Patrick Hutton states in his study on Halbwachs: "In remembering, we locate, or localize, images of the past in specific places. In and of themselves, the images of memory are always fragmentary and provisional. They have no whole or coherent meaning until we project them into concrete settings. Such settings provide us with our places of memory" (1993, 78). It is the imaginary inhabitation of such places, Gaston Bachelard foregrounds in *The Poetics of Space*, that allows subjects to repossess disappeared psychological dwellings and, with them, "an unforgettable past" (1969, xxxii). Through his theories of "topo-analysis," which he defines as "the systematic psychological study of the sites of our intimate lives," Bachelard establishes analogies between houses and books, to maintain that "we 'write a room,' 'read a room,' or 'read a house'" (8, 14). Hence it is significant that, in Chacel's literary reappropriation of an avant-garde cultural history, she deploys specific topographies of memory, centered on the house and the city, key spaces for modernist configurations of the world. Chacel's fictional recreations of the avant-garde context not only enable writer and reader to reenter, through the imagination, its historical and cultural spaces. They also critique traditional paradigms of modernist history and culture.

Studies on modernist movements have invariably stressed their androcentric orientation.[43] Given that modernism was premised on the free circulation of creators and intellectuals in a public sphere culturally designated as proper only to men, upper- and middle-class women were, as within Acuña's context, ideally associated with and consigned to the domestic realm. Modernism, then, as Lynne Walker notes, was defined against domesticity, and masculine reason against feminine sentiment (2002, 827).

Such arguments are confirmed by other feminist cultural critics, such as Rita Felski (1995) and Griselda Pollock. In her essay, "Modernity and the Spaces of Femininity," Pollock examines modernist visual representations of space to elucidate how "[s]exuality, modernism or modernity are organized by and [*sic*] organizations of sexual difference. To perceive women's specificity is to analyse historically a particular configuration of difference" (1988, 56). Spaces of femininity, she continues, are "those from which femininity is lived as a positionality in discourse and social practice. They are the product of a lived sense of social locatedness, mobility and visibility, in the social relations of seeing and being seen" (84). It is this kind of positionality in social practice and discourse that Chacel consistently foregrounds to renegotiate gender and class discrimination.

Although the barriers that rendered difficult women's equal participation in Spanish modernist cultural circles were repeatedly acknowledged by Chacel herself in diaries and interviews,[44] in essays such as "Comentario tardío sobre Simone de Beauvoir" [Overdue Commentary on Simone de Beauvoir] she avows that culture is not an exclusive, masculine domain: "Toda mujer, en toda época y en todo país pudo siempre proponerse por medio de proyectos como una trascendencia" [All women, in every historical period and in all countries, were always able to envisage personal transcendence through creative endeavor] (1993c, 506). Despite such pronouncements, in "La mujer en galeras" [Woman in the Galleys] Chacel elaborates on the sociocultural and political mechanisms of power that control access to culture for all groups constructed as other, including women (1993k). Where Chacel's preoccupation with women's access to equal educational and cultural resources most comes to the fore is in novels like *Memorias de Leticia Valle, Barrio,* and *Acrópolis.* These texts question the naturalized consigning of women by masculine cultures to the domestic sphere and reframe a national narrative of female disenfranchisement to argue for women's active participation in cultural matters. Such a stance also challenges a literary canon that, with few exceptions, has denied women producers their rightful place in cultural histories.[45] As Pollock affirms, "the discourse of phallocentric . . . history relied upon the category of a negated femininity in order to secure the supremacy of masculinity within the sphere of creativity" (1999, 5).

Chacel's critique of women's exclusion from valued social and cultural spaces, discourses and practices is highlighted from the very beginning of *Barrio,* when the illegitimate, lower-class Isabel rings the doorbell to Elena's upper-middle-class home. The doubt experienced by Isabel at the closed door is indicative of her anxiety on seeking to cross barriers of class, just as the initial denial of entry to her by Elena's grandmother, Eulalia, manifests the latter's conservative, exclusionary perspective on class: "El timbre delataba el titubeo, la duda de quien lo oprimía temiendo que no respondiese la persona llamada . . . —¿Vienes a ver a Elena? . . . —Pues Elena no está: salió con sus amiguitas. Entonces una despedida banal, torpe, evasiva como de quien es cogido en falta . . ." [The doorbell betrayed the hesitancy, the uncertainty of the person pressing it, fearful that the person called on would not answer . . . —Have you come to see Elena? . . . —Well, Elena isn't home: she's gone out with her little friends. Then a banal, awkward goodbye, evasive as if someone were being caught out] (Chacel 1981, 7).[46] As Isabel later recounts to Elena, "a tu abuela le pareció que yo no debía estar allí" [your grandmother was of the opinion that I shouldn't be there] (17).

The notion of barrier presented by the door is reinforced when Eulalia does not include Isabel among Elena's upper-middle-class friends; a reminder of inequality that causes Isabel to question her identity: "Entonces, ¿quién soy yo? ... Si ellas, las otras—¿qué otras? —son sus amiguitas, yo ¿qué soy? ... Yo ¿quién soy?" [Then, who am I? ... If they, the others—what others?—are her little friends, what am I? ... Who am I?] (7). Nevertheless Isabel is permitted to enter the home when she agrees to draw threads for Eulalia, who thereby affirms the class boundaries that she considers proper to their respective social stations (8). In Isabel's case, her lower-class status is intensified by her gender, to emphasize, as Lerner puts it, that "[c]lass is genderic" and that oppression in terms of one category is inseparable from oppression in the other (1997, 136, 143). Consequently, in Chacel's opening episode, class and gender discrimination is highlighted by foregrounding the difficulties faced when characters such as Isabel pass from assigned sociocultural contexts to other, disallowed ones. Isabel's discomfort on attempting this transition can be related to Henrietta Moore's comment that "[t]o leave certain spaces and pass into others is to know in your body what . . . differences involve; it is to know oppression and discrimination intimately in a way which does not allow for the separation of the physical from the mental" (1994, 81).

That the house in *Barrio* is not only a physical space but also an entity representative of society, culture, and their discourses is developed in a sequence almost immediately subsequent. Isabel's incomprehension of what it means to be likened by one of Eulalia's friends to a Carreño painting is described in terms of being enclosed within a prison or "calabozo," the door to which has been tightly shut: "[Y] se cierra la puerta" [And the door closes] (Chacel 1981, 16). These connotations are further reinforced when Isabel later recalls the episode, comparing cultural knowledge to the key that can unlock and illuminate the dark enclosure or figurative prison that terrifies the ignorant mind: "[L]a palabra que me aterró a mí era como un cuarto oscuro para el que no podía entrar en ella, pero para los que tenían la llave no era nada medroso" [The word that terrified me was like a dark room for those who could not enter it, but for those with the key it was not frightening at all] (39). Consequently on the eve of her visit with Elena and Elena's father to the Prado, to view paintings by Carreño, Isabel portrays the upper-middle class and culture to which she has access through her friendship with Elena in terms of a luxurious house that is not hers and into which she can only look from the outside until she has acquired sufficient light or knowledge to enter it: "[L]o que yo veo es como si mirase por una ventana una casa que no es la mía ... ; una casa lujosa, con espejos y lámparas de cristal, y viera que hay esas cosas que yo no estoy dentro, pero puedo verlas . . . tengo que dormir como si fuera a entrar en la casa que no es la de todos los días ... Hasta que haya luz ... " [I see it as if I were looking through a window into a house that doesn't belong to me ... ; a luxurious house, with mirrors and crystal lamps; it's as if I saw that there exist things that I don't inhabit but can see . . . I have to sleep as if I were to enter the house that isn't my usual abode... Until light comes] (30–31). Conversely once Isabel is familiar with the paintings by Carreño and other works in the Prado, their names and creators are likened to open curtains and windows that allow insight into formerly closed spaces: "Nombres como cortinas que se descorren, como ventanas abiertas" [Names like curtains that are opened, like open windows] (130).

Clearly, therefore, Chacel represents culture as habitats or spaces underpinned by issues contingent on gender, class, and access to education. The masculine gendering of modernist culture as antithetical to the domestic sphere and its assigned values is continually countered in *Barrio* by cultural artifacts being brought into the domestic sphere, where their virtues are debated. Thus Elena and Isabel visit the home of their friend, Felisa Olmedo, to see an edition of Dante's *Divine Comedy* purchased by Felisa's father and discuss the engravings that illustrate the work (171–76). Depicting souls in terms of bodies, the illustrations embed the abstract or transcendental in the material: "Las almas, para ser visibles, captables, audibles, tienen que hablar con la forma de sus cuerpos" [In order to be visible, apprehended, audible, souls must speak with their bodily forms] (173). Similarly, on discussing operatic pieces played on the Olmedos's gramophone, the young women privilege the emotions produced by the music, considering that they facilitate understanding through senses unerring in their logic: "[L]o comprehende [cualquiera] con los sentidos que no fallan nunca en la lógica" [Anyone can comprehend it, with a sensorial logic that never errs] (175). Consequently not only does Chacel's narrative firmly revindicate a cultural practice located within the domestic sphere. It also proposes that culture is transmitted and understood through elements traditionally deemed inimical to cultural transcendence through their identification with the feminine: namely, bodies and emotions.

The frameworks of exclusion that pertain to the early episodes in *Barrio* examined above are also proper to the gendered relationship of modernist cultural producers with the city. Male modernist artists and writers perceived cities as feminized entities that willingly offered up their sights to an objectifying and distanced creative gaze.[47] Not surprisingly, in keeping with this paradigm, frequent modernist subjects in male-authored works were women as objects of sexual desire and exchange, reflecting a sociocultural economy from which lower-class women were excluded as autonomous subjects and within which upper- and middle-class women were marginalized through their real and imaginary positioning as domestic angels. Consequently, as Pollock observes, "the social process defined by the term modernity was experienced spatially in terms of access to the spectacular city which was open to a class and gender-specific gaze" (1988, 84).

Chacel's work critiques such a discriminatory gaze and the aesthetics that accompany it. In her essay "Madrid en el recuerdo" [Remembering Madrid], published in 1986, Chacel comments that, in her trilogy, representations of the city cannot be divorced from its inhabitants, their habits and their vital spaces: "[C]omo novelas, consisten los tres . . . en un continuo diálogo entre habitantes—sus hábitos y sus habitáculos como personas dramáticas—de Madrid" [Like novels, the three entities are constituted . . . by a continuous dialogue among Madrid's inhabitants—whose habits and vital spaces are akin to dramatic characters] (1993m, 613). The masculine modernist gaze establishes a relationship of distance and detachment with a feminized city, on which the artist or writer imposes his vision. Conversely, as apparent in the following quotation from *Acrópolis,* Chacel's portrayal of the city there reveals that she conceives of it as a living, dynamic body that constitutes a diverse sociohistorical and philosophical text created by those who inhabit it:

> [E]l hábitat urbano [es] tan realmente natural como cualquier madriguera, topinera o cubil, que es expresión, semblanza, impronta del bicho que lo habita . . . Los barrios están apersonados en un estilo, color, olor, temperatura, se distinguen, incanjeables ... Igualmente las casas, cada una de ellas. Empezando en sus ladrillos como miembros del barrio y luego entregando sus órganos, vísceras. . . . (1984, 153)
>
> [The urban habitat (is) truly as natural as any burrow, molehole or lair, which expresses and bears the likeness and imprint of the animal that inhabits it . . . City districts are characterized by a particular style, color, smell, and temperature; their differences are not exchangeable ... The same applies to houses, to each and every one of them. Beginning with their bricks, like members of the district, and then surrendering their organs, their viscera.]

In keeping with this stance, in *Acrópolis* Chacel's narrative voice perceives Madrid's quarters in terms of their social histories. In the case of the Maravillas District, it is described according to the different sociocultural histories that feed into its pre–Civil War narrative present and continue to inform the authorial post-Franco present, as exemplified in the following quotation:

> Gran Mercado: culmina la realidad, el movimiento de lo que nutre —ya muerto, ya inmóvil—a lo que vive y come y anda. . . . La plaza, plaza hoy día encuadrada por casas que, en sólo un siglo, crecieron y envejecieron. Crecieron sobre un campo de guerra, de triunfo . . . Y en seguida—siglo bendito, hoy ostentando en la gloria sus gloriosos pecados—, en seguida vino el albañil con su ladrillo y llana, vinieron los cristaleros y fumistas, . . . acudieron los carboneros . . . Se formaron hogares a su medida. . . . (Chacel 1984, 38)

> [The Great Market: it crowns reality, the movement from what it nourishes—whether dead or unmoving—to what lives and eats and walks. . . . The square, the square today framed by houses that, in only a century, proliferated and aged. They sprouted in a field of war, of victory . . . And immediately—blessèd century, today showing off in glory its heavenly sins—, immediately there arrived the bricklayer with his bricks and trowel, the glaziers and stove repairers, . . . there came the coalmen . . . Homes were formed befitting their needs].[48]

This kind of representation recalls Lefebvre's proposal that "the city is an *oeuvre*, closer to a work of art than to a simple material product. . . . The city has a history; it is the work of a history, that is, of clearly defined people and groups who accomplish this *oeuvre*, in historical conditions" (1996, 101). At stake in Lefebvre's concept of oeuvre is the theoretical right of all inhabitants to participate in and use the physical and symbolic resources of the city, as explained by Eleonore Kofman and Elizabeth Lebas: "The right to the *oeuvre* (participation) and appropriation (not to be confused with property but use value) was implied in the right to the city" (1996, 20).

Undoubtedly the city constitutes the physical and figurative space clearly identified by Chacel as that within which subaltern others might acquire greater opportunities for sociopolitical protagonism and cultural advancement. Her emphasis on the city not only concords with the fact that modernism was, as Williams has indicated, inseparable from a specific relationship of intellectuals and cultural producers with the metropolis (1989, 44). It was the city, as Chacel declared in a critique of Federico García Lorca's rural dramas, that held out the challenge for Spain to leave behind its traditional identity as romanticized landscape and achieve the transition from "pueblo," connotative of a rural class and the people of a backward national economy, to *polis* or democracy:

> La vivaz presencia del pueblo en su obra [de Lorca] es la de un pueblo-paisaje, lleno de los dramas de la vieja tradición—dramas que para nosotros eran ya paisaje, . . . que quedaban al margen de nuestra vida urbana . . . La ciudad era el tendido donde el pueblo tenía que afrontar el envite de la era moderna, la era que, dándole al pueblo más valor, más relieve, más espacio vital que ninguna otra época le dio . . . le pone en el trance de dejar de ser pueblo. (Chacel 1993w, 238)

> [The vibrant presence of the village people in his (Lorca's) work is characteristic of a people-landscape, replete with dramas from the old tradition—dramas that for us were already landscape, . . . on the margins of our urban life . . . The city was the bull-ring where the people had to confront the charge of the modern era, the era that, giving the people greater value, presence and vital space than any other . . . sets them the challenge of ceasing to be the masses.][49]

The obstacles that hamper Spain's effective transformation from underdeveloped nation to modern democracy are repeatedly couched in *Barrio* and *Acrópolis* in terms of a hierarchized, engendered opposition between two classes—the one socially privileged, the other disadvantaged—and their corresponding ways of seeing. In *Acrópolis,* Chacel's description of a Sunday excursion from Madrid to Toledo by several of Elena's and Isabel's middle-class male friends premises a dynamics of seeing that, turning on the motif of landscape, highlights the differences that impede Spain's advancement. On the tram journey through Madrid to Atocha station Chacel's narrative voice stresses the distance between classes through positioning the young men as seated opposite impoverished workers, "trabajadores de domingo, . . . irredentos, encadenados a pequeños servicios sin domingo. . . . apenas cubiertos con vestigios de indumentarias no adecuadas a ninguna faena..." [Sunday workers, . . . without redemption, condemned to odd jobs without holidays. . . . barely covered in rags unsuitable for any work] (1984, 177).

Such possibilities for women to engage in formerly proscribed cultural activities are overwhelmingly evident in *Acrópolis*, where the constant excursionism in which characters delight is to urban cultural centers such as museums, art galleries, theaters, and cafés. In these sites where culture is displayed, debated, and contested, Chacel's texts affirm the assiduous participation of young women, like her characters Elena and Isabel, in cultural critique and production.[50] At the same time, the experiences had by Chacel's coprotagonists seem more to incarnate exceptions to the rule or a utopian vision of what might be, rather than the reality of daily life for the average young woman of middle-class background or aspirations in the period depicted.[51] Perhaps more than representing a common reality, Chacel's Elena and Isabel embody the dream of a modern cultural and sociopolitical economy that had yet, in the early decades of the twentieth century, to materialize fully. Nevertheless their engagement with culture emphasizes that the construction of this economy, as another of Chacel's characters suggests, requires integrating aesthetic practice into daily life, so that it becomes second nature: "No, . . . esta gran ciudad que queremos no ha nacido. Está apuntando por otros barrios, . . . No está trazada, está brotada o producida por hábitos ... " [No, . . . this great city that we desire hasn't been born. It's sprouting in other districts, . . . It isn't already laid out but blossoms or is produced through habitual actions] (Chacel 1984, 71–72). It is such a practice of culture that has the power to set the stage for a more egalitarian participation by a nation's inhabitants in sociopolitical life. For Chacel's Elena and Isabel, it is through practicing culture that different questions can be asked of society and history, as I now explore in the ensuing section.

Viewing "from 'Elsewhere'": Female Spectatorship and the Interrogation of History

The questioning of consecrated traditions that informs avant-garde works is evident in *Barrio* and *Acrópolis* on the many occasions that Elena and Isabel consider artistic and literary works that constitute a masculine canon. However, their contemplation of these masterpieces imbues them, once again, with embodied, "feminine" values.

In this sense, Elena and Isabel revindicate what Pollock has termed "the particularity of the female spectator—that which is completely negated in the selective tradition we are offered as history" (1988, 85). By foregrounding the perspectives of female spectators and their situatedness in masculine space, Chacel's texts enact Pollock's thesis of "the rearticulation of traditional space so that it ceases to function primarily as the space of sight for a mastering gaze, but becomes the locus of relationships. The gaze that is fixed on the represented figure is that of equal and like . . ." (87). What is stressed is "phenomenological space," which does not perceive space as determined by sight alone but rather, encompasses other senses as well, according to the always diverse, contingent values held by viewing subjects within specific sociohistorical contexts (65).

The renegotiation of cultural space so that it might serve to promote egalitarian relationships is privileged in *Barrio* on the aforementioned visit to the Prado that Isabel makes in the company of Elena and her father. In contrast to the door to Elena's house, through which Isabel could only pass in her allotted social place, the main door to the Prado is revolving, guaranteeing easy and equal entry to all: "[L]o fácil que es pasar por una puerta, una puerta giratoria, una puerta que parece que se mueve por sí misma, . . . ella sigue girando y otros vienen detrás, otros que tienen que pasar igualmente . . ." [How easy it is to go through a door, a revolving door, a door that apparently moves all by itself, . . . it keeps on turning and others enter behind, others who have to enter on an equal basis] (Chacel 1981, 33).

Whereas Elena's father appreciates the paintings for their canonical value and wishes his charges to do the same, Elena wants Isabel to view them according to more personal, affective criteria, as the latter relates:

> De cuando en cuando [Elena] echa una ojeada a su padre . . . A veces él nos indica cualquier cosa para que no dejemos de verla. Pero Elena quiere que yo vea, ante todo, sus amores.
>
> —Lo que son los cuadros, los pintores, las épocas ya lo irás aprendiendo, ahora tienes que ver los personajes que son sólo para enamorarse. (34–35)

> [From time to time (Elena) glances at her father . . . Sometimes he points something out to us that we simply have to see. But above all, Elena wants me to see what she most loves.

—What paintings, painters and epochs there are, you'll learn little by little; now you must see the personages that you can't help but fall in love with.]

In particular, Elena's appreciation of the sculpture of Ariadne takes the form of a ritual encompassing music and dance, modes of expression that disrupt the paradigm of distanced spectatorship adopted by her father:

> Elena canturrea, dando vueltas alrededor de Ariadna . . .
> Elena sigue cantando y rodeando a Ariadna, su padre deja de mirar el retrato del rey o del caballo y lanza a Elena una mirada indefinible ... Una mirada burlona y al mismo tiempo enternecida, una mirada de connivencia. . . . (35–36)
>
> [Elena sings softly, circling around Ariadne . . .
> Elena continues singing and moving around Ariadne, her father stops looking at the study of the king or horse and gives Elena an undefinable look ... A mocking yet tender look, a complicitous look.]

Elena's song and dance around the sleeping statue introduce movement and change into that mythologized, static cultural context. The dormant Ariadne, called on by Elena to awaken—"¡Despierta ... , abandonada! ... " [Awaken ... , abandoned one!] (Chacel 1981, 36)—becomes representative of the need for all those culturally constructed as other to awaken from their slumber and engage actively with their context.

A comparable instance, also occurring in *Barrio*, foregrounds Isabel's interaction with a painting in the Prado of Doña Margarita of Austria by a disciple of Velázquez, Juan Bautista Martínez del Mazo (c.1610–67).[52] Yet again, it is pertinent that Chacel's ekphrastic representation focuses on the fact that the abstract, transcendental themes of life and death depicted in the painting are symbolized by the domestic space of the house and its adjoining rooms. Thus, in one section of the work, the queen, already dead, is laid out enshrouded in her bedroom: "Ella está muerta en la alcoba, tendida en la cama . . . está con un sudario blanco . . ." [She is dead in the bedroom, laid out on the bed . . . wrapped in a white shroud] (132). In another section, she is presented in an adjacent room, taking leave of life: "[M]ientras las otras rezan, ella está aquí, en esta otra habitación, pensando, despidiéndose de todo. . . . tiene en la otra mano, en la que apoya en el respaldo del sillón, . . . un gran pañuelo blanco, como para hacerle aletear en la despedida" [While the other women pray, she is here, in this other room, thinking, taking leave of everything. . . . in her other hand, resting on the back of the armchair, . . . she is holding an enormous white handkerchief, as if for fluttering in farewell] (132–33).

On Isabel's contemplation of the scene the work exceeds its material and temporal frames. Her reading of this visual text brings her to formulate questions regarding the subject of the painting and the process of its creation: "¿En qué reina se ve un peinado así[?] . . . en el retrato que Mazo pintó—¿Cuándo? ¿Antes o después de muerta? ¿Posó ella para el pintor aquí[?]" [What queen ever had such a hairstyle? . . . in the portrait by Mazo—When? Before or after her death? Did she pose for the painter here?] (133). Isabel's interrogation of the painting brings to mind the paradigm of spectatorship elaborated by Michael Ann Holly, for whom art historians are placed by their historical artifacts in specific "grammatical relationships," made manifest in the form and style of their narratives (1995, 84).

In Chacel's texts, it could be said that the grammatical position most taken up by her intradiegetic spectators or readers is that of the question, as exemplified by Isabel's queries above. Often symbolized in Chacel's works by the open door,[53] the question places the reader neither inside nor outside a bounded context, but in a hybrid space of transition. Questions, as Pollock affirms in the context of art history, allude to "a more radical departure from . . . [its] paradigms. Instead of art history's study of 'looked at objects' . . . [a] different agenda is proposed when . . . we ask: why were they looking? What were they looking at? What pleasures or anxieties in looking had to be managed?" (1995, 41). The mark of interrogation that inhabits Chacel's texts signals an engagement with cultural artifacts that does not address them as finished products but as ongoing processes that awaken curiosity and the desire to understand in their contemporary viewers/readers. By reading Martínez del Mazo's painting in a way that addresses the sociohistorical processes that potentially influenced its composition, Isabel's musings stress this dynamic interdependence between culture and society.[54]

Following the questions cited above, Chacel's text moves from external features to internal ones, considering that the figure of Margarita leads Isabel to imagine the psychological circumstances surrounding her death: "Su mirada es muy triste como si no estuviese preparada para la muerte . . . Tal vez sin testamento; sin confesión no es probable porque eso no se lo habrían consentido. . . . Tendría muchas más joyas, además de esos azabaches, y tal vez quisiera dejárselas a alguna de sus damas, doncellas o amigas ... " [She looks very sad, as if she weren't prepared for death . . . Perhaps she died without a will; it's unlikely that she died without confessing, because that would never have been allowed. . . . She would have a great many more jewels apart from those jet pieces, and she probably wished to leave them to some of her ladies-in-waiting, maids, or friends] (1981, 133). Rather than concentrating on the philosophical or political themes that canonically would inhere to the representation of a queen's death, Isabel's focus is on the personal and the interrelational, and on the embodiment of history in subjects with whom empathy can be established. Indeed it is as a result of Isabel's interaction with Martínez del Mazo's work that she incorporates into her own person the two plaits observed on the queen in the painting: a legacy that in turn enables her to explore previously undiscovered aspects of her identity, as in the sexually charged exchange with Luis that immediately follows (133–35).[55]

The dynamics present in the readings offered by Elena and Isabel of artistic works constitute what Teresa de Lauretis has called a "view from 'elsewhere,'" understanding "elsewhere" as what is disregarded in contemporary hegemonic discourses but which remains present in "the chinks and cracks of the power-knowledge-apparati" (1989, 25). For Lauretis, such a view constitutes the crux of the feminist project, which must represent the forgotten or deliberately omitted through "a movement from the space represented by/in a representation, by/in a discourse, by/in a sex-gender system to the space not-represented yet implied (unseen) in them" (26). Elena's and Isabel's interactions with cultural artifacts consistently foreground elements associated with the feminine, represented by masculine discourses as other to and therefore outside culture and history, and show them to be integral to the meanings of the work.

Chacel's emphasis on a cultural poetics engaged with contemporary contexts is reiterated through other characters, such as the philosopher Manuel and the art critic Martín. Valid artistic expression, Martín ponders in *Acrópolis*, should not consist of still lifes that arrest or even deny historical movement, like "un puchero de Zurbarán" [one of Zurbarán's pots] (Chacel 1984, 129).[56] On the contrary, art should exceed its frames of time and space by furnishing practical truths that might continue to be relevant to the present day:

> Esas intenciones son reales, son momentos de realidad, que no están quietos como pucheros, sino que están realizando ... Por eso me empeño . . . en comprobar sus resultados prácticos, que serían algo así como la demostración de que no eran fantasmas, flatulencias de la mente, del genio artístico, sino palabras verdaderas, verdades. Y, si son verdad, ¿qué más podemos pedirles? ... Que sigan siéndolo ... . (129)
>
> [Those intentions are real, they are moments in reality that aren't still like pots but are making ... That's why I insist . . . on verifying their practical results, which would be similar to showing that they weren't ghosts, mental flatulence, of the creative spirit, but real words, truths. And, if they are true, what more can we ask of them? ... That they continue to be so]

The avant-garde debate as to what roles culture should indeed perform in society and national life occupies a prominent space in Chacel's *Barrio* and *Acrópolis*, and it is to this subject that my next and concluding section is dedicated.

Art as Immortal Temple or Sociopolitical Forum?

Arguably, the most debated issue regarding avant-garde cultural production has been its positioning with regard to sociohistorical issues. On the one hand, due to its formal aesthetics, it has been judged apolitical, hermetic, and deliberately distanced from social problems. On the other, revisionist critics like Eduardo Subirats have revindicated its utopian, revolutionary thrust: "The pioneers of the avant-garde proposed a revolutionary aesthetics under the aegis of rupture and emancipation, simultaneously linked to the most noble and utopian of social values and to hope" (1985, 17).[57] Such a focus holds for Chacel's case, because, as already underlined, she constantly foregrounds in her trilogy and other writings the importance of innovative culture for Spain's democratic transformation and the vital role to be played by cultural producers in that process. Hence she questions in 1937, during the Civil War, if "la parte a quien está confiada la actividad más explícita, la que ha de conducir al pueblo hacia lo que es su objeto, esto es, los creadores de cultura, los intelectuales, estamos en realidad cumpliendo con nuestro verdadero deber" [those entrusted with the most explicit activity, those of us charged with leading the masses toward their objective, that is, we creators of culture, the intellectuals, are really fulfilling our true duty] (1993e, 372). Several decades later, in her essay "Aclaración, no polémica" [Clarification, Not Controversy], written in 1962, Chacel declares her literary production to be socially responsible, choosing the adjective "responsable" over "comprometido" [committed], a word that, she states, lacked currency forty years earlier (1993a, 213).

By the early 1930s, with the coming of the Second Republic and growing tension in Spain and Europe polarized around socialism and fascism, the relationship of culture with society, literature with politics, had come under intense scrutiny. Within such a climate, avant-garde writing occupied an ambiguous position: on the one hand, it was attacked for its preoccupation with aesthetic form, seemingly at the expense of addressing sociopolitical issues; on the other, it was hailed as the ideal medium for expressing social commitment, due to its rejection of bourgeois institutions and markets, and its revolutionary formal attributes.[58] Chacel's trilogy retrospectively endeavors to bridge the gap that opened up between avant-garde literature and the social novel of the 1930s, reclaiming the former as an antitraditionalist force with the potential to inaugurate new ages. As stated in my introduction to this study, it was precisely that combination of avant-garde aesthetics with historical engagement that was yearned for in the 1970s and 1980s, in a literary context weary of a formal experimentation generally lacking in historical awareness and of a light literature manufactured for a market driven by consumer values.

The historical avant-garde debate as to whether art should serve to immortalize beauty or intervene in society and politics is paramount in Chacel's *Barrio* and *Acrópolis,* and especially evident in her representations of the art museum. In *Barrio,* the Prado is initially depicted as a repository for the allegedly eternal beauty of culture. Hence the museum is described by Elena as a secular temple and as "el pueblo de Apolo" [Apollo's abode] (Chacel 1981, 37, 258). Such a concept is developed by Isabel, for whom to go to the museum is

> [p]asar a mejor vida . . . lo fácil que es pasar por una puerta . . . no hay que abrirla, sino que hay que . . . entregarse a tiempo . . . y uno pasa y entra en otro mundo . . . Uno está viendo, está oliendo un

> aire que no ha olido nunca, está oyendo un silencio como una quietud, una luz, un brillo en el suelo ... Hay que andar por ese suelo que nos refleja . . . imposible romper la quietud, imposible ir más allá porque no se concibe nada mejor que esto, lo que está ahí delante, que parece infinito, que parece que no puede cambiar. . . . (32–33)
>
> [to pass to a better life . . . how easy it is to pass through a door . . . you don't have to open it but . . . surrender at the right moment . . . and you pass through it and enter another world . . . You're seeing, you're smelling an air that you've never smelled before, you're hearing a silence like a stillness, a light, a gleam on the floor ... You have to walk on that floor that reflects us . . . it's impossible to shatter the stillness, impossible to go beyond, because you can't conceive of anything better than this, than what is there before you, seemingly infinite, seemingly unchangeable.]

The insistence here on abandoning the self to art as a timely act of faith—"entregarse a tiempo"—on culture as an unchanging, perfect world that confirms an illusory stability, and on art as a timeless entity apparently removed from historical turmoil recalls Nora's theorization of the *lieu de mémoire* as a kind of sanctuary or "*templum*": "Unlike historical objects, *lieux de mémoire* have no referents in reality; or, rather, they are their own referents—pure signs. This is not to say that they are without content, physical presence, or history—on the contrary. But what makes them *lieux de mémoire* is precisely that which allows them to escape from history" (1996a, 20, 19). In this sense, the museum acts, as Jessica Evans states, as a space seemingly outside the reach of historical change that can thus preserve a national cultural heritage and, with it, the illusion of a stable national identity and united community. At the same time, however, the museum is also inserted within precise historical circumstances, as its purpose from the late nineteenth century onward was the edification and democratization of the public in a government-directed process of nation formation (1999, 6–8). All these factors underwrite Chacel's representation of the museum as the guardian of the nation's cultural heritage.

Accordingly Chacel also portrays that same space as a forum for sociopolitical debate, or, as Duncan Cameron puts it, as a site for "confrontation and experimentation" (1972, 198). Explaining further, Cameron specifies that "the forum is where the battles are fought, the temple is where the victors rest. The former is process, the latter is product" (199). This notion of art as forum in *Barrio* is channeled through the character of Máximo Montero, a neo-Romantic figure of mysterious origin.[59] In comparison with his mentor, the philosopher Manuel, who tends toward an Ortegan position on the desired objective neutrality of the intellectual, Montero embodies the principles of an avant-garde that perceives the need for a more committed sociohistorical stance. Consequently his visits to the Prado are not to admire an artistic canon but to discuss politics behind the statue of the Dama de Elche (Chacel 1981, 260).[60] By mentioning this work in connection with Montero, Chacel suggests that "pure" beauty is never neutral but always acts as a screen for political agendas.

Neutrality is challenged on a political level when Montero leaves to join the Allied forces in World War I, despite Spain's official stance of nonbelligerence: "El que es consecuente consigo mismo, se va consigo mismo. . . . el discípulo se va, saliendo del nublado, dejándolo allí, como si el único medio de desafiar la tormenta fuese asumirla: ser tormenta, llenarse de tormenta" [He who is faithful to himself, leaves with his self. . . . the disciple departs, leaving behind the rain clouds, leaving them there, as if the only way of braving the storm were to take it on: be the storm, fill oneself with storm] (274). Thus Montero can be read as incarnating the generalized support by Spanish intellectuals of the Allies from 1915 onward, which, Francisco J. Romero Salvadó asserts, equated to "opting for a future Europeanized Spain, modern, secular and democratic, in place of the tradition-ridden, priestly, oligarchical Spain that was" (1999, 13). Consequently World War I was a watershed event that dominated intellectual opinion in Spain and problematized any modernist affirmation of the autonomy of art.

The question posed by Chacel in *Barrio* as to whether cultural space, as symbolized by the Prado, should serve as allegedly neutral temple or sociopolitical forum is afforded greater contextualization when Elena and Isabel are labeled "estetas" [aesthetes] and "decadentes" [decadents] by their detractors for embracing ideals of beauty seen as removed from reality.[61] This position of perceived aesthetic decadence or lack of commitment is contrasted with another that supposedly stands for a socially redemptive culture. Among the characters whom Chacel casts as adopting this second stance are Montero, Ramón, and Manuel, with the latter describing himself as belonging to "la especie zoológica—o será a la especie lógica, de nuestros logos didácticos—, los que hemos nacido maestros, vocacionalmente . . ." [the zoological species—or rather, to the logical species, of our didactic logos—, those of us who were born to teach, for whom teaching is our calling] (1981, 267). Such an opposition between an allegedly pure aesthetics and didactic social engagement evokes the differentiation between generational positions explored by María Dolores Dobón in Spanish writers and intellectuals of the early twentieth century. The *esteta*, Dobón affirms, was identified with an individualistic modernism seen as preoccupied with formal aesthetics. Conversely the *sociólogo* [sociologist], or Manuel's "zoological species," who proclaimed to employ the *logos* or word in the service of society, was equated with those who shared the collectively oriented sociopolitical commitment of the Generation of 1898 (1996, 58).

The aesthetics propounded by the *sociólogos* and *estetas* respectively are explored in *Barrio* in two juxtaposed passages. Both kinds of aesthetics, however, are shown to challenge the distinctions noted by Dobón, in that they are equally critical of bourgeois values and conservative sociopolitical structures, in keeping with avant-garde concerns. The passage identified with the *sociólogos* pertains to Joaquín Dicenta's 1895 drama, *Juan José*, acclaimed by the 1898 Generation. Whereas in Dicenta's work tragedy is precipitated by the illiteracy of its working-class protagonist, Juan José, Chacel's narrative voice broadens the proportions of that tragedy to set it within the context of Spain's stunted intellectual development. This national disgrace is caused not so much by lack of education as by the massification of the literary market at the expense of quality, with Manuel commenting: "En primer lugar, la ignorancia no es tan grande porque saben leer y hay cerros de libros a peseta ... ¡Saben leer! ¡Fíjate! Ahí tienes un conflicto, una llaga nacional que duele de verdad" [First, the extent of their ignorance is not so serious because they can read and there are masses of books dirt cheap ... They can read! Just imagine! There you have a conflict, a national wound that really hurts] (1981, 224). It is due to this absence of literary quality, represented in terms of diseases common in underdeveloped countries, that Spain is unable to compare favorably with its northern European neighbors: "Es lo que padece nuestro terruño: se nos ha encanijado ... no sé qué raquitismo zambo, qué escrófula vergonzante es lo que le aqueja . . . esas cosejas que vais a aplaudir como un solo hombre, ¿podrían pasar unos kilómetros arriba de la frontera?"

[That's what is wrong with our nation: it has become puny ... I don't know from what variety of knock-kneed rickets it is suffering, from what kind of embarrassing scrofula . . . those aberrations that you all applaud unanimously, could they occur a few kilometers north of the border?] (224).

As a play, *Juan José* anticipates the avant-garde defiance of aesthetic and social conventions, as it breaches theatrical canons by dignifying a working-class protagonist for the first time (Ruiz Ramón 1980, 364). Hence, as one of Chacel's characters comments to Laura, Elena, and Isabel: "Es una cosa muy diferente de esas que veis vosotras. No tiene nada de reyes ni de espadas en alto ... Es enteramente otra cosa" [It's something very different to what you usually see. There aren't any kings or drawn swords ... It's something completely different] (Chacel 1981, 209). Nevertheless a literary work with a lower-class protagonist does not necessarily make the play mass culture. When Dicenta's work is compared with a work of "high" canonical culture, Shakespeare's *Romeo and Juliet,* it is the latter that is judged to cater to bourgeois expectations and values in its deployment of a typical romantic plot: "[C]uando los dos acaban a puñal y veneno, el amor queda en buen lugar..." [When the two die from dagger and poison, love is as it should be] (219). In contrast, Juan José "no se comporta como todos los demás, como el montón" [doesn't behave like everyone else, like the rest] (218).

The other passage, associated with the *estetas,* portrays the corner of a garden loved by Elena and Isabel, which belongs to their bourgeois friend, Piedita. Inhabited by the crane, a "princesa en exilio" [princess in exile] (230) that recalls the poem "Sonatina" by Rubén Darío (1985, 180–81), considered the father of Spanish modernism, the autumnal garden epitomizes a unique, naturalized modernist beauty that hides the ugliness of encroaching urban development: "Construcciones más altas habían ido cercándolo y quedaba encajonado, pero los árboles, los arbustos—lilas, celindas que todavía, en el otoño, no habían perdido la hoja, le daban una oscuridad que ocultaba los paredones de cemento ... " [Taller buildings had gradually surrounded it, boxing it in, but the trees and shrubs—lilacs, syringas that even in autumn still had not lost their foliage, lent it a shade that concealed the cement walls] (Chacel 1981, 230). As the following quotation highlights, this declaredly sacred aesthetic space stands in opposition to a tasteless capitalist consumption of culture symbolized by the married Piedita's house, which overflows with interchangeable, reproducible objects, easily forgotten: "El fondo del jardín, el rincón de la grulla era algo sagrado . . . era, en su profundidad, la única elevación posible sobre el nivel trivial de la casa brillante. De la casa y sus cosas. . . . Llegaban cosas nuevas y se situaban en el primer plano . . . hasta que eran suplantadas por otras que las relegaban al olvido" [The bottom of the garden, the crane's corner, was quite sacred . . . its profoundness afforded the only possible means of rising above the triviality of the glittering house. Of the house and its things. . . . New things would arrive and occupy the foreground . . . until replaced by others that consigned them to oblivion] (231).[62]

Thus modernist values that privilege lasting quality, and hence promise the preserving of cultural memory, are contrasted with an indiscriminate bourgeois consumerism, reliant on a constant substitution of items according to fashion. While this latter process appears to make culture more accessible to a wider public, the democratic ethos that such consumption seemingly promotes is fictitious, as Jean Baudrillard remarks: "Fashion—more broadly, consumption—masks a profound social inertia. It is itself a *factor* of social inertia, insofar as the demand for real social mobility frolics and loses itself in fashion, in the sudden and often cyclical changes of objects, clothes and ideas. And to the illusion of change is added the illusion of democracy" (1981, 50). Nevertheless, although the avant-garde, characterized by its constant drive for innovation, is not exempt from its creations being associated with passing fashion, it is that very innovation that often makes its products incompatible with accepted tastes, reducing their appeal to a broader public. For Chacel, the development of a strong nation clearly hangs on eschewing a literature subject to market demands. Hence, in her essay "Lo nacional en el arte" [National Identity in Art], first published in 1949, her rhetorical question as to "¿Qué es lo nacional que puede manifestarse en las producciones del espíritu?" [What can be revealed about national identity in creative works?] is answered as follows: "Sin duda la obsesión más funesta para la obra del espíritu es ésta, ¡tan corriente hoy día! de pretender adivinar lo que el público quiere . . ." [Undoubtedly, the most unfortunate obsession for creative production, and so common nowadays!, is to claim to guess what the public wants] (1993l, 287). This tension between market demand and literary quality continues to be of great relevance in contemporary Spain, as will be discussed in the conclusion to this book.

Concepts of "natural" original and mass-produced copy, evident in the above descriptions relating to Piedita's garden and house, are also engendered notions, placed in a corresponding hierarchy of values. The character of Piedita and the frivolous spaces with which she is associated reveal Chacel's rejection of the bourgeois massification of culture, engendered as feminine. Whereas the fear of mass culture was usually symptomatic of a sociopolitical elite's fear of disenfranchized masses or marginalized others, Chacel, like Ortega, clearly associates mass culture with crass bourgeois taste.[63] This feature both implies the commitment to disadvantaged classes inherent in Chacel's work and also foregrounds her avant-garde attack on bourgeois culture.[64] At the same time, however, the devalued term continues to be represented as feminine, in keeping with masculine modernist rhetoric. Gendered constructions such as these are aptly explained by Huyssen when he comments on the modernist fear of "being devored by mass culture through co-option, commodification, and the 'wrong' kind of success," while it clings to "the persistent gendering as feminine of that which is devalued" (1986, 53). Chacel's discourse is no exception in this respect.

Whereas for one strand of the avant-garde, that of the *estetas* embodied by Elena and Isabel, the so-called original is held to guarantee a quality capable of surviving historical change, for another strand, associated with the *sociólogos,* that same model is unequivocally aligned with a modernism deemed effeminate and incapable of regenerating society and the nation. Hence Ramón, representative of the *sociólogos,* critiques Elena's and Isabel's pursuit of cultural beauty, equating them and their aesthetics with breasts, feminine body parts that cannot represent the general body politic: "Hemos sacado en consecuencia que sois *estetas, tetas, tetas* . . . vivís dedicadas a eso de la estética, de la es-tetica [*sic*] . . . No sabéis jugar con las cosas serias . . . No servís para camaradas . . ." [We've concluded that you're *aesthetes, teats, teats* . . . your lives are devoted to aesthetics, aes-teatics . . . You don't know how to approach serious issues . . . you're no good as comrades] (Chacel 1981, 276–77).

Ramón contrasts the girls' position with that adopted by himself and Montero:

> No somos de los que se saltan una página y siguen leyendo. Ampliamos la teoría un día que [Montero] os encontró dibujando la amazona. Fue precisamente el día que él había tomado la decisión de

> irse allá. Las noticias eran atroces: ya habían invadido Bélgica. . . . Vosotras no os enterabais de nada. . . . Y los periódicos asegurando que España seguirá neutral . . . Ya veréis si podéis seguir en la higuera ... (279)
>
> [We're not the kind to skip a page and continue reading. We expanded the theory the day that Montero came across you both sketching the Amazon. It was the very day that he had made up his mind to go there. The news was atrocious: Belgium had already been invaded. . . . You had your heads in the clouds. . . . And with the newspapers affirming Spain's ongoing neutrality . . . You'll soon see if you can continue in the clouds]

Ramón considers that the young women have yet to put into practice the combative stance symbolized by the Amazon that they were sketching; an attitude that premises transformation on the sacrifice of their breasts or aesthetics and on a radical shift in mentality: "¿O no entendéis que tenéis que cortaros *dentro de la cabeza* todo lo que os estorba el movimiento? ¿No comprendéis que eso quiere decir pasar por el aro: ser otras, pensar de otro modo, hablar de otro modo?" [But can't you understand that you have to cut off *inside your head* everything that hampers movement? Can't you understand that that means knuckling under: being different, thinking differently, speaking differently?] (279). The alleged avoidance of political matters in the cultural production equated with the *estetas* is here explicitly paralleled with Spain's neutrality vis-à-vis the European conflict; both aesthetics and nation, Ramón suggests, partake of a "feminine" stasis by supposedly refusing to engage with the times.[65]

Ramon's views, therefore, demonstrate how a modernist master narrative of sociopolitical progress, equated with the masculine, constructs itself against national backwardness, gendered as feminine. Such strategies of engendering typify the processes of legitimation and discrediting common to literary movements and groups, anxious to demarcate their respective identities. Correspondingly, as Kirkpatrick remarks, the 1898 Generation defined itself as virile and ethical against the supposedly soft, superficial aesthetics of early modernism, viewing with special suspicion the latter's "'decadent' tendency to blur the lines between the genders" (1999, 119).[66]

Significantly Chacel's text disrupts the privileging of socialist ethics over "pure" aesthetics to argue for a reconciliation of the two elements of this gendered dichotomy. The imagined possibility of such a fusion is posited when, on Montero's departure for the war, he addresses Isabel and Elena as "camaradas" [comrades], provoking Elena's query as to whether there might not exist "camaradas decadentes" [decadent comrades]:

> —¿Por qué nos habrá llamado camaradas, cuando siempre se ha hartado de llamarnos decadentes?
> —Precisamente por eso: para borrarlo, para que no tengáis mal recuerdo de él.
> —Sí, eso es. Yo lo sentí así y se me pasó por la cabeza decirle ¿Puede haber camaradas decadentes?
>
> (Chacel 1981, 275)
>
> [—Why on earth has he called us comrades, when he's always called us decadents to his heart's content?
> —Precisely for that reason: to erase it, so that we don't remember him badly.
> —Yes, that's right. I thought the same thing and it occurred to me to ask him: Can there be such a thing as a decadent comrade?]

Consequently, I maintain, Chacel's characters represent an avant-garde position that does not see experimentation in aesthetics as incompatible with sociopolitical transformation. Indeed Chacel's belief that great literature can only be created through direct engagement with the nitty-gritty of life is underlined in her 1937 essay, "Cultura y pueblo" [Culture and the People]: "¿[C]ómo se atreve a llamarse camarada el intelectual que es ciego a la vida de la calle, que no ha sabido crear nada profundamente arraigado en la realidad circundante? . . . Hay en la gran literatura mesas que no pueden haber sido vistas desde la puerta . . ." [How can an intellectual dare call himself comrade if he is blind to life on the streets, if he has not succeeded in creating anything deeply rooted in the reality around him? . . . In great literature there are tables that cannot have been seen from remaining in the doorway] (1993e, 375). Within the modernist context, formal experimentation did not necessarily presuppose the autonomy of art from lived experience. On the contrary, as Felski asserts, "[f]or a variety of [European] avant-gardes, this defamiliarizing potential allowed artistic innovation to acquire an integral connection to social change" (1995, 23).

That aesthetic neutrality is impossible and cannot be divorced from politics or gender is foregrounded by Chacel in the concluding section of *Barrio*. Here her narrative persona takes issue with modern Spanish thought that has failed to engage satisfactorily with sociohistorical dilemmas. The passage in question suggests that Spain's official neutrality in World War I is entrenched in conservatism and the desire to preserve a status quo, summarized by Manuel as "nuestra proximidad con lo que no pasa" [our closeness to what doesn't happen] (1981, 262). It is the very proximity of the war and Spain's distancing from it that accentuates the latter's negatively defined differences from northern Europe, with these damningly calibrated in terms of provincialism, backwardness, and figurative exile: "[P]or sentirlo tan próximo que nos quita el aliento, es precisamente por lo que nos sentimos tan lejanos, provincianos, peninsulares, que es como ser ciudadanos de un jirón, de un pingajo geográfico ... Aparece la idea geográfica como confinamiento. Eso es sentirse extraño porque se está al margen" [For precisely the same reason that its very proximity takes our breath away, we feel so remote, so provincial and peninsular, like citizens of a tatter, a geographical rag ... The geographical factor is akin to exile. You feel foreign because you are on the margins] (266).

The "Disaster" of 1898, which defined Manuel's generation, provoked in its intellectuals two modes of action. As evident in the following quotation, one was to look inward to address the internal ills of the nation, epitomized in the expression "sweeping out the house"; the other, that chosen by Manuel, was to look outward to Europe: "Desapareció la hiperbólica extensión sin puesta de sol y cogieron la escoba . . . Otros, más provincianos todavía . . . arrastramos nuestro rincón, llevamos a cuestas nuestra madriguera. Salimos a dar un paseo y miramos las góndolas, . . . los bulevares con sus cenáculos, sus núcleos de presente ... " [The hyperbole of the empire where the sun never sets vanished and they picked up the broom . . . Others of us, even more provincial . . . dragged our piece of home with us, bearing our lair on our backs. We went out for a stroll and contemplated the gondolas, . . . the boulevards with their literary gatherings, their nuclei of modernity] (266). However, this attempt at Europeanization, Manuel judges, was unsuccessful, because intellectuals persisted in clinging to figments of an obsolete, parochial notion of Spanish identity, symbolized by Castile: "[Y] no entramos, no ingresamos . . . Y nos volvimos a nuestra madriguera tan provincianos como habíamos salido y elegimos con obstinación —¿o con cobardía, con encastillamiento[?], ¡son tan bellos los castillos!, y es tan fácil vivir a su sombra" [And we didn't enter, we didn't gain entry . . . And we returned to our lair as provincial as when we had left and we stubbornly made our choice—or were we cowardly, taking refuge in our castle fortification?, castles are so beautiful!, and it's so easy to live in their shadow] (266–67).

Here Chacel's narrative voice, in its critique of an inward-looking, centralized vision of the nation, recalls certain aspects of Unamuno's writings, who, in his 1902 study, *En torno al casticismo*, extolled Castile as "el país de los castillos" [the land of castles] (1986, 55). This inference is strengthened through Manuel's subsequent references to "[l]a provincia, la cátedra fácilmente alcanzable" [the province, the University professorship easily within reach] (Chacel 1981, 267), reminiscent of Unamuno's chair in provincial Salamanca.[67] What is more important, however, is the emphasis in the above passage on the failure to enter or be admitted to Europe: "[Y] no entramos, no ingresamos" [And we didn't enter, we didn't gain entry]. This comment indirectly alludes to Spain's inability then to enter the intellectual "school" and modern democracy represented by northern nations, as intimated by Chacel's statement, quoted earlier, from "Volviendo al punto de partida": "[S]abíamos que para entrar en ella [la escuela] teníamos que . . . pasar por un examen de ingreso: esto es, de conciencia" [We knew that to enter it (the school) we had to undergo conscientious preparation and pass an entrance exam: that is, an examination of conscience] (1993z, 283–84).

Similarly debated and challenged in *Barrio* are recognizable aspects of Ortega's thought. Reflecting on the ideal relationship of philosophy with history, or theory with life, Manuel initially adopts an Ortegan stance by advocating distance from political concerns,[68] considering that excessive proximity yields a perspective contaminated by subjective passions and theoretical inconsistencies: "¿[Q]uién es el que ve más claro, el más próximo o el más lejano? . . . La proximidad arrastra impurezas. Las mejores cosas, las pasiones, las intimidades más verdaderas arrastran impurezas teóricas. . . . Solo [*sic*] los que lo vemos desde lejos lo vemos puramente, inconsolablemente" [Who sees more clearly, the one who is nearest or farthest away? . . . With proximity come impurities. The best things, passions, the truest intimacies, bring with them theoretical impurities. . . . Only those of us who can see from afar can see purely, inconsolably]

(Chacel 1981, 262–64). However, Manuel reasons, such a distance is itself ethically impossible to maintain, as those same concepts intended by intellectuals to liberate humanity are also deployed to legitimate wars: "[N]o estamos libres de culpa los que trabajamos solo [*sic*] con papel, *nosotros* somos todos los que hacemos algo, tanques, entre otras cosas . . . todo nos incumbe a los que pertenecemos a esta casta de los liberadores" [Those of us who work with just pen and paper are not blameless, *we* are all those who make something, such as tanks . . . those of us who belong to this breed of liberators are responsible for everything] (265–66).[69] The unfulfilled challenge facing theory or philosophy, Manuel states, is for it to be put into practice and lived by those unable to theorize: "Mientras tanto llegan los hechos y los otros, los que quedan al margen de lo teórico, que es para quienes estaba teorizado lo teórico, . . . siguieron sin oírlo . . . arrastrados por sus pasiones triviales y reales . . ." [Meanwhile events unfold and the others, those who remain on the margins of theory, for whom theory was theorized, . . . still didn't hear it . . . swept along by their trivial, but real, passions] (264). As he reminisces, that ideal remains a still pending issue: "[L]o que querríamos es que lo teórico fuese práctico, practicable, y no lo fue" [What we wanted was for theory to be practical, able to be practiced, and it wasn't] (263–64).

For Manuel, those who survive the trauma of war and emerge from its dark vortex of catastrophe face two possibilities: either the pessimism of existentialist theory or remaining committed to the remembrance of the past. As he states: "Y cuando uno . . . ha pasado el túnel, no le queda más que dos salidas: la de la amargura . . . la del pesimismo sistematizado, teorizado y envasado en seductores recipientes teóricos o la salida que no es salida. . . . Lo que sale es lo eternamente encadenado. . . . Sin olvidarse, ¡eso nunca!, todo menos olvidar" [And when you've . . . passed through the tunnel, you're left with just two options: either bitterness . . . pessimism systematized, theorized and presented in seductive theoretical wrappings or the way out that is a cul-de-sac. . . . What does come out is enchained for all time. . . . Without forgetting, never that! anything but forgetting] (264–65). It is this imperative never to forget the past and pursue its unfulfilled dreams that is at the crux of Chacel's trilogy and its significance for post-Franco Spain.

Likewise, in the final pages of *Acrópolis,* history takes centerstage in the form of an allegorical female figure. Nevertheless, even while her "paso primaveral—abrileño" [spring step, typical of April] (Chacel 1984, 359) connotes the April advent of the Second Republic in 1931, her revolutionary promise is weakened by her configuration according to classical models, as Chacel's ekphrastic representation of Republican iconography makes clear: "Ahora se pinta en la mente de todos el paso de la Historia . . . Pasa grandiosa, con su corona de laureles, de la que se escapa la larga cabellera . . . Va ingrave, esbelta, lleva el gran mamotreto inconcluso—que no le pesa—y la pluma—de águila—en la mano derecha" [Now on the minds of all the passage of History is painted . . . She passes by, grandiose, crowned with laurel leaves, from under which her long hair escapes . . . She floats by, slender, bearing the great, unfinished volume—which does not weigh her down—and the feather—an eagle's—in her right hand] (358–59).[70] The ultimate failure of the Republic to resolve the demands of class conflict is noted by Chacel's narrative persona as a historical repetition of the same, in that its revolution was unable to avoid reproducing the bloodshed of the past: "Verla callejear es raro, pero cuando aparece—cuando se deja ver—recorre hasta los suburbios, por eso la han pintado a veces en crónicas sombrías, miserables, sangrientas: contratando con las otras efigies conocidas . . ." [You rarely see her in the street, but when she does appear—when she lets herself be seen—she is even in the slums; that is why she has sometimes been depicted in gloomy, depressing, and bloody chronicles: entering into a pact with the other familiar images] (359). The inadequacy of sociopolitical structures, even under the Republic, to put into practice the ideals of Chacel's avant-garde generation is summarized by Manuel's devastated reference after the Civil War to "la nueva era, de la que sólo se puede asegurar que *no era eso*" [the new era, about which you could only affirm that *it wasn't that*] (357).

Although this concluding section of *Acrópolis* refers to the era of the Second Republic, it also constitutes an authorial meditation on Spain's past from the contemporary present of 1984, the year in which the work was published and two years into a socialist government.[71] The reiterated allusions to smoke, fire and holocaust, and the somber, relentless leitmotif of the theme of guilt (1984, 356–66), all contribute to inviting the novel to be read as a retrospective critique of the context that led up to the Civil War and the ensuing dictatorship. That earlier time has given way to an uncertain present of calm, which, the narrative voice hopes, might be the beginning of an era of peace, symbolized by the divine dove of the Holy Spirit: "Eras de inseguridad en las que mandaba el Padre. Luego, veinte siglos mandando el Hijo. ¿Será posible que al fin, ahora que nos ven—quien nos vea—en medio de nuestro desamparo, se haga cargo de nosotros el Espíritu? ... " [Eras of uncertainty governed by the Father. Then, twenty centuries governed by the Son. Might it be possible, at last, now that they see us forsaken—whoever sees us—for the Holy Spirit to look after us?] (367). The materialization of that hope of lasting harmony is one of the challenges that Chacel's avant-garde ethos presents to post-Franco Spain.

Conclusion

Chacel's novels of memory, published after Franco's death, are dedicated to recovering the cultural history of her avant-garde generation and its engagement with the liberal transformation of Spain. Yet these works, fictionalized reconstructions of generational consciousness, speak more eloquently perhaps of Chacel's desire for how their history might have been rather than of the contradictions and tensions within modernist principles and groups. As Nora has elucidated, generational consciousness is a retrospective invention, and a generation itself a site of memory, created through the interaction of memory, history, and the desire to bear witness to the ethos of an age. Moreover, as outlined at the very beginning of this study, the timing of the publication of the novels also intersected with the desire in post-Franco democratic Spain to reclaim lost liberal traditions that, ostensibly focused on cultural values, appeared comfortingly removed from the atrocities of the Civil War. Chacel's texts, therefore, seem highly appropriate for a sociopolitical context that urged amnesia and forgiveness regarding Spain's recent contentious past.

Without doubt, Chacel's *Barrio de Maravillas* and *Acrópolis* constitute probing interrogations of the multifaceted culture and history forged by modernist generations throughout the first third of the twentieth century, and revindicate their unfulfilled project for national transformation, truncated by the Civil War and Franco dictatorship. In Acuña's context, education is premised as the key to transforming Spain into a European nation. In Chacel's avant-garde context, education takes on a still wider purview, to refer not only to a scholastic system but to the practice and integration of culture into daily affairs, so that it might provide the values for an informed national community to participate effectively in democratic life. Chacel's trilogy, denominated the "School of Plato," encapsulates this ideal of intellectual preparation through its constant emphasis on places of education and acculturation, mentors, educators, and students.

The pitfalls undermining this desired national transformation derive, Chacel's works insist, from discriminatory practices in terms of gender and class, and from a lack of traditionally ascribed feminine values in society and its politics. The engendered divisions between domestic and public spheres that underlie patriarchal culture are also endemic in masculine modernist culture. Chacel's novels reveal that the discrimination practiced in the public sphere against feminized others begins in the home, where denial of equal access to physical spaces is concomitant with closing off emancipatory cultural discourses and practices, and with reserving a sociopolitical and cultural history for a very few.

Hence hegemonic paradigms that seek to transcend spaces and values associated with the feminine, whether this be the home, bodies or emotions, are consistently challenged in Chacel's *Barrio* and *Acrópolis.* Not only is the home in *Barrio* a privileged site for the practice of culture. In both texts dominant tropes for referring to culture and the nation are those associated with the home, especially culinary metaphors. Similarly the modernist city, theoretically premised on a masculine gaze that preserves class and gender differences, is shown to be an inadequate model for transforming Spain from backward nation into modern *polis.* Chacel's texts displace such a paradigm of vision by insisting on a mode of seeing that endeavors to establish relationships with others premised on understanding rather than mastery, and thus allow disregarded perspectives to inform individual and collective psyches.

Above all, Chacel's works argue for a cultural production both cognizant of its responsibilities to society and its future, and equally committed to breaking new ground in its aesthetic practice. Behind the historical avant-garde's emphasis on writing a "new novel" that would combine aesthetic innovation with lasting quality was its critique of an indiscriminate bourgeois capitalism, guilty of creating a cultural market ill-equipped to educate appropriately the general population. It was perhaps this issue that most contributed, albeit for counterposed reasons, to the oblivion of members of the cultural generation whose memory Chacel's works seek to recover. Lambasted by defenders of the social novel in the 1930s, and later by the social realists in the 1950s, for allegedly eschewing social commitment, the historical avant-garde was also, contradictorily, seen as a threat to an immovilist status quo, resulting in it being conveniently forgotten by conservative elements during the Franco régime.

Today, as Chacel herself has stated, the challenge is to read and understand the works of her generation from within the specificities and constraints of their sociohistorical circumstances. To do otherwise, is to impose on them classificatory principles foreign to their revolutionary potential and to distort their profound engagement with liberal history, society, and national transformation. It is this sociohistorical commitment, and the values underpinning it, that make the remembrance of the Spanish historical avant-garde not only vital for understanding Spain's past, but also imperative for navigating the shoals of its present and future.

Conclusion: Materializing Liberal Histories: Spain as Democracy, “Federation,” and European Nation

> Y, ¿cómo saber si es honrá la muchacha a quien quiere la serenidad objetiva, la muchacha futuro, la juventud de la gran patria sin fronteras?
>
> —Chacel 1984, 103

> [And, how can you tell if the young girl loved by serene objectivity is honorable, the young girl that is the future, the youth of the great nation without borders?]

VITAL FOR THE FORMATION OF IDENTITIES ARE THE NARRATIVES THAT individuals and societies relate to each other. Consequently one of the questions that has pervaded this study is how the stories told by Rosario de Acuña, Ángela Figuera, and Rosa Chacel can shed light on understanding Spanish cultural and national identities in the past. More pertinent still, perhaps, is how their literary works might contribute to the constantly evolving social, cultural, and political identities in Spain today. Bhabha's concept of nation as narration, whereby nations are shaped through the discourses of their diverse constituencies, signals the importance of telling histories differently. Redrawing narrative parameters can redefine established social, cultural, and political identities, and help produce new subjectivities. Highlighted throughout my discussion of Acuña, Figuera, and Chacel have been the engendered identities at stake in the visions of democracy elaborated by the three writers, their representations of the relationships between unity and diversity within cultural and national communities, and the position of Spain vis-à-vis Europe. In the conclusion that follows, I will address these issues both within the writers' contexts, where applicable, and also with regard to present-day Spain.

In the Spanish nineteenth century the dominant liberal historiographic model privileged the unity of the nation-state over and above more localized interests. Acuña's theater, however, only partially conforms to such a paradigm. The traditional metaphor of the nation as family, based on ties of kinship and love, is invariably present in Acuña's dramas. Nevertheless this family is also shown to be divided by conflicting interests, in turn conditioned by opportunism, "race," religion, class, and gender. On most occasions, attempts to negotiate contrasting views founder, as in *Amor á la patria*, where Inés is not successful in persuading Pedro to abandon the French troops and defend his homeland, and in *El Padre Juan*, with Isabel unable to discourage Ramón from his course of action. The others against which Acuña creates her vision of the Spanish nation are not so much the racial others of an imperial Spain as those of ignorance, uncontrolled capitalism, and religious prejudice. Spain, her works argue, cannot form part of an allegedly more advanced northern Europe unless far-reaching changes in education, the economy, and spiritual tolerance are implemented.

Nineteenth-century Spain conforms to the model of traditional nation-state born toward the end of the eighteenth century with the French Revolution, as explained by Guibernau (1999, 150), and which Anthony Smith describes as a "civic kind of nationalism . . . of order and control" (1996a, 363). The regional roots of such nations are revealed in Acuña's *Amor á la patria* through her equation of Spanish patriotism with the Aragonese. Comparable to the "ethno-symbolic" component of revolutionary potential stressed by Anthony Smith in the construction of nations (362), this factor becomes modified in Acuña's work to emphasize small regional groups whose ideals are at variance with a centralized power and its form of government. Consequently Sorolla's Germanía in Valencia, from *Tribunales de venganza*, and Ramón's visionary project in Asturias, as in *El Padre Juan*, are at odds with a hegemonic order, whether that be an imperial monarchy or Restoration government, considered not to fulfil their obligations to their people. In this sense, Acuña's representations underline a national model in which certain regional groups are cast as offering potentially more viable options than a centralized state. If the current order within which Acuña writes is that of a Moderate Restoration government in conjunction with the monarchy, the alternative model that she promotes, most visible in *Tribunales*, is an independent republic founded on the sovereignty of the people.

Furthermore the sociopolitical model of liberal governance envisaged in Acuña's works rests on the voluntary alliance of an enlightened upper class with the lower-middle classes, as evident in *Amor á la patria* in the noble Inés's renouncing of class privileges to marry her artisan husband. The new nobility is no longer to be determined by lineage and inherited wealth but by the acquisition of spiritual riches through a scientific education, which has the power to eliminate class and gender differences. Whereas in *Tribunales* it is Sorolla who embodies this self-made model, in *El Padre Juan* access to education is extended to women, represented by Isabel, and is about to be made available to the villagers through Ramón's planned construction of the school.

Fundamental for the formation of such interclass alliances is associationism. Illegal for much of the nineteenth century, associationism is apparent in Acuña's dramas in the emphasis placed on communities such as the Germanía in *Tribunales* and the importance of the movements of freemasonry and freethinking in *El Padre Juan*. The association of classes behind common goals is also related to the socialist thrust of Acuña's works, which prophesy that the demand by the disadvantaged for social justice will produce a new history, free from old tyrannies. In this sense, Acuña shows herself acutely aware that, as Guibernau points out, cross-class support is essential if any nationalist movement is to achieve power (1999, 94).

Nevertheless, while Acuña's works advocate the agency of a common people, the composition of this people is ambiguous and changes over time. In *Amor á la patria* the common people is identified with small landholders and the peasantry, whose love of the land is fundamental for their opposition to the French invader. In the later *El Padre Juan*, these same small landholders have become contaminated by materialist bourgeois values and are equated with the entrenched isolationism and conservative beliefs that impede Spain's effective modernization. Within this paradigm, Acuña's production advocates a return to the land informed by technological knowledge, so as to produce a moral regeneration away from consumerism. Acuña's works, therefore, oppose a rampant capitalism seen as exacerbating class divisions.

Within Acuña's contemporary context the lack of success of her models for national development is patent in the unlucky ends suffered by her male protagonists, such as Sorolla and Ramón. Their fates are due as much to the rigidity of the dominant orders that they contest as to their inability to devise appropriate action to overturn the status quo. Consequently Acuña's historical actors suggest that, whether the changes sought come from the lower or upper classes, they cannot be based on violent revolution. Here Acuña moves away from socialist revolution to recommend a more gradual transformation wrought by culture and education, in consonance with Krausist philosophy. The individual and national identity desired by Acuña is one that balances reason with emotion and passionate exaltation with pragmatic realism, thus overturning subjectivities founded on engendered dichotomies.

Invariably the survivors of historical upheavals in Acuña's dramas are women, who remain either as exemplars for patriotic emulation or as ideals to which to aspire. This representational significance accorded to women flies in the face of their virtual nonpresence in national histories and hegemonic political spheres in late nineteenth-century Spain. Acuña's works, therefore, implicitly revindicate the full integration of women into the political realm, as vital actors in national histories. Her later theater and essays lay the blame for women's contemporary invisibility at the door of liberal thought itself, which privileges a social contract open only to men due to its engendering the public sphere as masculine and the domestic sphere as feminine. Acuña's critique of hierarchical systems of governance that cannot admit or accommodate differences therefore extends into the domestic realm, to advocate a complete revolution in gendered politics and the politics of gender.

Today, in the early twenty-first century, such a battle still has not been won. Although, as Mercedes de Grado indicates, judicial and legal frameworks guarantee theoretical equality between men and women, real equality continues to be a chimera (2004, 25). Accordingly Grado revindicates a contemporary strand of feminism of equality in Spain known as "illustrated feminism," which, arising out of the socialist feminism of the 1970s and rooted in the democratic principles of the Enlightenment thinkers, has never been fully implemented. The reason for this unfinished project, Grado explains, echoing Acuña's critique, is the betrayal of those theories by modern revolutions such as the French Revolution, the premises of which, equality, liberty, and fraternity, were never inclusive of women (35). Spain today, Grado maintains, effectively constitutes a patriarchy by consensus, because, while there exists legal equality, this parity does not extend to all aspects of social, political, economic, and symbolic activity, a principle essential for illustrated feminism (38–39). Above all, Grado considers that the paradigm defended by a feminism of equality is not at odds with the positive recognition of differences. The right to difference presupposes equality, in that the differences intrinsic to each individual are seen by others as worthy of equal respect (45).

The emphasis in Acuña's work, therefore, on the failings of liberal thought, on the need to acknowledge differences and on women's equal participation in the public sphere makes her corpus still highly relevant for Spanish society today. Indeed Jacqueline Cruz remarks that equality for women in the Spanish political arena is practically nonexistent, with one of the principal culprits for such a situation continuing to be, as Acuña herself lamented almost a century and a half ago, the different socialization of men and women, with the latter not being educated to aspire to positions of power. As in Acuña's context, women in politics still tend to occupy symbolic positions, so as to enhance the progressive image of parties and attract the female vote (Cruz 2004, 73, 77, 80).

The importance of memory for national identity, as patent in nineteenth-century liberalism, is systematically underscored by scholars of nationhood (Gellner 1983; Llobera 2004; Tusell 1999). Anthony Smith is no exception when he affirms that, without memory, there is "no identity; no identity, no nation. . . . Identification with a past is the key to creating the nation, because only by 'remembering the past' can a collective identity come into being" (1996b, 383). Acuña, Figuera, and Chacel all premise their constructions of the Spanish nation on particular rememberings of Spain's liberal past. However, after *Tribunales de venganza*, Acuña, disenchanted with mainstream Moderate liberalism and its historiographic enterprise, abandons rewriting the past to focus directly on contemporary problems, such as those present in *El Padre Juan* and *La voz de la Patria* [The Nation's Voice] (1893). In Chacel's work, to which I turn shortly, remembering a liberal cultural past is vital for fashioning a post-Franco democracy. Regarding Figuera's poetry, which champions the perspective of the Republican defeated, the trauma that resulted from the Civil War and from the Franco dictatorship made remembering not only an extremely difficult task but also an ethical imperative, in order to dislodge then hegemonic versions of history.

Consequently, to a greater extent than in Acuña's and Chacel's works, Figuera's corpus highlights the importance of common symbols and mythologies for the construction of a nation, while displacing symbolic elements essential for the National Catholicism of the Franco dictatorship. In order to define its exclusive concepts of citizenship and nationhood, Nationalist and Francoist Spain promoted closed-off, mythical times and figures, and especially those of Christ and Mary, molded according to masculine principles of self-sufficiency and invulnerability. In contrast, Figuera's poems confuse the rigid identities on which the dictatorship rests, so as to open up space for the articulation of silenced, dissident histories.

Engaging with a National(ist) narrative of origin, Figuera's work continually contrasts official renditions of the historical past and present with the experiences lived by the defeated in her contemporary moment. Such a reinscription constitutes what Bhabha has called the "double-time of the nation" (1990a, 294). Representatives of this double-time are Figuera's Mary and Christ, bearers and incarnations of the word, who become, through the writer's pen, both one and the other, straddling and mediating the fissures and divisions in national identity and historical memory. Not only the authoritative linchpins of Francoist National Catholicism and the models for its idealized sociocultural identities, Christ and Mary are also potent symbols of reconciliation and identification with those who suffer.

This kind of disjuncture is addressed by Bhabha in terms of a tension between a nationalist pedagogy and its authoritative discourse, on the one hand, which sees the people as its historical object, and, on the other hand, the people's strategic, redemptive performance of national life as "a repeating and reproductive process" (1990a, 297). Bhabha posits that it is at the borderlines where pedagogy meets performance that the people as nation emerges, as this split constitutes the site of negotiation and action for historical subjects: "It is through this process of splitting that the conceptual ambivalence of modern society becomes the site of *writing the nation*. . . . The people are neither the beginning or the end of the national narrative; they represent the cutting edge between the totalizing powers of the social and the forces that signify the more specific address to contentious, unequal interests and identities within the population" (297).

Such concepts are made tangible in Figuera's poetry through her deployment of the symbol of the wound, the cut in Spain's sociopolitical body that speaks of the struggle between historical closure and openness, cultural and political homogeneity and heterogeneous inclusivity, official amnesia and continued remembrance. The wound represents the unresolved trauma wrought by the Civil War and systematically cultivated thereafter by the regime, and demands recognition of the pain inflicted on the national body. It resists the vaunted Francoist narrative of one united nation by highlighting the divisions ongoing in the latter and defies the assimilation of dissident narratives into univocal historical accounts.

In Figuera's poems, the refusal of the past to be disappeared and the need for dissident histories to be heard render her messages especially applicable to Spain in the early twenty-first century. Spain's transition to democracy since the death of Franco in 1975 was premised on a collective pact of silence about the recent past in order not to reopen national divisions. The republican ideal, embraced by the three writers in this study, was eliminated as a viable option for rebuilding the nation, in that it was considered a return to a past associated with the Civil War. Consequently dates associated with the Second Republic, such as April 14, have been avoided for national commemoration (Aguilar and Humlebæk 2002, 143, 150), unlike Figuera's strategic emphasis on dates to oppose and break with Francoist history. Thus the restoration of democracy was not accompanied by a resurrection of the past so as to confront it and establish a dialogue with it. On the contrary, democracy depended, in many ways, on the continuation of a former order and on the encouragement of collective amnesia (Cardús i Ros 2000, 25); indeed to do otherwise would have necessitated, Aguilar and Humlebæk contend, "refounding the nation around different references, for which there was no consensus" (2002, 150). Figuera's poetic work provides a model for reconciliation in present-day Spain within politically sensitive limits,[1] and claims a space for the hearing, judgment, and reparation of historical wrongs. The full materialization of this process in contemporary Spanish society and culture is still pending, although it is now facilitated through organizations such as the national Asociación para la Recuperación de la Memoria

Histórica [ARMH, Association for the Recovery of Historical Memory], founded in 2000, and legislation such as the Ley de Memoria Histórica [Law of Historical Memory].

Acuña's image of the nation as a close-knit community formed by the association of like-minded individuals is also present in Chacel's post-Franco novels of memory. Departing from the philosophical legacies of the Institución Libre de Enseñanza and Ortega, Chacel privileges a "high" culture that can be rendered accessible to a general public through appropriate education and exposure. This process is enacted by the friendship between her coprotagonists, the middle-class Elena and working-class Isabel, and the access to culture that the former and her extended family grant the latter. Furthermore, while in *Barrio de Maravillas* and *Acrópolis* Chacel implements Ortega's theories regarding formal revolution in the novel, her aesthetic practices also exploit the sociopolitical implications of that revolution. Her works therefore stress that subjects must engage with cultural works as processes, not products, to consider the pertinence of historical pasts to the present moment and, in so doing, critique and transform national life.

In *Barrio* and *Acrópolis,* Chacel's recreation of the early twentieth-century modernist generations, including her own, constitutes both a recuperation of their liberal values and heritage and also a reinvention and reinterpretation of their cultural histories in alignment with the challenges facing post-Franco Spain in its transition to democracy. Chacel's reelaboration of modalities of modernist generational consciousness, therefore, acts as a significant site of memory in which the interests of present generations might find common ground with those of past ones,[2] so as to bridge past and present and take the nation forward into a truly democratic future. Indeed Chacel's model of nationhood bears comparison with Nora's concept of a cultural nation, forged on embracing and commemorating its heritage or patrimony.[3] With regard to Spain, José-Carlos Mainer stresses that the concept of cultural patrimony, historically linked to the formation of the liberal, middle-class citizen, gathered fresh impetus in Spain from the 1978 Constitution onward, which guarantees, in Article 44, that the state will foster access to culture, to which all are entitled (2001, 161, 165).

Such a transition to a cultural nation, Chacel's novels of memory contend, requires shifting former paradigms of vision, reliant on the detached objectification of others by hegemonic subjectivities, to other ways of seeing that foreground interdependence and empathy in forming national communities. Here aesthetic considerations associated with paradigms of spectatorship are shown to be deeply implicated in social politics. Like Acuña's work, Chacel's takes issue with the patriarchal division between public and domestic realms, which associates the public with masculine culture and the domestic, with feminine nature. These barriers, Chacel's narratives imply, are part and parcel of a similar division established between a so-called pure aesthetics conceived of as feminine and a "masculine" culture ostensibly committed to transforming its sociopolitical context. Chacel's production, ever attentive to discriminatory configurations of engendered difference, argues for the full participation of feminized others in cultural and national life, and the importing of values associated with those others into aesthetic and, by extension, political principles.

Consequently Chacel's texts, with their emphasis on cultural quality and ethical considerations, condemn change driven by market values and indiscriminate bourgeois consumerism. In this sense, her criticism of a capitalist market has much in common with Acuña's. In that a consumer-ruled market produces a present disconnected from both past and future, this ahistorical present, Resina declares, "not only destabilizes subjects and entire communities but itself becomes a modality of time out of time, an eternal transition blind to its origins or destination" (2000b, 93). In contrast, Chacel's novels speak for a transition in Spanish history that, in order to stabilize the national community, needs to bear in mind both origins and destination. Key for Spain becoming a democratic European nation, her work argues, is a committed culture governed by quality rather than by market pressures.

The insistence in Chacel's works on Spain producing a European cultural economy was arguably fulfilled in the Transition years, with Fusi, following political historian Ignacio Sotelo, remarking that Spanish culture was then "a culture installed in Europeanness" (2004, 121). However, Chacel's critique of a literature driven by market pressures is perhaps even more current today than it was in the context of the historical avant-garde. Mainer, for example, signals that in the cultural state that Spain constitutes today, the subsidization of culture sits uneasily with cultural independence, while making culture popular neither ensures quality nor effective access to artistic products (2001, 168). Similarly José Luis Martín Nogales sees Spanish literature in the 1990s as a product of commercial forces, in which editorial empires, canny distribution strategies and marketing techniques play decisive roles in facilitating a writer's success (2001, 179–81). For his part, Javier Aparicio Maydeu remarks on a Spanish publishing world that has gone into overdrive, producing too many books with a very short life-span on the shop-floor, before being substituted by the next echelon of "new" releases (2002, 27).

Regarding the positioning of female writers within the contemporary Spanish literary market, they continue to be exposed to similar problems to those experienced by Acuña, Figuera, and Chacel, as the following statement by Christine Henseler makes evident: "The publishing panorama that women writers faced in the 1990s displayed characteristics similar to those of the late nineteenth century and the first three decades of the twentieth century." Among those characteristics are the gender prejudices revealed by a still largely male establishment on evaluating the work of women writers (2003, 3, 11). In this vein, and echoing the labeling of most nineteenth-century women writers as mere *literatas*, allegedly unable to reach the benchmark of a literature that had to be "manly," is Clara Obligado's reference to the stereotypical view that women produce an inferior literature to that of men and that women who are considered to write as well are seen as exceptions to their sex (2003, 78). The gendered politics of exclusion and invisibility that Acuña, Figuera, and Chacel all contended with and address in their works continue current in Spain's present-day literary context, with Obligado (2003, 82) and especially Laura Freixas (2000, 55–66) providing telling commentaries on this issue.

With respect to Spanish nationalism today, it has seen a return to a more open nineteenth-century model, away from the centralizing intolerance that, beginning in the early twentieth century, culminated in the Franco regime (Granja, Beramendi, and Anguera 2001, 210).[4] That more inclusive paradigm is evident in Acuña's works, where the privileged national model, consonant with Acuña's Progressive liberalism, is that of a federation of peoples. Recognizing diversity in unity, such a model constitutes an extension at state level of the principles of associationism. Moreover it is in keeping with the utopian nationalism of radical liberalism, which envisaged the absence of borders as reflecting an epoch of increased cooperation and harmony among different peoples. If the success of a federation can be gauged from its ability to negotiate conflict through democratic processes (Guibernau 1999, 53), Acuña's plays, which endeavor to create consensus among opposing views, may be seen as constituting a step toward this political model. Indeed, as Tusell indicates, what is important for achieving democracy is a political system that is "consociacional," based on consensus or agreement among its diverse members, given that the desire for consensus demands confronting issues regarding plurality and difference (1999, 165).

The pertinence of the federal model to Spain's current political configuration continues to be debated in contemporary writings. On the one hand, for a nation to be considered a federation, the federal principle must, strictly speaking, be inscribed in its constitution. On the other hand, while this does not apply to Spain, the fact remains that Spain's configuration as a "nation of nations," composed of autonomous regions, renders it a hybrid entity straddled between centralization and federalization.[5] The desire that Spain adopt a federal structure is most evident among the regional nationalisms within Spain, which also support the recreation of the European Union as a "Europe of peoples," thus reducing the dependence of their regions on the Spanish state (Granja, Beramendi, and Anguera 2001, 201, 208).[6]

The entry of Spain into the European Union on January 1, 1986, brought to fruition the hopes of Acuña and Chacel for the Europeanization of Spain, and, to a certain degree, fulfils all three writers' desire for a world without discriminatory borders. As from 2002 there exists for the majority of EU countries a single monetary economy, while in 1995 the Schengen Agreement erased frontiers between its signatories, refocusing attention on issues of national sovereignty (Guibernau 1999,159–60). At the same time, this removal of frontiers has increased concern regarding the integrity of the borders of the European Union. As a result, Spain, at the southern extreme of this supranational body, is once again caught between Europe and Africa, and engaged in unrelenting surveillance of its Mediterranean borders to preserve its own national integrity, and that of Europe. Moreover, with Spanish enclaves still in Ceuta and Melilla, and significant African and Muslim populations living within its borders, Spain's position vis-à-vis the Orient bears comparison with the challenges surrounding the presence of racial and religious others in Acuña's works.[7]

Today Spain constitutes what Guibernau terms a "post-traditional nation-state," a democracy whose good health depends on negotiating the multiple identities that make up its culturally diverse state (1999, 158, 164). Such a nation, as imagined by Chacel's narrative persona in the epigraph to this conclusion, is a youthful woman with the assured strength, if not virtue, to emerge from the divisions of the past. The stories told by Acuña, Figuera, and Chacel unsettle hegemonic discourses of Spanish cultural and national identity to emphasize the heterogeneous, contested evolution of the Spanish liberal nation and the ongoing nature of this project.[8] Through their production, the past is revealed as part and parcel of contemporary identities.

There exist many histories on Spain as a nation-state, identified clearly as an object for analysis. However, scarce on the ground are histories on the Spanish nation as a dynamically evolving sovereign subject, despite the intimate connections between these two kinds of history (Granja, Beramendi, and Anguera 2001, 267). The literary representations of Acuña, Figuera, and Chacel contribute to writing just such a history of Spain as nation, permitting enhanced understanding of its multifaceted aspects. If balanced cultural and national histories are to emerge, women's accounts must be acknowledged as also seriously participating in writing the nation. Otherwise they remain, like all forgotten others, within history yet absent from it, returning to haunt the present until granted due recognition within the cultural narratives that conform national identities.

Notes

Introduction

1. Throughout this book all translations of titles of works and Spanish quotations are my own. I only give the original quotations in Spanish for primary works by Rosario de Acuña, Ángela Figuera, and Rosa Chacel, and on limited occasions for other authors when warranted for stylistic reasons.

2. Regarding my use of the term *modernity*, I also draw on Rita Felski, who explains that modernity distinguishes between "traditional societies, which are structured around the omnipresence of divine authority, and a modern secularized universe predicated upon an individuated and self-conscious subjectivity" (1995, 13).

3. With respect to this premise, see Gerda Lerner (1997, 131–98) and Joan Wallach Scott (1988, 15–27).

4. The literature on the concept and formation of *nation* is vast. Anthony D. Smith, for example, defines *nation* as "a named human population sharing a historic territory, common myths and memories, a mass, public culture, a single economy and common rights and duties for all members" (1996a, 359). For Javier Tusell, a nation is "a community whose members are united by a sense of solidarity, a common culture and national consciousness" (1999, 56). See also Homi Bhabha (1990b), Montserrat Guibernau (1999), and Josep R. Llobera (2004).

5. For an excellent critique of studies on "inventing" a nation, see Tusell (1999, 56–61, 90–91).

6. I place "race" within quotation marks to indicate that it is an ideological construct (see Henry Louis Gates 1986b and Lerner 1997, 184–97).

7. Tusell also pinpoints the importance of human desire in constructing a nation in modern times (1999, 91).

8. Thus Francisco Giner de los Ríos stated in 1862 that literature is a "universal mentor, that reproduces the past for us, explains the present, and enlightens and educates us regarding the unknown possibilities of the future" (1876, 170). With respect to this point, see also Sandie Holguín (2002, 25).

9. See, for example, the 1933 publication, *Rosario de Acuña en la Escuela*, which features homages to Acuña by prominent writers and intellectuals associated with the Second Republic. There Acuña's work is described as "literature by she who dreamed for you the highest seat of honor in the Republic" (*Rosario de Acuña* 1933, 7).

10. Although, during the 1960s, dissident Spaniards exiled in Mexico intended to publish a book on Acuña, this project remained unfulfilled. Within Spain, it was only in February and March 1969 that a series of articles by Patricio Aduriz on Acuña's life and works appeared in the Gijón newspaper, *El Comercio.* In contrast, since the advent of democracy in Spain, Acuña's name has been bestowed on streets in Madrid, Pinto, Santander, and Gijón, a Gijón Summer School dedicated to feminist issues, a Gijón secondary school, a Masonic lodge, and a proliferation of women's societies (Fernández Riera 2005, 136–40).

11. For valuable overviews of Acuña's work, see José Bolado (Acuña 2007a, 399–463), Luciano Castañón (1986), Macrino Fernández Riera (2005), Elvira María Pérez-Manso (1991) and María del Carmen Simón Palmer (1989, 1993). For historical accounts of Acuña's links with freethinking and freemasonry, see María Dolores Ramos Palomo (1999, 84–89) and Pedro F. Álvarez Lázaro (1985, 179–88). Apart from *Rienzi el Tribuno* and *El Padre Juan,* Acuña's plays have not been republished. Her essays and newspaper articles, however, have recently been collected and republished by Bolado (Acuña 2007a, 2007b) and Fernández Riera (2005).

12. To date, the only book-length literary studies on Figuera's compelling corpus are those by Jo Evans (1996) and José Ramón Zabala Aguirre (1994), enabled by the republication of Figuera's poetry undertaken by Roberta Quance (1986). For overviews of Figuera's work, see María Payeras (2002, 17–60), Janet Pérez (1996, 100–6), John Wilcox (1993; 1997, 173–96), and the studies in the special edition of the journal *Zurgai* in December 1987.

13. For overviews of Chacel's corpus, see Catherine Davies (1998), Shirley Mangini (2001), María Pilar Martínez Latre (1994), Cora Requena Hidalgo (2002), and Emilio Salcedo (1983), as well as the journal publication *Rosa Chacel: La obra literaria* (1988). Many studies have focused on issues of gender, with particular emphasis given to Chacel's 1945 novel, *Memorias de Leticia Valle,* and *Barrio de Maravillas* (1976). Other texts that have received much attention are Chacel's avant-garde novels, *Estación: Ida y vuelta* (1930) and *La sinrazón* (1960). Few studies exist on her essays (see Mangini 1998) and fewer still on her poetry (see Catherine Bellver 2001).

14. Indicative of Chacel's only relative inclusion in the canon is the scant space dedicated to her in recent volumes on contemporary Spanish literature. Francisco Umbral (1995), for example, provides no entry for her, while *The Cambridge History of Spanish Literature* edited by David Gies (2004) mentions her merely in passing in various articles there. In the extensive review of studies on the construction of the "Generation" of 1927 by Andrew Anderson (2005), it is evident that very few include Chacel.

15. Regarding Moderates and Progressives, see also Raymond Carr (1982, 158–63).

16. For the importance of Krausist philosophy and the Institución Libre de Enseñanza in forging Spanish liberalism, see Holguín (2002, 20–25). Regarding the principles of Krausist thought and its development in nineteenth-century Spain, see Raquel Vázquez Ramil (2001, 25–31).

17. Regarding the different forms of republicanism associated with liberalism in Spain in the late nineteenth and early twentieth centuries, see Manuel Suárez Cortina (2003b). For federalism, see Guibernau (1999, 50–54).

18. As Ángel Bahamonde and Jesús A. Martínez affirm, "the birth of history as a scientific discipline was given expression in liberal discourse, which recovered and gave order to a past that would be protagonized by the nation. In this way 'history' was born linked to the study of the Spanish nation" (2001, 497). With respect to the relationship of historical writing and nation formation within the more general context of nineteenth-century Europe, see also Carolyn Boyd (1997, 67).

19. Regarding the obstacles preventing national unity, see Tusell (1999, 102–7).

20. For Anthony Smith, a state is "a legal and political concept; states can be defined as autonomous, public institutions of coercion and extraction within a recognised territory. States are not communities" (1996a, 359). Regarding the concepts of nation and state in the Spanish context, see also Guibernau (1999, 13–14), Clare Mar-Molinero and Ángel Smith (1996), and Tusell (1999, 53–120).

21. Significant among the many events honoring the writers of Chacel's "Generation" of 1927 are the homages in 1977 to commemorate its fiftieth anniversary, especially that held at the Madrid Institute of Hispanic Culture, in which Chacel participated, and the homage to Corpus Barga in the Madrid Atheneum in 1979. Rafael Alberti was awarded the National Prize for Theater in 1981 and the Cervantes Prize in 1983, while María Zambrano received the Cervantes Prize in 1988. It should also be remembered that Vicente Aleixandre was granted a Nobel Prize in 1977.

22. I here quote from the abstract of Silvina Schammah Gesser's paper entitled "What to Do with a Distressing Past: the Spanish Civil War in Commemorative Exhibitions and Catalogues," presented at the international conference, "War Without Limits," University of Bristol, July 19, 2006. Regarding such a "recuperation industry," see also José-Carlos Mainer (2004, 689).

23. For Víctor Pérez Díaz, Spain's transition to democracy had concluded with the referendums on the Constitution in 1978 and on the Basque Statute of Autonomy in 1979. He sees the new political order as consolidated during the first Socialist government, from 1982 to 1986. At the time of publication of his study, however, in 1987, he considers that the institutionalization and internalization of the democracy by governing bodies and general society were still pending (Pérez Díaz 1993, 3–4).

24. In her essay, "Presencia II," Chacel similarly laments the contemporary abandoning and discrediting of memory (1994, 13).

25. References to drafting *Barrio de Maravillas,* entitled in its embryonic state "El callejón de las negras," can be found in Chacel's diaries from 1940 to 1966, published as *Alcancía (Ida)* (Chacel 1982a), on pages 44, 109, 176, 186, 214, 307, and 370, and in her diaries from 1967 to 1981, entitled *Alcancía (Vuelta)* (Chacel 1982b), on pages 88, 164, 212, 248, 261, 296, 307–9, 320, 332, 347, and 357. References to *Acrópolis* are given in *Alcancía (Vuelta)* (Chacel 1982b) on pages 384, 387, 427–28, 430, 432, 434, 436, and 439, while *Ciencias naturales* is mentioned on pages 251 and 402.

26. Furthermore aware that she could not rely entirely on personal experience and notes for an adequate representation of the sociohistorical contexts of her novels, Chacel also alludes in her diaries to researching data in historical studies

and literary texts pertaining to the periods, and mentions meeting with others who lived through the events depicted (see Chacel 1982b, 307–8, 434).

Part 1. Representing the Nation

1. Susan Kirkpatrick describes the discrimination against women who did write theater and historical novels as follows: "Women should not attempt to write theater or historical novels, as these genres require knowledge of a conflictive, harsh public reality" (1990, 37). Nevertheless defying this cultural proscription are the many female dramatists contemporary with Acuña mentioned in *Autoras en la Historia del Teatro Español.* Almost 80 percent of their works were published, with 60 percent being staged (Alvear 1996, 616). For Acuña, see Alvear (1996, 621–30).

2. *Las Dominicales del Libre Pensamiento,* founded in 1883 by Ramón Chíes and Fernando Lozano, became the foremost freethinking publication in Spain (Fernández Riera 2005, 27).

3. Acuña's letter and reactions to it are reproduced in José Bolado (1985, xix–xxiii).

4. With respect to Acuña's life, see Fernández Riera (2005) and Bolado (Acuña 2007a, 23–399).

5. Regarding the "Angel in the House" paradigm, see Bridget Aldaraca (1982).

6. Acuña's initial adherence to "safe" subjects is exemplified by *Ecos del alma* (Acuña 1876).

7. As Maryellen Bieder explains, "*literatas* were feminine women, who consistently took a normative approach when inscribing themselves within feminine discourse and within the sociosexual construction of Woman current in their day" (1998, 78). As for the term *varonil,* Bieder specifies: "Since virility is the hallmark of men's writing, it necessarily comes to encode literary merit. . . . To read a woman . . . as exclusively feminine is not a sign of admiration for her but of her exclusion from literary value. To find that her writing verges into the territory of the masculine becomes a sign of her approximation to value" (1995, 108).

8. Thus, in her "Preludio" to *La siesta,* Acuña writes: "Sin unidad de tiempo ni de acción, sin carácter, ni originalidad, ni estilo, estas hojas, que pudieran muy bien pasar como escritas con tinta de adormideras, te ofrecen una colección de artículos, formados siempre como las pompas de jabón . . ." [Lacking in unity of time and action, and devoid of character, originality and style, these pages, which could very well be seen as written in sleep-inducing ink, offer you a collection of articles, invariably formed like soap bubbles] (1882f, xii). Similar sentiments are expressed in her prologue to *Tiempo perdido* (Acuña 1881c, 5–6).

9. Carole Pateman explains that, within the Greek *polis,* "citizenship was upheld by the *phratries,* the brotherhoods, which were crucial for the sense of communal identity." However, she stipulates that "[i]n the modern world, citizenship, for the first time, is (ostensibly) universal, and thus civil fraternity extends to all men *as men,* not as inhabitants of particular cities" (1988, 80). It is in keeping with these more universal nuances that Acuña employs the concept of brotherhood.

10. For Antonio Jiménez García, Krausism was the most important philosophical and social movement of contemporary Spain, standing for "*rationalism* in philosophy, *liberalism* in politics and *reform* in social matters" (1985, 188).

11. José Álvarez Junco notes that "the canonization of the conflict of 1808–14 as the War of Independence ended up producing an almost perfect national myth, because, after having been created by the liberals, it succeeded in remaining untouched by political divisions . . . . Once that conflict had ended in victory, it would become, as the century progressed, the most solid foundation for collective pride and the cornerstone of the mythology used by the emerging nation-state to crown itself with glory" (2004, 144).

12. The importance of Zaragoza for the construction of the concept of an autonomous Spain is underlined by José María Jover and Guadalupe Gómez-Ferrer, who signal that French occupation of eastern Spain was initially unsuccessful due to the heroism of Zaragoza (2001c, 22).

13. Álvarez Junco observes that by 1820, the beginning of the three-year period of the liberal Constitution, the term *pueblo* was synonymous with nation, in the sense of "the community of citizens who, without benefiting from special differences, income or jobs, make a living from their work" (2004, 139).

14. All quotations from Acuña's works are cited parenthetically in the text. When quoting, I have elected to follow the original accentuation rather than modernize it.

15. Likewise Inés again exhorts Pedro: "[¡]y al noble son de tus cantares pátrios / lucha como español en las murallas!" [and to the noble sound of your patriotic songs, / fight like a Spaniard on the city walls!] (Acuña 1877, 24).

16. With respect to the relationship between the nation and the language of kinship and home, Benedict Anderson remarks that the latter "denote[s] something to which one is naturally tied. . . . the family has traditionally been conceived as the domain of disinterested love and solidarity. . . . Just for that reason . . . the state can ask for sacrifices" (1991, 144).

17. Thus Modesto Lafuente affirms: "Suddenly social hierarchies disappeared, because the *patria* to be defended was not that of nobles or commoners; the *patria* belonged to all, was the mother of all" (quoted by Paloma Cirujano Marín, Teresa Elorriaga Planes, and Juan Sisinio Pérez Garzón 1985, 193; original: Lafuente 1889, 18:86–87).

18. Regarding the defense of Zaragoza, John Lawrence Tone notes that "each house [became] a fortress that had to be taken in hand-to-hand combat or pounded into dust" (1999, 262).

19. Ramos Palomo signals that Acuña again privileges patriotic over maternal love in her subsequent drama, *La voz de la Patria* (1893), in which Aragonese women send their sons off to fight in the contemporary war in Morocco (1999, 87). For an analysis of this play, see Christine Arkinstall (2006), Mary Lee Bretz (2001, 218–19), and Esther Zaplana (2005, 48–51).

20. Acuña's women thus resemble those in Benito Pérez Galdós's historical novel, *Zaragoza*, from his *Episodios nacionales*, published three years earlier in 1874. Galdós's female characters not only embody a nation in need of defense but, more importantly, a nation empowered to defend itself (Tone 1999, 267–68).

21. During the period of 1854–56, when the Progressive liberals were in government, their reform of the Constitution in 1856, although never made law, clearly established that sovereignty no longer resided in king and Parliament but in the nation; thus Article 1 states that "all public powers emanate from the nation, in whom sovereignty essentially resides; for that same reason, it is the exclusive prerogative of the nation to establish its fundamental laws" (quoted by Jover and Gómez-Ferrer 2001d, 183).

22. Regarding the importance placed on decentralization in later nineteenth-century Spain, see José Luis Aranguren (1981, 114). As for the Comuneros, they are perceived by nineteenth-century Spanish liberals as historical models and their struggle becomes identified with "the people's struggle against the monarchy, with freedom against absolutism" (Pérez 2001, 237, 239). The uprising of the Comuneros was also a key myth during the Spanish Second Republic, with Prime Minister Manuel Azaña recasting it as the first modern revolution, with middle and working classes united in a common democratic endeavor (Juliá 2004, 205).

23. Described as "the last of the warrior-prelates of Castile, and the most formidable of them all," Antonio de Acuña sided with the rebels after being expelled from Zamora by those who questioned his right to his diocese. He was captured after the defeat of the Comuneros at Villalar and executed five years later at Simancas (Elliott 1970, 157–58). For a detailed account of his role in the uprising of the Comuneros, see Joseph Pérez (2001, 114–20).

24. Published between 1850 and 1867, Lafuente's thirty volumes, the indispensable reference until the Second Republic, consolidated the notion of a Spanish people defined by permanent characteristics and linked to a specific geographical location or nation (Álvarez Junco 2004, 201, 204).

25. Elliott notes that the status of the *moriscos* or converted Moors was particularly acute in the kingdom of Valencia. By 1609 they constituted about a third of the population there and were known as the "nation of new Moorish Christians" (1970, 305–6).

26. Acuña's depiction is in keeping with the fact that the Valencian Arabs were principally dedicated to agriculture, with a deep-rooted attachment to the land (Elliott 1970, 306).

27. For an account of the Spanish liberals and African colonization, see Cirujano Marín, Elorriaga Planes, and Pérez Garzón (1985, 195–203), as well as Miguel Martín (1973, 11–17).

28. This analogy between the lion and the lower classes is strengthened by Acuña's identification of the lion with the common people in her essay, "Valiosísima adhesion": "[U]n pueblo que despierta, . . . un pueblo que desperezándose, como el leon arto [*sic*] de míseros despojos, lanza los candentes hierros sino logra, con su vigorosa fuerza, romper las cadenas que lo aprisionan" [A people that awakes, a people that, stretching its limbs, like a lion tired of miserable scraps, shakes its burning irons to succeed in breaking, with its prodigious strength, the chains that imprison it] (Acuña 1992e, 56).

29. The association of the lion with collective sovereignty is evident in posters pertaining to the later Second Republic, where the allegorical female figure of the Republic is invariably depicted with a lion (see posters 217, 218, and 219 in Jordi Carulla and Arnau Carulla [1997, 1:102]).

30. This association is strengthened when Sorolla later declares to Cabanillas: "¡Si teneis las entrañas de la fiera / y el alma por el vicio emponzoñada!" [But your innermost being is beast-like / and your soul, poisoned by vice!] (Acuña 1880, 46) and "del amor del tigre no me fío" [I don't trust a tiger's love] (47).

31. Not coincidentally, in "Valiosísima adhesión" Acuña associates the socio-cultural evils besetting the working classes of contemporary societies with the tiger: "[E]l verdadero mónstruo apocalíptico, representación terrible de todas las ignorancias, las rutinas, las supersticiones, los egoismos, las vanidades, las envidias, las sensualidades y las soberbias; esa esfinge de cien cabezas que afianza sus garras de tigre en . . . los proletarios de las sociedades contemporáneas . . ." [The true monster of the Apocalypse, the terrible representation of all ignorance, routine, superstition, egoism, vanity, envy, sensuality and pride; that Sphinx of a hundred heads that sinks its tiger's claws into . . . the working classes of contemporary societies] (Acuña 1992e, 67–68).

32. Regarding honor as symbolic of "the quest for an appropriate marriage of liberty and order" in nineteenth-century Spain, see Sarah White (1999, 233).

33. This opposition between taxpayers and nobles is repeatedly stressed in Acuña's play; for example, Andrea asks Sorolla: "¿Serás al fin agermanado? Á veces / cuando medito á solas en la causa / que mueve á los pecheros de Valencia / contra esos nobles de orgullosa raza, / siento en mi corazón algo que grita / pidiendo se castiguen sus infamias" [Will you, then, become a brother? Sometimes / when I ponder alone the cause / that inspires the Valencian taxpayers to rise up / against those nobles of proud race, / I hear in my heart a cry that calls out / for their infamous deeds to be punished] (Acuña 1880, 14).

34. Arising from the theories of Fourier, Owen, and Cabot, associationism aimed to transcend individual egoism and promote humankind's fulfilment of its potential through communities that collectively owned the means of production (Artola 2001, 388).

35. For a full account of the variable fortunes of associationism outlined here, see A. Bahamonde Magro and J. Toro Mérida (1978, 68–94, 155–58).

36. Regarding federalism in relation to Acuña, see Arkinstall (2006).

37. For women in Spanish freemasonry, see Natividad Ortiz Albear (2005).

38. In "¡Yo, en la Academia!" Acuña refers to this rejection as mutual: "[Y]o rompí con ella [la sociedad] para siempre y radicalmente, y ella me descalificó ... (e hizo bien, porque ninguna de sus leyes, costumbres, ni fines fueron nunca acatados, ni siquiera respetados por mí) y yo la descalifiqué a ella para meterse conmigo, ni para mal ni para bien . . . Entre ella y yo no puede haber ningún acomodo" [I broke with society radically and forever, and it ostracized me ... (and it did well to do so, because I never followed or even respected any of its laws, customs or objectives . . . and I shunned it to keep my own company, neither for evil nor good . . . Between society and myself there cannot be any *rapprochement*] (Acuña 2000b, 56; original: *El Noroeste*, Gijón, January 31, 1917).

39. For an account of this scandal, see Simón Palmer (1989, 32–34).

40. According to Daniel Palacio, Acuña's ascent of the Evangelist was carried out in 1890, just prior to her writing the play (1992, 12). The spatial coordinates frame Acuña and her play within a liberalism open to northern Europe and fed by freethinking, freemasonry, and religious feeling unfettered by Catholic dogma;

the Evangelist not only connotes the figure of John the Baptist, Christ's forerunner, but was also, as José Antonio Ferrer Benimeli notes, one of the patron saints of medieval freemasonry (Ferrer Benimeli 2001, 17).

41. Regarding Carlism and the Carlist wars, see Carr (1982, 184–95, 337–40) and Tusell (1999, 109–10).

42. Acuña elaborates more fully on these "tipos intermediarios" in her 1881 satirical essay, "Los intermediarios (Boceto)." There she singles out priests (Acuña 1881b, 52–53) and politicians, casting the latter as ineffective and lacking in insight: "Los tenemos patricios: estos son los que más daño suelen causar porque ocupan un sitio que acaso quitan á verdaderos racionales . . ." [We have the patricians: those who usually do the most harm because they occupy a place that they perhaps take away from those who are truly rational] (145).

43. Contributing to the strength of anticlericalism in Spain was the emphasis placed by liberal reformers on scientific discovery and development, as well as the ripple effect of secularizing legislation in France under the Third Republic (Jover and Gómez-Ferrer 2001f, 397).

44. This admiration is palpable in Acuña's essay "El amigo Manso," where she praises Galdós's novel of the same title and remarks that his literary work is "un monumento de gloria para él y para la patria" [a monument of glory to him and the nation] (Acuña 1882a, 87). Similarly, in "Carta a un soldado español," she refers to Galdós as the "luz literaria de la España contemporánea" [literary beacon of contemporary Spain] (Acuña 2000a, 67). Another of her essays, "Pipaon (Biografía)" (Acuña 1882e), is dedicated to one of Galdós's characters from his *Episodios nacionales.*

45. However, although Galdós's *Electra* aroused a social and political scandal comparable to that caused by Acuña's play, performances were allowed to continue. This difference was perhaps due to Galdós's more established literary reputation as well as to contemporary prejudices against women writers.

46. The reconciliation of these two factors was impossible. Despite the fact that the 1812 liberal Constitution defended the right of Spanish citizens to education—"so as to form true Spaniards, upright men who love their country"—the reality was that too few resources were dedicated to this aim, with the state budget eaten up by military salaries and by support to the Catholic Church. With some fifty years of the nineteenth century under conservative governments, religious education was seen by politicians as necessarily guaranteeing respect for authority (Álvarez Junco 2004, 548).

47. Regarding the Institución, see Boyd (1997, 30–36) and Vázquez Ramil (2001, 39–50).

48. With respect to Catholic traditionalists and their position on Spanish education and history, see also Boyd (1997, 99–121).

49. Apart from Acuña's philosophical beliefs, more tangible proof of her involvement with the Institución can be seen in her essay, "Educación agrícola de la mujer," published in *La Gaceta Agrícola* in 1883 and commented on by José Ontañón, an *institucionista* (Vázquez Ramil 2001, 62).

50. Fear of the Catholic Church's hold over women was later palpable during the Second Republic, in the opposition from many on the left to women being granted the vote in 1931. In 1933, in the first elections in which women could

vote, there was a swing back to the center-right with a conservative socialist coalition (Scanlon 1986, 274–80).

51. Manuel Pedregal and Cañedo's words, part of a speech delivered to the Círculo de la Unión Mercantil in 1880, are quoted by Gómez Molleda (1966, 148); original: *Revista España* (1881): 551.

52. Jesuit influence on Spanish education and society was evident in the founding of the Catholic university of Deusto and in the hold of Jesuit confessors on upper-class youth, denounced in the publication, *The Empire of the Jesuits,* in the 1890s (Carr 1982, 467). The Jesuit influence on women is the object of Acuña's censure in her "Discurso," a speech given to a feminist meeting of the Republican Union in Gijón in 1917 (*El Noroeste* 21 [7309] June 6, 1917: 2).

53. With regard to the need to educate Spain, Boyd points out that in 1897 some 60 percent of Spaniards were illiterate, two-thirds of whom were adult women (Boyd 1997, 8). For statistics regarding literacy levels in Spain at the turn of the twentieth century, see also Rosa María Capel Martínez (1986, 369–70).

54. Although universal male suffrage was passed by law in 1869, it was abolished in 1875 with Cánovas's *turno pacífico,* the alternation of political power by peaceful agreement between the political parties. It was not reinstated until 1890 under Sagasta, also a freemason (Carr 1982, 350, 359).

55. The association of freemasonry with socialism in the late nineteenth century and early decades of the twentieth foundered in 1936 when the Socialists proclaimed the incompatibility of freemasonry with socialism, considering the former a fundamentally bourgeois institution. Ironically a short time later, Spanish freemasonry was persecuted under the Spanish right and Franco, who identified it with marxism and communism (Ferrer Benimeli 2001, 180).

56. The emphasis on Luis as Ramón's spiritual brother is apparent in Luis's following statement: "Ramón es para mí más que un amigo, un hermano; . . . no es al amigo de Ramón, es a su hermano a quien habla" [For me, more than a friend, Ramón is a brother; . . . Ramón isn't speaking to his friend, but to his brother] (Acuña 1989c, 175). Likewise Ramón tells Luis: "[T]e estimo con afecto de hermano" [I love you like a brother] (183–84).

57. Exploring the vexed meanings attached to country and city, Raymond Williams states: "On the country has gathered the idea of a natural way of life: of peace, innocence, and simple virtue. On the city has gathered the idea of an achieved centre: of learning, communication, light. Powerful hostile associations have also developed: on the city as a place of noise, worldliness and ambition; on the country as a place of backwardness, ignorance, limitation" (1973, 1).

58. Fever as a metaphor for the rampant growth of capitalism in Spanish cities is best exemplified by the "fever for gold" in Catalonia (Jover and Gómez-Ferrer 2001b, 286).

59. Again, in "Una peseta," Acuña urges the curbing of excessive consumption to combat poverty and hunger (1992d, 86–87). The excessive luxury with which the Madrid upper classes lived is borne out by an article that appeared in *La Época,* February 20, 1884, entitled "La alta burguesía madrileña y el comercio de lujo," reproduced in Bahamonde Magro and Toro Mérida (1978, 242–43).

60. The intellectual and social regeneration of the bourgeoisie, Acuña states in her essay, "Los deportes del porvenir," can be partially achieved through physical

exercise, such as that afforded through agricultural work: "El cerebro ha intensificado por demás su labor, y la especie humana, en sus castas directoras, degenera . . . La ciencia lo dispone: hay que desentumecerse, tonificarse; . . . hay que equilibrar el alma con el cuerpo . . ." [Mental activity has become excessive, and the human species, in its ruling classes, is degenerating . . . Science stipulates that the body must be stretched and toned; . . . the soul must be brought into harmony with the body] (Acuña 1992b, 95).

61. Acuña rightly attributes the rejection of technology in agriculture to fear of loss of jobs, wages, and social status (1882b, 157–58).

62. At the time Acuña wrote "El lujo," Spain was beginning to suffer the effects of the great European depression, partially manifest in cheaper foreign products flooding internal markets. As a result, there was a fall in income for the owners of agricultural properties and their workers, with all the accompanying social problems, together with a lack of investment in agricultural infrastructure (Jover and Gómez-Ferrer 2001b, 295–97). It is relevant that Acuña perceives the vice of luxury more as an issue of class rather than gender, moving away from the typical association of women with luxury spending, as elucidated by Theresa Ann Smith (2006, 81–82, 185).

63. Spain's perceived image of backwardness and economic stagnation in the late nineteenth century is also contested by Carmen Iglesias (2000).

64. With respect to nineteenth-century representations of Pelayo, see Álvarez Junco (2004, 217–19).

65. The parallel arose when subsequent mythifications of the Visigoths cast them as a power unlawfully displaced by foreign invaders: in their case, the Moors (Álvarez Junco 2004, 40).

66. María makes a similar comparison when she tells Isabel: "[E]vocas en mí el recuerdo de aquellas mujeres godas, tan apasionadas como enérgicas" [You evoke in me the memory of those Visigoth women, as passionate as they are energetic] (Acuña 1989c, 165).

67. Reinforcing this idea was the cultural renaissance that Asturias enjoyed after Pelayo under Alfonso II and III (*Libro de Asturias* 1975, 89–92).

68. Hence Ramón refers to the villagers in terms of wild beasts, cave bears, and stultified intelligence, echoing Acuña's previously cited comparison of Spanish society with beings between monkey and man: "[E]scuché vuestros aullidos de fiera . . . me figuraba penetrar en vuestros cerebros, colindantes con el del oso de las cavernas . . . Todo el pasado tenebroso impío, le veía yo estampado en vuestras rudas inteligencias, momificadas en un quietismo de sepulcro, al desarrollarse lejos de toda civilización ... " [I heard your beast-like howls . . . I imagined penetrating your minds, similar to the cave bear's . . . I saw all the dark, impious past imprinted on your primitive intelligences, mummified in a tomb-like quietness due to developing far from all civilization] (Acuña 1989c, 200–1).

69. Scanlon indicates that the Republican Federal Party expressed its desire to reform the legal code so as to grant greater rights to married women (and garner their political support), but that these intentions never became law (1986, 137–38).

70. Regarding this pedagogical policy of revolution from "on high," see Gómez Molleda (1966, chap. 13).

71. With respect to the importance of Gijón for the growth of socialism and the trade union movement in the late nineteenth and early twentieth centuries, see Pamela Beth Radcliff (1996).

72. For Acuña's defense of socialist beliefs, see her essays "El 1° de mayo," "Cuartillas de una mujer" and "¡Justicia! ¡Justicia! ¡Justicia!" (Fernández Riera 2005, 151–52, 170–71, 235–37).

73. For a general discussion of the New Woman and her significance for fin-de-siècle Western culture, see Elaine Showalter (1990, 38–58). For models of the same by nineteenth-century Spanish women writers, see Lou Charnon-Deutsch (1994, 141–85).

74. The existence of these prejudices, even among male supporters of the Institución, is documented by Vázquez Ramil (2001, 53). Wendy S. Jones points to the presence of a similar paradigm of split masculinity in eighteenth- and nineteenth-century England, whereby man could be a "ruthless capitalist" in the masculine public sphere and a "feminine" Christian in the home (2005, 61). Regarding Acuña's stance, see also Zaplana (2005, 46).

75. The tensions inherent in Ramón's attitude toward Isabel are palpable in Isabel's following account of her education by Ramón, which stresses feminine docility and conformity to masculine will: "[P]ara alzar mi inteligencia hasta la suya me bastó docilidad, 'Lee ese libro, me decía' y en vez de arrojarle con el usual desdén femenino, estudiaba todas sus páginas teniendo orgullo en contestarle: 'He aquí el libro que me diste, sé lo que encierra.' Así, poco a poco, llegó el día en que nuestras inteligencias se hallaron tan unidas como nuestros corazones" [To raise my level of intelligence to his, all I needed was docility. "Read that book," he would tell me and, instead of casting it aside with typical feminine disdain, I would study each and every page, taking pride in responding: "Here is the book that you gave me, I know its contents." In this way, little by little, our minds became one with our hearts] (Acuña 1989c, 164–65).

76. As Susan Moller Okin remarks: "Most nineteenth- and early twentieth-century feminists did not question or challenge women's special role within the family. Indeed, they often argued for women's rights and opportunities . . . on the grounds that these would either make them better wives and mothers or enable them to bring their special moral responsibilities, developed in the domestic sphere, to bear on the world of politics" (Okin 1998, 123). Regarding the debates surrounding women's education in nineteenth-century Spain, see Scanlon (1986, 15–50).

77. Acuña also critiques the contemporary masculine ideal of Woman in "Algo sobre la mujer" (Acuña 1881a), while prejudices against women's tertiary education are highlighted in "La Jarca de la Universidad": "¿A quién se le ocurre ir á estudiar á la Universidad? ¡Dios nos libre de las mujeres letradas! ¿A dónde iríamos á parar? ¡Tan bien como vamos en el machito! ¡Pues qué! ¿Es acaso persona una mujer?" [Who would think of studying at university? May God keep us from educated women! Where will it all end? When we're going so well with chauvinists! Indeed! Is a woman even a person?] (Acuña 1992a, 20). In a letter written to the Masonic lodge, "Constante Alona," on July 3, 1885, Acuña represents the state of women in terms of slavery, referring to her "condición de mujer (es decir, de esclava)" [condition of womanhood (that is, of slavery)] (quoted by Álvarez Lázaro

1985, 340; the entire letter is reproduced 339–40). This last statement cannot help but recall Mary Astell's impassioned question in 1700: "If *all Men are born free,* how is it that all Women are born slaves?" (1996, 18).

78. An even more forceful criticism of women's education is leveled in 1892 by Emilia Pardo Bazán, who maintains that differences in education between the sexes are greater than those between the different social classes (Scanlon 1986, 28).

79. Regarding these issues, see Alison Jaggar (1983, 33).

80. With respect to Ramón, Acuña draws on Romantic topoi. Like other Romantic heroes, such as the Duque de Rivas's Don Álvaro and José Zorrilla's Don Juan, he lacks identifiable origins, rebels against social and religious conventions, and is perceived as a Satanic figure by conservative villagers. Regarding such formulations of the Spanish Romantic hero, see Kirkpatrick (1991, 101–30).

81. It is not irrelevant for Isabel's revolutionary dreams that in June 1870, with the Republican reforms emerging from the Glorious Revolution, civil marriage was declared the legal form of union for all, a law overturned with the subsequent Restoration (Scanlon 1986, 146).

82. It is pertinent to contrast Acuña's scenario with the ending of Pardo Bazán's *Memorias de un solterón* (1896), where Fe and Mauro both undergo a transformation to embark on a companionate marriage (see Charnon-Deutsch 1994, 151–63). Similarly Galdós's *Electra* ends with the promise of Electra's and Máximo's future union, with religious fanaticism finally conquered by love. Galdós's drama, then, is more conventional than Acuña's, given its topical ending in terms of gender and his inability to visualize more empowering sociocultural alternatives for women.

Part 2. The Spanish Civil War

1. For a reproduction of the Fresco, see Michael Richards (1998, 8, fig. 1).

2. With regard to the use of myth by Francoist historians, David Herzberger explains that "the authentic history of Spain as a nation is postapocalyptic. . . . it suggests the end of transformation through the final epiphany of truth" (1995, 34).

3. As Rafael Tranche and Vicente Sánchez-Biosca indicate: "The reconstruction, therefore, is the proof of Victory; they are equivalent events" (2002, 231).

4. Regarding the influence of censorship on her work, see Figuera's answers to the survey carried out by Johannes Lechner (1975, 143–44).

5. A reading of Figuera's work in line with Francoist ideals is that offered by Rafael Bosch: "Motherhood in dire hardship is noble, despite the burden of monotony, work and poverty. Motherhood for the fatherland is pleasurable, even though offspring may kill each other" (1962, 6). Regarding the regime's insistence on Woman as mother, see María Teresa Gallego Méndez (1983, 161–74).

6. The import of Figuera's maternal politics is also developed by Emilio Miró (1987, 314–17).

7. For detailed accounts of Figuera's life, see the biographical studies by María Bengoa (2002) and José Ramón Zabala Aguirre (1994, 37–80).

8. Serge Salaün states that in Spanish society, historically marked by Catholicism, Christian references constituted an instantly available tool for conveying Republican dissidence, establishing a linguistic complicity (1985, 245). Regarding the use of biblical language to express opposition to the Franco dictatorship, see Mónica Jato (2004).

9. As Carr notes, Article 26 of the Republican Constitution, establishing the separation of church and state, split the Cabinet (Carr 1982, 606).

10. I here draw on Lois Parkinson Zamora, who states that "the ending of Revelation . . . does not . . . [represent] a return to Eden . . . it responds to it, encompasses it, supplants it metaphorically" (1993, 17).

11. Quoted by Julio Rodríguez Puértolas (1987, 410); original: Pedro Laín Entralgo, "Por un orden lúcido. En la agonía del separatismo," *Arriba España*, May 13, 1937.

12. Quoted by Alun Kenwood (1993, 58); original: *ABC*, July 23, 1936. That resurrection constituted the thematic heart of the Nationalists' concept of the nation is demonstrated by Ernesto Giménez Caballero's following statement from *Los secretos de la Falange* (1939): "How can we talk about 'national resurrection' if we forget that the word 'nation,' . . . like 'spirit,' like the 'life' of a country, has as its etymological root the cherished key of 'to die' so as 'to be reborn'?" (quoted by Rodríguez Puértolas 1987, 1014).

13. Dionisio Ridruejo's comment, from a radio broadcast on November 15, 1938, is quoted by Rodríguez Puértolas (1987, 476). The equivalences created between the martyred José Antonio and the crucified Christ are evident in the 1943 commemoration of the former's death in No-Do, where the landscape is configured according to the Stations of the Cross (see the video of No-Do compiled by Tranche and Sánchez-Biosca 2002).

14. Quoted by Rodríguez Puértolas (1987, 992); original: Manuel García Morente, *Ideas para una filosofía de la historia de España* (1943).

15. Quoted by Rodríguez Puértolas (1987, 452); original: José Pemartín, "El Caudillo hace la Historia," *Qué es lo nuevo . . . Consideraciones sobre el momento español presente* (1938). Similarly Giménez Caballero declares in a radio broadcast on November 20, 1938: "José Antonio's Work came down in the form of the Holy Spirit to anoint our Leader's head with continuity and blessings" (quoted by Rodríguez Puértolas 1987, 398).

16. Quoted by Rodríguez Puértolas (1987, 919); original: José María de Arrese, *La revolución social del nacional-sindicalismo* (Madrid: Nacional, 1940).

17. Such a calendar is visible in the dating of Jorge Villén's prologue to his *Antología poética del Alzamiento, 1936–1939*, written in March 1939, as "March of the Third Triumphal Year" (Lechner 1968, 275).

18. Regarding Christ's wounds as roses, see Leo Steinberg (1996, 374).

19. All subsequent quotations from Figuera's poems are cited parenthetically in the text.

20. For the left-wing political utilization of Christ as carpenter, see Nicholas Perry and Loreto Echeverría (1988, 108).

21. As Paloma Aguilar comments, the economic crisis reached its most critical point at the end of the 1950s (2002, 114).

22. One of the ways in which the Franco regime manifested its authority was by controlling material supplies to the population. This procedure, as Richards explains, "both guaranteed the overriding preoccupation of most of society with personal survival rather than political protest, and ensured that the sacrifices to be made during the long period of economic crisis . . . would be overwhelmingly made by the working class" (1998, 24).

23. Regarding this celebration, see Tranche and Sánchez-Biosca (2002, 428–32). Figuera critiques the Francoist rhetoric of peace in "Esta paz," from 1950 (1986, 114–15).

24. With respect to the Munich conspiracy, see also Aguilar (2002, 102–7) and Rafael Gómez Pérez (1986, 95–98).

25. Examples of such sentences are the executions of the communist Julián Grimau on April 20, 1963 and of the anarchists Joaquín Delgado and Francisco Granados in August that same year (Gómez Pérez 1986, 99).

26. Regarding the miners' strikes, see Gómez Pérez (1986, 117–20).

27. Figuera reiterates similar sentiments in "Ya que no baja el ángel": ". . . Mil novecientos sesenta y dos trabajos / pasaron como tropa de indómitos corceles, / sobre la patria donde los muertos se levantan / uno a uno, y aprenden de nuevo a estar erguidos" [One thousand and sixty two tasks / passed like a herd of unbroken steeds, / over the motherland where the dead rise up / one by one, and learn again to stand erect] (1986, 325).

28. For the importance of May 1 as a figurative site of remembrance for those Republicans and anarchists killed during the Civil War and the Franco dictatorship, see also Aguilar (2002, 90n.78).

29. The words are José María Pemán's, quoted by Santos Juliá (2004, 294). For a discussion of the Francoist appropriation of May 2, see Richards (2002, 97) and Aguilar and Carsten Humlebæk (2002, 127, 134–37).

30. According to Richards, violence was methodically programed and implemented by the Nationalists. In contrast, the Republicans never deployed violence in a systematic fashion (1998, 32–33).

31. As Jo Labanyi explains, drawing on Jacques Derrida (1994), "ghosts are the traces of those who were not allowed to leave a trace; that is, the victims of history and in particular subaltern groups, whose stories—those of the losers—are excluded from the dominant narratives of the victors" (2002, 1–2).

32. For this equation of the axe with fascism, see León Felipe's long poem, *El Hacha (Elegía española),* from 1939.

33. The poets to whom Figuera refers are most likely Miguel Hernández, Jesús López Pacheco, Antonio Machado, Blas de Otero, Gabino Carriedo, Ángel Crespo, Gabriel Celaya, and José Agustín Goytisolo, many of whom were her friends and correspondents for years (Bengoa 2002, 102, 106).

34. See Celaya's composition, "La poesía es un arma cargada de futuro" (1986, 92–94).

35. Regarding the ambiguity surrounding this monument and whose dead it was supposed to honor, see Aguilar (2002, 81–85).

36. Richards declares that during the Civil War thousands of Spaniards disappeared through Nationalist executions never officially placed on historical record. Many common graves similar to those described in Figuera's poems were

not disinterred until after Franco's death in the late 1970s. It was only then that, in some areas, more than 50 percent of the Civil War fatalities effected by the Nationalists were finally recorded (1998, 31, 38, 198n.101). Today locating as many mass graves as possible from the Civil War and identifying the remains of victims is the avowed mission of the national Asociación para la Recuperación de la Memoria Histórica (ARMH, Association for the Recovery of Historical Memory).

37. Ricoeur defines prescription as "a prohibition against considering the criminal consequences of the action committed, including the right and even the obligation to begin criminal proceedings. . . . it is refusing . . . to move back up the course of time to the act and to its illegal or irregular traces. The traces are not erased: it is the path back to them that is forbidden" (2004, 471–72).

38. In "No quiero," from *Toco la tierra* (1962), Figuera writes: "No quiero / que la tierra se parta en porciones, / que en el mar se establezcan dominios, / que en el aire se agiten banderas, / que en los trajes se pongan señales" [I don't want / the earth to be divided up into bits, / the sea to be made territory, / flags, waved in the air, / garments, marked] (1986, 274).

39. These "wolves" reappear elsewhere in Figuera's poems, as exemplified in the following verses from "Culpa"—"Si los lobos consiguen mantenerse robustos / consumiendo la sangre que la tierra no empapa" [But the wolves manage to remain robust / consuming the blood that the earth cannot absorb]—and from "Creo en el hombre": "Porque se ríe a diario entre los lobos" [Because you laugh every day in the midst of wolves] (1986, 181, 279).

40. This notion of totalitarian reordering is echoed in Figuera's "Mundo concluso," which refers to the impossibility of imagining anew in a world "ya fabricado, rígido, / archisabio, ahito [*sic*] de mapas y de fórmulas" [already fashioned, rigid, / overly wise, satiated with maps and formulas], a world that is "definitivamente / desoladoramente total y rematado" [definitively / desolately complete and finished off] (1986, 148).

41. For a critique of Spain's autarky and the need to build figurative bridges, see also Figuera's poem, "Puentes," from 1958, which begins: "Estamos encerrados en la isla / (una islita de nada)" [We are imprisoned on the island / (a tiny island, barely nothing)] (1986, 241).

42. Franco's refusal to contemplate a third position is evident in his following proclamation: "He who thinks of mediation proposes a broken, materialist, divided, wretched and subdued Spain . . . A peace for today and another war for tomorrow" (quoted by Richards 1998, 150).

43. In other compositions, Figuera (1986) depicts Spain as a prison ("La cárcel" 193), an "estación sin nombre" [a nameless station] full of displaced persons ("Estación" 194), and a sterile land where it is impossible to sow new seed ("Regreso" 196–97).

44. It is likely that Figuera's allusion to "such pretty sonnets to the rose" criticizes the uncommitted poetry, typical of that published in the literary journal *Garcilaso* from 1940 to 1955, which viewed Franco's Spain through rose-tinted lenses. Regarding *Garcilaso*, see Lechner (1975, 22–30).

45. The association here of the rose with poetry and bloody destruction recalls Blas de Otero's poem, "Crecida," from *Ángel fieramente humano* (1950): "Traigo

una rosa en sangre entre las manos / ensangrentadas. Porque es que no hay más / que sangre" [I bear a bloody rose in my hands / bloodied. Because there is nothing else / but blood] (1992, 72). Regarding Figuera's possible awareness of the poetry of Gertrude Stein, who wrote "Rose is a rose is a rose is a rose," from her poem "Sacred Emily" (1993, 187), Figuera did translate into Spanish a critical work on Stein, published by Gredos in 1962 (Bengoa 2002, 118).

46. The original text is by Juan Pablo Fusi, "Para escribir la biografía de Franco," *Claves de Razón Práctica* 27 (November 1992): 9.

47. On December 8, 1936, in full Civil War, the feast of the Immaculate Conception was declared a national holiday in the hope that Mary, as "the pacifier of the world," would bring peace to a war-torn Spain (Perry and Echeverría 1988, 215).

48. For such Nationalist imagery, see posters 1920 and 1959 in Carulla and Carulla (1997, 2:533, 547). Rafael Abella declares that "soldiers, and with them, the great majority of the armed forces, paraded the scapular of Jesus's Sacred Heart, which bore the following inscriptions: 'Halt, bullet; Jesus's Heart is with me' or 'Stop, foe, Jesus's Heart is with me,' the latter with even greater protective powers" (1973, 172).

49. For examples of such images, see posters 727 and 744 in Carulla and Carulla (1997, 1:231, 234).

50. Quoted by Perry and Echeverría (1988, 163); original: *Palabras del Caudillo: 1937–42* (Madrid, 1943): 149.

51. For Mary as mediator between heaven and earth, see Marina Warner (1985, 285–86).

52. Regarding these two poems, see also Jo Evans (1996, 44–45, 72–75, 92–97).

53. The struggle of Figuera's poetic voice with the Angel may be read as an internal struggle with the *alter ego* of Ángela, a being endowed with wings through her written word and name: ". . . las seis letras / –alado laberinto– de mi nombre" [the six letters / –winged labyrinth– of my name] ("Esta que soy," 1986, 152). For readings of this poem, see also Jo Evans (1996, 93), Payeras (2002, 26), and Wilcox (1993, 187). Figuera's reference in "Vencida por el ángel" to the absence of the sword also suggests the imagined defeat of a militaristic ethos of censorship and repression, often represented by Franco's crusading sword (Boyd 1997, 263).

54. My reading here differs from that of Jo Evans, who presents the poetic subject's "dawning of social awareness" as "a necessary form of violation," a kind of rape fantasy (1996, 94).

55. Regarding the long-established correlation between Christ and Mary as Holy Mother, see Caroline Walker Bynum. The feminization of Christ is not new among dissident Spanish poets, with León Felipe, in "Diré cómo murió" from *Ganarás la luz* (1945), likening the dead motherland to the crucified Christ: "Sola y en cruz ... España-Cristo, / con la lanza cainita clavada en el costado, / sola y desnuda, / . . . / sola sobre mi calvero y mi calvario" [Alone and on the cross ... Spain-Christ, / her side pierced by the Cainite spear, / alone and naked, / . . . / alone above my clearing and my calvary] (Felipe 1990, 197).

56. For an overview of the figure of the *Mater Dolorosa* in Republican poetry during the Civil War, see Juliá (2004, 271–74).

57. While the process envisaged in Figuera's work is to be realized within the boundaries of democratic law, for the regime the Day of Judgment demanded the summary eradication of all others antagonistic to its order, with death by execution referred to as "final judgement" (Aguilar 2002, 94). Similarly Juliá describes the Nationalists as advocating a policy of "extermination and annihilation, similar to how the angels will proceed on Judgment Day" and cites the Jesuit Félix G. Olmedo, who in 1938 propounds: "We accomplish through war what the angels will do on Judgment Day: separate the wheat from the chaff" (Juliá 2004, 291).

58. As Giesen argues with regard to the recognition by the German nation of its Nazi past, such a process requires that crimes be atoned for by an innocent figure (2004, 131–33).

59. Regarding Figuera's fears of thematic repetition and lack of originality, see Quance (1986, 18).

60. Hence, in Figuera's poem "Libertad," the symbol of the cross is used to refer to censorship and the elimination of dissident others: "A tiros nos dijeron: cruz y raya. / En cruz estamos. Raya. Tachadura. / Borrón y cárcel nueva. Punto en boca" [Under fire they told us: that's the end of that. / We're on the cross. Crossed out. Erased. / A clean slate and another prison. Full stop on our mouths] (1986, 219).

61. Imagery in verses such as these is not unlike that in a poem entitled "A los jóvenes dolorosos" (1937), by Falangist Ramón de Basterra: "Oh, joven doloroso, joven triste / que sufres como yo del mal de España / y que una negación honda, en tu entraña / tienes, clavada, contra todo lo que existe" [Oh, suffering youth, sad youth / who suffers like me from Spain's ills / with deep-seated rejection, to your innermost being / nailed, of all that exists] (quoted by Rodríguez Puértolas 1987, 9).

62. This Francoist narrative of the 1960s was developed by Richards, "The Spanish Civil War 70 Years On: Public and Personal Memories of the War as Social History" (keynote address at the international conference, "War without Limits," University of Bristol, July 17–19, 2006).

63. Regarding the sanctioning of killing in wartime, see Elaine Scarry (1985, 121–22).

64. The Tree of Life is the Tree of Jesse. Representing Christ's genealogy, it subsequently became linked to the Immaculate Conception (Stratton 1994, 12). One of the most famous associations of Christ with the grapevine is the 1469 painting belonging to the School of Friedrich Herlin, *Christ with Ears of Wheat and Grape Vine,* reproduced in Steinberg (1996, 368–69).

65. In this sense, Figuera's poetry resembles Pablo Neruda's *Tercera Residencia* and *Canto General,* which also deploy Christian symbols such as bread and wheat, and structure poems as litanies (Lechner 2:108). Figuera met Neruda in Paris in 1957, when she was there on a librarian scholarship (Bengoa 2002, 146).

66. Ample proof is provided by Lechner's analysis of dissident poetry written after the Civil War (1975, 102–11) and by Rodríguez Puértolas's recopilation of Nationalist works, exemplified by the following quotation from "Blasón del yugo y las flechas" by Ernesto La Orden Miracle: "¡Yugo de Dios y la Patria, / para orar y para arar! / . . . Ningún español se niegue / a uncirse y a trabajar / sobre esta

tierra baldía / que pronto será trigal" [Yoke of God and the Fatherland, / for praying and ploughing! / . . . Let no Spaniard refuse / to harness himself and work / this barren earth / that soon will be a wheatfield] (Rodríguez Puértolas 1987, 160; original: *Romancero Nacional*, ed. Luis Miracle [Barcelona, 1939]).

67. Likewise in Figuera's poem "No quiero," the poetic voice alludes to the Nationalists' "scorched-earth" policy: "No quiero / que el trigo se queme y el pan se escatime" [I don't want / the wheat to burn and bread to be scarce] (1986, 273).

68. Payeras also notes that Figuera's themes of sowing and harvesting relate to the present and future of Spain (2002, 40).

69. It is likely that here Figuera draws on Blas de Otero's following verses from "A la inmensa mayoría," in *Pido la paz y la palabra* (1955): "Yo doy todos mis versos por un hombre / en paz. Aquí tenéis, en carne y hueso, / mi última voluntad. . ." [I'll give all my verses for a man / at peace. Here you have, in flesh and blood, / my last wish] (1992, 102).

70. Aguilar stresses that in Francoist Spain "the real reintegration of the defeated would have meant giving them a voice and a vote, committing the Government to listening to their criticisms and granting them equal rights with regard to those enjoyed by the winning side" (2002, 148).

71. In contrast, the Francoist writer, Antonio Tovar, associates such healing measures with reactionary politics: "To call out for an 'iron surgeon' is revolutionary; the reactionary prefers healing medication and plasters" (quoted by Rodríguez Puértolas 1987, 1149; original: "Antígona y el tirano, o la inteligencia en la política," *Escorial* 10, 1943).

72. The reference to the elimination of serpents recalls Mary's conquest of the same creature, symbolic of "her victory over evil" (Warner 1985, 268).

Part 3. Recovering Cultural History

1. For Chacel's identification with the 1927 Generation, see her essay "Hablando de mí" (Chacel 1993i, 91). Among studies that place Chacel within that same generation are those by Catherine Bellver (2001) and Shirley Mangini, for whom she is the foremost female novelist of the avant-garde writers (2001, 146). The term "Generation of the Republic" is used by Miguel García Posada to extend membership of the 1927 Generation beyond its poets (1999, 20). Regarding the temporal boundaries of the avant-garde, Jaime Brihuega loosely fixes these between 1909 and 1936 (1981, 148), while for Guillermo de Torre they correspond to the years between 1918 and 1940 (1974, 2:275).

2. Chacel's intention that her trilogy constitute a biography of her generation is underscored in her essay, "Autobiografía intelectual" (Chacel 1993b, 71), as well as in her epigraph to *Acrópolis*, which opens with a quotation from Dámaso Alonso's chapter from *Poetas españoles contemporáneos* entitled "Una generación poética (1920–1936)": "[L]os recuerdo a todos en bloque, formando conjunto, como un sistema que el amor presidía . . ." [I remember them all as a whole, forming a group, like a system governed by love] (Chacel 1984, 7). Chacel refers again to Alonso's words in "Sendas recobradas" (1993x, 271).

3. Regarding the political commitment of those intellectuals associated with *El Mono Azul* and *Hora de España*, and for an analysis of the differences between these two publications, see Salaün (1985, 359–66).

4. For biographical information on Chacel, see Isabel Foncea Hierro (1999, 14–26), Cora Requena Hidalgo (2002, 8–11), and Ana Rodríguez Fischer (1988).

5. Among numerous other honors, in 1976 Chacel received the Critics' Prize for *Barrio de Maravillas*, in 1982 there took place in Madrid a symposium to celebrate her work, and in 1987 she received the National Prize in Spanish Literature (see Rodríguez Fischer 1988, 21–23).

6. Regarding discrimination in Chacel's contemporary context, see Teresa Bordons and Kirkpatrick (1992); Kirkpatrick (2003, 264, 269–70); and Mangini (1987 and 2001, 148–49).

7. Indeed, on remembering her visit to Spain in 1961, Chacel maintains that she did not meet with any political obstacles, despite being known as "desafecta al régimen" [opposed to the regime]. However, she was received coldly by intellectuals and writers, due to her association with "dehumanized" literature (Chacel 1993w, 249).

8. Ana María Moix attests to the *Novísimos*'s rediscovery of Chacel as follows: "It was the meeting of the beliefs of a new generation of readers . . . badly nourished . . . with the work already written (and how well!) of a writer who had begun almost half a century before. The meeting took place forty years late, but it did take place" (1994, 65). For Chacel's relationship with the Novísimos, especially Moix, Pere Gimferrer, and Guillermo Carnero, see *Alcancía (Vuelta)* (Chacel 1982b, 32, 248), and *De mar a mar: Epistolario* (Chacel and Moix 2003). Regarding the Novísimos's desire to renew the novel through recovering the Spanish and European avant-garde spirit of the 1920s and 1930s, see Santos Alonso (2003, 57).

9. Regarding Chacel's views on writers of the *Nouveau Roman*, see, for example, *Alcancía (Ida)* (Chacel 1982a, 198, 214), *Alcancía (Vuelta)* (Chacel 1982b, 107–8), and her essay on Michel Butor (Chacel 1993y, 259–69). For her allegiance to the "new novel" derived from Ortegan aesthetics, see Chacel's entry for January 27, 1970 in *Alcancía (Vuelta)*. There, while acknowledging that current aesthetic expectations for the novel are different from those in 1930, Chacel refuses to compromise her style in response to suggestions from the Novísimos and questions whether their abandoning of premises of that earlier aesthetics is because of different tastes or lack of ability (Chacel 1982b, 276). Chacel's fidelity to the premises of the avant-garde "new novel" can be observed in her statement that she cannot abandon the "1927 formula," because she does not consider that its full potential has yet been realized (428).

10. In *Alcancía (Ida)*, under her entry for October 12, 1961, Chacel expresses her fear that the cultural regeneration of Spain that Ortega's generation and her own hoped to effect might never be resumed due to the absence then of suitable circumstances (1982a, 265).

11. Christopher Soufas also blames conservative Spanish paradigms of literary criticism during the Franco era for the discrediting of Spanish modernism, declaring that "[w]hat happened after the Civil War . . . was an 'unmaking' of Modernism" (1998, 466).

12. Even in 1977 Chacel remarks that current literary critics do not attempt to evaluate the reasons for the existence of her generation ("no aquilatan el alma de la cosa" [they do not extract the soul of the matter]), but simply classify it (1993w, 251).

13. The haunting of the present by the past is encapsulated in *Barrio* in the allusion to the revenant (Chacel 1981, 222). This symbol becomes prominent in the last novel in the trilogy, *Ciencias naturales.*

14. Regarding the philosophical novel and its influence on Chacel's work, see Roberta Johnson (1993, 172–73, 178–80).

15. Nora observes: "*Lieux de mémoire* arise out of a sense that there is no such thing as spontaneous memory, hence we must create archives, mark anniversaries, organize celebrations, pronounce eulogies, and authenticate documents because such things no longer happen as a matter of course. When certain minorities create protected enclaves as preserves of memory to be jealously safeguarded, they reveal what is true of all *lieux de mémoire*: that without commemorative vigilance, history would soon sweep them away" (1996a, 7).

16. With the terms *modernist* and *modernism* I refer to a movement predicated on its desire to be modern and break with a tradition perceived as inadequate for the exigencies of an industrialized, technological, capitalist age. Although its temporal coordinates vary in different countries, they are generally considered to depart from the last decades of the nineteenth century and extend until 1939: the year that marks the end of the Civil War and the outbreak of World War II. The literature regarding Spanish modernisms is vast. Helpful studies are those by John Butt (1993) and Germán Gullón (1993); the volume edited by Monique Chefdor, Ricardo Quinones, and Albert Wachtel (1986), and that by Anthony L. Geist and José B. Monleón (1999b).

17. Geist and Monleón indicate that "Ortega's writings have all but disappeared from contemporary discussions about modernism, in spite of their being one of the first attempts at establishing a theory of the avant-garde" (1999a, xx). Regarding the Generation of 1927 as constituting a Silver Age, see Mainer (1983). Chacel herself refers to the 1920s as a golden decade or "década de oro" (1993h, 102).

18. Ortega is compared to Socrates by Fernando Vela, secretary of the *Revista de Occidente* in its first period (Llera 1991, 97). Apart from Ortega, many of the fictional characters in Chacel's trilogy are derived from real figures in modernist generations, such as Miguel de Unamuno, Ramón Gómez de la Serna, and Máximo José Kahn, the minister for the Spanish Republic in Athens and a character in *Ciencias naturales.* Kahn, an exile like Chacel in the post–Civil War years, gave Chacel the notebook with which she initiates her diary, *Alcancía (Ida)* (1982a, 13).

19. Also defending in qualified tones the term *generation* is Francisco Ayala, a member of Chacel's cultural generation: "This concept of generation is very controversial. I consider that it is a real, solid concept, but it needs to be used flexibly" ("Memoria viva" 1993, 11).

20. For Chacel's viewpoint on the avant-garde, expressed in 1930, see "Respuesta a la encuesta sobre 'la vanguardia'" (Chacel 1993t, 229).

21. For studies on the Generation of 1898, see José Luis Abellán (1973), José Luis Bernal Muñoz (1996), María Dolores Dobón (1996), and Donald L. Shaw

(1975), as well as the volume edited by John P. Gabriele (1999). Particularly valuable for developing my own position on Chacel's work have been those discussions of her avant-garde context and her relationship with contemporary intellectuals by Bordons and Kirkpatrick (1992), Tatjana Gajic (2002), Johnson (2003, 210–23), Reyes Lázaro (1994), María Carmen López Sáenz (1994), Mangini (1987, 1993, 1998, 2001), and Rodríguez Fischer (1993, 1999).

22. In her essay, "Invitación a la Escuela," Chacel refers to the importance for her generation of World War I: "El maremagnum que revolvió la sangre de Europa en el catorce nos arrastró a todos definitivamente, todos tomamos partido . . ." [The tsunami that churned up Europe's blood in 1914 swept us all away, we all took sides] (1993j, 327). The homage to Góngora features in *Acrópolis* (Chacel 1984, 230–34) and is examined by Gajic (2002, 247–49, 251–57).

23. Nora reiterates that, at the same time that "[a] generation is a product of memory, an effect of remembering," memory is also "the linchpin of definitions of generation" (1996b, 522, 527).

24. Chacel again equates a historical epoch with the concept of nation in "Réplica a una entrevista," referring to "nuestra patria mística, nuestro tiempo" [our mystical nation, our time] (1993s, 221).

25. Such notions also pertain to Julius Petersen's elaboration of what constitutes a cultural generation. Among the factors considered essential are a common spiritual date of birth, the participation in common life experiences, which create affinity among its members, and modes of expression peculiar to that generation (Torre 1974, 1:59–60).

26. Further explaining the association of "installation" with history, Ortega's disciple, the philosopher Julián Marías, states: "Spain's reality is, rather, a way of installation, understood, of course, vectorially; I mean, that from which every projection begins. . . . it is made in history, takes place historically" (Marías 1992, 45).

27. All subsequent quotations from *Acrópolis* are cited parenthetically in the text.

28. With respect to "climate," Ortega declares: "Eras enact the role of moral climates, historical environments to which nations are subject. However great the differences between nations, their shared era bestows on them certain similarities" (1981d, 14–15).

29. The connotations of "clan" can be observed in the following quotations from *Barrio* (Chacel 1981): "Magdalena ha muerto se desgarra la armonía del clan la armonía que a veces existe . . . principalmente la armonía fraternal, camaradería de la sangre, del tiempo, sobre todo ... " [With Magdalena's death the clan's harmony is destroyed, the harmony that occasionally exists . . . mainly a fraternal harmony, a comradeship of blood and, above all, of time] (154) and "¡Nosotros! es una alcoba, . . . es una guarida, es un clan" [We! The word is an intimate room . . . a lair, a clan] (161).

30. Scholars who have noted the importance of art and cultural creation in *Barrio de Maravillas* and *Acrópolis* are Clara Janés (1994), Wilma Newberry (1988), and Kirkpatrick (1992, viii).

31. Whereas the term "gente nueva" was identified with the 1898 Generation (Dobón 1996, 61–63), the designation "gente novísima" originally came from an 1897 article by Clarín of the same title. There he distinguishes between the

"gente nueva" [new people], seen as disdainful of his Generation, and the "gente novísima" [very new people], whom he describes as follows: "Generally, they are more respectful, . . . more humble, and know what being a disciple is all about" (quoted by Dobón 1996, 62–63; original: *Los Lunes* de *El Imparcial*, May 4, 1897).

32. Chacel acknowledges Ortega's influence on her work in essays such as "Ortega" (1993p) and "Ortega a otra distancia" (1993q). In "Respuesta a Ortega," published in 1956, she remarks: "[M]e considero actualmente como uno de los discípulos más jóvenes de Ortega" [Nowadays I consider myself one of Ortega's youngest disciples] (1993u, 369). For the influence of Ortega's aesthetics on Chacel, see López Sáenz (1994). Among other Spanish writers whom Chacel recognizes as impacting on her literary formation are Pío Baroja, Ramón Gómez de la Serna, Juan Ramón Jiménez, Unamuno, and Ramón del Valle-Inclán (see Chacel 1993h, 102–8).

33. Thus Ortega writes: "The select minorities constitute an open class in which all Spaniards can participate, as the only way to free their conscience of prejudices and rusty partisanships. . . . The minorities, by virtue of their role and mission, are duty bound to take all measures to perfect democracy, which, because it contains the great and infinite principle of freedom, will always be a system continually in the making . . . Ensuring that democracy respects freedom is the responsibility of the nation's minority, who must, should the contrary occur, sound the alarm" (quoted by Llera 1991, 172–74).

34. Intergenerational respect is confirmed by Luis García Montero: "Another thing that stands out is the respect toward the maestros. It was an era characterized not only by originality and innovation, but also by great generosity of spirit toward the maestros" ("Memoria viva" 1993, 16). Although Chacel does acknowledge personal difficulties with the group formed around Ortega's *Revista de Occidente*, as well as with Ortega himself, she stresses that disagreements do not invalidate adherence to common ideals (see Chacel 1993z, 278).

35. Giner states: "Everything is disintegrating, in tatters; the nation is falling apart, not only morally but in real terms. . . . What can be more spiritual than sweeping out a nation, teaching it the religion of cleanliness—by cleanliness, I mean integrity, fastidiousness . . . passion set free!" (quoted by Pijoán 1927, 18).

36. In "Sendas perdidas" Chacel alludes to the enormous influence of the Institución in the early twentieth century, calling it an "escuela de maestros" [school of maestros] and indeed, "*la escuela*" [the school] (1993w, 243–44).

37. By "school" Chacel also means a specific literary movement that looked outward to the best of European culture (1993h, 105). Chacel's entry for June 1960 from *Alcancía (Ida)* again emphasizes that her generation's "school" was impeded by historical circumstances from coming to full fruition: "Se trata de una escuela que empezaba entonces, en el veintitantos, que provenía de Proust y de James Joyce, y que en España apuntó superficialmente en muchos, pero sólo en mí con verdadera solidez y adhesión. Naturalmente, fue estrangulada" [It was a school that began then, in the 1920s, having originated in Proust and James Joyce. In Spain its presence in many was superficial, and it was only in me that it really took root and blossomed. Of course, it was suffocated] (1982a, 214). Similar notions are reiterated in her entry for November 12, 1961 (1982a, 265).

38. In her 1937 essay, "Cultura y pueblo," Chacel, referring to the characteristics of the Republican revolution, states: "[S]i llegamos a comprender qué es lo que se salda en ella verdaderamente original y decisivo, tendremos que convenir en que es, precisamente, la posición del pueblo respecto a la cultura y de la cultura respecto al pueblo" [If we succeed in understanding what turned out to be truly original and decisive about it, we would have to agree that it is, specifically, the positioning of the people vis-à-vis culture and viceversa] (1993e, 369).

39. The purpose of higher education, the philosopher Manuel declares in *Barrio*, is the intellectual mentoring of a new generation, described in terms of shepherding a flock: "[L]a cátedra no es nada si uno no la ha hecho apacentando el hato de una generación" [A University Chair is nought if it has not served to shepherd the flock that is a generation] (Chacel 1981, 268). Regarding the association of culture with farming work, see Zygmunt Bauman (1987, 94).

40. Significantly the metaphors that inform these debates are present to a remarkable degree in Ortega's imaginary dialogue between Baroja and Azorín in "Diálogo sobre el arte nuevo" from 1924: "Why not imagine that generations are human crops and that suddenly a mutation appears in one of them? . . . 'an emerging evolution,' or rather, an evolution with sudden offshoots of originality. In that way, unexpected changes in artistic tastes could be explained. You and I, unexceptional beans, are now witnessing the birth of an outstanding literature."—"The same stew!"—"No, the stew is not the same; what will surely be the same is the indigestion" (1981a, 136).

41. In *Barrio* it is significant that Laura's widowed brother, Manolo, buries his wife Magdalena in a civil cemetery, in a gravesite without a cross (Chacel 1981, 211).

42. In "Volviendo al punto de partida" Chacel refers to the positive benefits derived from such immigration, particularly highlighting the influence of foreign female intellectuals on Spanish women writers, herself included (1993z, 288).

43. Regarding the misogynist character of modernism, see, in particular, Felski (1995) and Huyssen (1986, 44–62).

44. See, for example, Alberto Porlan's interview with Chacel (1984, 21).

45. Chacel alludes to this kind of discrimination in "Volviendo al punto de partida" from 1964, where she highlights that her inclusion in José Aranguren's 1931 study on the 1927 Generation was purely on the basis of sexist criteria (1993z, 289–90).

46. Subsequent quotations from *Barrio de Maravillas* are cited parenthetically in the text.

47. Regarding this masculine engendering of the modernist city, see Shari Benstock (1989, 27) and Griselda Pollock (1988, 71).

48. This type of urban description is reiterated elsewhere in *Acrópolis* (see Chacel 1984, 136–37, 211–12).

49. As noted by Michael Ugarte (1996), Madrid was seen by its liberal intellectuals as the "cradle of culture" that would nurture a modern nation still in its infancy.

50. In *Acrópolis* alone (Chacel 1984), references are made to works by Boecklin (98), Chagall (202), Delacroix (97), Durero (361), El Greco (179), Géricault (96), Goya (95–98, 301, 361), Gros (76), Leonardo da Vinci (28), Madrazo (98), Miura

(220), Zuloaga (337), Zurbarán (129), the French impressionists Maurice Denis, Monet, and Puvis de Chavannes (82), as well as avant-garde artists like the Catalan Anglada-Camarasa (49–53).

51. It is relevant that in 1930 only 0.1% of women had access to higher education (Capel Martínez 1986, 387).

52. I have been unable to locate this painting in catalogues of Martínez del Mazo's works. The most similar is one entitled *Doña Mariana de Austria, viuda.* It is thus uncertain whether Chacel here refers to an actual painting, to a work inaccurately remembered, or to a fictionalized construct.

53. In *Acrópolis* the representation of philosophical questions as open doors is evident in Manuel's stream-of-consciousness dialogue with himself: "La cuestión había quedado abierta, pero cuanto más abierta, más asfixiante. . . . Pero ¿quién abrió la cuestión? Ya se sabe que cuando le dicen a uno, 'te has dejado la puerta abierta,' eso quiere decir, 'anda a cerrarla'" [The question had remained open, but, the more open it was, the more suffocating. . . . But, who opened the question? It's common knowledge that when you say to someone, "you've left the door open," it means "go and shut it"] (Chacel 1984, 127).

54. Similar premises privileging the sociohistorical processes that influence cultural production are visible in other ekphrastic descriptions in *Acrópolis,* such as when Manuel considers Antoine-Jean Gros's painting, *Bonaparte Visiting the Plague Victims of Jaffa* (1804) (see Chacel 1984, 76).

55. Elena is also represented as advocating this ethos of incorporation when she states in *Barrio*: "Quiere uno casarse con la cosa, zambullirse en la cosa" [You want to become one with the thing, jump right into it] (Chacel 1981, 137).

56. The importance of dynamic movement for modern art and literature is also stressed in *Barrio* when Elena wants Isabel to use a live mouse as model in her attempts at modern art: "[Q]uería que Isabel llegase conociendo ya un plan más moderno. Quería [Elena] ponerle un modelo vivo, un modelo con movimiento. . . ." [She wanted Isabel to acquire knowledge of a much more modern system. (Elena) wanted to assign her a live model, a model that moved]. The death of the mouse converts it into a still life, which Isabel no longer wishes to copy (Chacel 1981, 128–29). For a different interpretation, see Gajic (2002, 228–30).

57. Similarly Geist maintains that the Spanish historical avant-garde set out to challenge a notion of art as an autonomous bourgeois institution by reinserting it into lived social practices and foregrounding the processes that informed its creation (1993, 57–58).

58. For expositions of diverse perceptions of the Spanish avant-garde, see Juliá (2004, 227–60) and Rodríguez Fischer (1999, 30–45). The alliance between a radical formal art and sociopolitical radicalism was recognized by José Díaz Fernández (1930, 50), who affirmed that the revolutionary style of the avant-garde would be the most suitable for creating a truly social literature.

59. The name Máximo evokes the male protagonist of Galdos's anticlerical play *Electra* (1901), considered to mark the birth of the 1898 Generation and mentioned in relation to Acuña's *El Padre Juan.* Regarding Chacel's Máximo, see also Kirkpatrick (1992, xiv–xv).

60. Today this statue is held in the National Arqueological Museum in Madrid.

61. Examples from *Barrio* pertaining to Elena as "decadente" are as follows: "Eso de las cigüeñas no era lo mejor. No era malo, no, pero hubo otras cosas. Hubo una que yo elogié mucho y Montero se sonrió: me dijo, '¡Decadente!'" [The depiction of the storks wasn't the best. It certainly wasn't bad, but there were better things. There was one that I praised highly and Montero smiled, calling me "Decadent!"] and "[C]on ese aliento de las fieras también se ha deleitado otro decadente.—'Otro ¿tan decadente como yo?'—Más o menos" [Another decadent has also taken pleasure in those beasts' breath.—Someone as decadent as me?—More or less] (Chacel 1981, 239, 251).

62. Chacel continues to critique the senseless bourgeois consumption of art through the antique dealer in *Acrópolis*: "Todas vienen a ver quién se lleva la [cosa] más cara porque no tienen pinta de entender mucho" [All the women come to see who among them can buy the most expensive object, because they don't appear to be connaisseurs] (1984, 208).

63. In *La deshumanización del arte* (1925), Ortega signals that avant-garde "dehumanized" culture, envisaged as a radical redrawing of modes of perception and representation, proves unpopular with both a bourgeoisie habituated to an unchallenging consumption of culture and also the lower classes, who lack sufficient education to understand its meaning. Thus Ortega's concept of "masa" [masses] cuts across class divisions to refer to all those who are unprepared, whether through unreceptiveness or inadequate education, to engage with avant-garde culture: "The masses are opposed to new art and that will always be so. . . . An avant-garde work . . . splits the public into two groups: a minority, made up of a small number receptive to the work; and another, the great majority, who are hostile to it" (1981c, 13).

64. In "Sendas perdidas" Chacel refers to the meanings that *bourgeois* held for her generation: "Entonces, *burgués* no tenía el sentido exclusivamente político que tiene ahora: burgués era un ente social antipático, antiestético, aburrido, retardatario" [Then, the term *bourgeois* did not have the exclusively political meaning that it has today: to be bourgeois was to be socially disagreeable, lacking in aesthetic taste, boring, conservative] (1993w, 243).

65. Kirkpatrick also discusses this same episode but does not explore its political implications (2003, 79–80).

66. For a more general discussion of the engendering of cultural and national discourses among fin-de-siècle European and Spanish intellectuals, see Kirkpatrick (2003, 89–93).

67. Nevertheless Chacel also describes Unamuno as one of her maestros (1993i, 92), analyzing his work extensively in *La confesión* (1980, 93–157).

68. According to Luis de Llera, Ortega aimed to promote a culture "less conditioned by national circumstances that, desiring to be more universal, became increasingly pure . . . The first maxim was to remove oneself from all politics or partisanship, preserving intellectual distance" (1991, 176). Regarding this issue, see also Juliá (2004, 158–78).

69. These same concepts are reiterated shortly afterward: "El camino de los intelectuales, de los maestros, los artistas, los científicos creadores ... , de los que no van por una senda estrecha, sino que la suya se dilata por toda la tierra y son ellos—los de la espada . . . los que la desenvainan por las palabras que otros pro-

nunciaron, crearon, entronizaron ... " [The path of intellectuals, maestros, artists, creative scientists ... , of those who do not follow a narrow path but one that encompasses the whole earth, and it is others—the ones who bear swords . . . who unsheath them according to the words that the former uttered, created, held up on high] (Chacel 1981, 273).

70. For a visual depiction of the Republic as here described in Chacel's *Acrópolis,* although without the imperial eagle's plume, see the jacket cover of this book, which reproduces poster 219 in Carulla and Carulla (1997, 1:102).

71. The collapsing of the Republican era on to that of a contemporary present is suggested in *Acrópolis* by textual allusions to the "época actual" [present era], to the "esplendente libertad" [splendid freedom] and to the avalanche of foreign tourism to Spain (Chacel 1984, 358).

Conclusion

1. Aguilar and Humlebæk remark on "the limited space of maneuver between remembrance of the Civil War and reconciliation" (2002, 127).

2. In this context, it is relevant that the beginning of democracy in Spain coincided with the celebration of the one-hundredth anniversary of the so-called Generation of 1914, with celebrations around members of the 1927 Generation following shortly afterward (Mainer 2001, 175).

3. Commemoration, Nora clarifies, is "a secular form of expression associated with the tradition of the Enlightenment, the [French] Revolution, and the Republic," while patrimony is "a constituent part of a subgroup identity, of a social category perceived exclusively in terms of its cultural dimension" (1998, 629, 632).

4. However, for Eduardo Manzano Moreno and Pérez Garzón, present-day Spain also continues to wrestle with issues inherited from the nineteenth century, such as regional nationalisms, the relationship of education with a localized versus national history in forming Spanish citizens, and the ethical and political implications of this matter for historical memory (2002, 274–76).

5. Nevertheless scholars like Edurne Uriarte consider that Spain has already adopted a federal model through its autonomous communities (2003, 213ff.).

6. This ideal is sustained by the creation of the Committee of the Regions within the European Union.

7. Regarding the Spanish in Melilla, claimed by Morocco since 1961, Hastings Donnan and Thomas Wilson state the following: "Although in most ways Melilla is their city, they feel caught between many worlds. They are literally on the border between Spain and Morocco, but are also squarely placed in the frontier between Europe and Africa, between the Christian and the Muslim worlds, between, in their eyes, civilisation and barbarism, and between order and chaos" (1999, 68).

8. With respect to this evolution and its contemporary relevance, see Antonio Morales Moya (2001).

Works Cited

Abella, Rafael. 1973. *La vida cotidiana durante la guerra civil.* Barcelona: Planeta.

———. 1984. *La vida cotidiana bajo el régimen de Franco.* Madrid: Temas de Hoy.

Abellán, José Luis. 1973. *Sociología del 98.* Barcelona: Península.

Acuña, Rosario de. 1876. *Ecos del alma.* Madrid: A. Gómez Fuentenebro.

———. 1877. *Amor á la patria. Drama trágico en un acto y en verso.* Madrid: José Rodríguez.

———. 1880. *Tribunales de venganza: Drama trágico-histórico en dos actos y epílogo, original y en verso.* Madrid: José Rodríguez.

———. 1881a. Algo sobre la mujer (Apuntes). In Acuña 1881c, 61–89.

———. 1881b. Los intermediarios (Boceto). In Acuña 1881c, 109–65.

———. 1881c. *Tiempo perdido.* Madrid: Manuel Minuesa de los Ríos.

———. 1882a. El amigo Manso. In Acuña 1882d, 87–92.

———. 1882b. El lujo en los pueblos rurales. In Acuña 1882d, 139–64.

———. 1882c. Influencia de la vida del campo en la familia. Madrid: Montegrifo.

———. 1882d. *La siesta: Colección de artículos.* Madrid: G. Estrada.

———. 1882e. Pipaon (Biografía). In Acuña 1882d, 25–39.

———. 1882f. Preludio. In Acuña 1882d, vii–xiii.

———. 1893. *La voz de la Patria: Cuadro dramático en un acto y en verso.* Madrid: R. Velasco.

———. 1917. El Discurso de doña Rosario de Acuña, leída en el mitín feminista de Unión Republicana de Gracia. *El Noroeste,* year 21, no. 7309, June 6, 1917, 1ff.

———. 1989a. Apuntes de estudio para los tres papeles más importantes del drama. In Acuña 1989c, 233–36.

———. 1989b. Dedicatoria. In Acuña 1989c, 133–37.

———. 1989c. *Rienzi el Tribuno. El Padre Juan. (Teatro).* Edition, introduction, and notes by María del Carmen Simón Palmer. Madrid: Castalia / Instituto de la Mujer.

———. 1992a. La Jarca de la Universidad. In *Rosario de Acuña: Homenaje* 1992, 19–21.

———. 1992b. Los deportes del porvenir. In Bolado 1992b, 95–101.

———. 1992c. Testamento. In Bolado 1992b, 45–51.

———. 1992d. Una peseta. In Bolado 1992b, 81–87.

———. 1992e. Valiosísima adhesión. 1884. In Bolado 1992b, 53–70.

———. 2000a. Carta a un soldado español voluntario en el ejército francés durante la Gran Guerra. In Bolado 2000a, 58–68.

———. 2000b. ¡Yo, en la Academia! In Bolado 2000a, 55–57.

———. 2007a. *Obras reunidas, 1: Artículos (1881–1884).* Edited by José Bolado. Oviedo: KRK.

———. 2007b. *Obras reunidas, 2: Artículos (1885–1923).* Edited by José Bolado. Oviedo: KRK.

Aguilar, Paloma. 2002. *Memory and Amnesia. The Role of the Spanish Civil War in the Transition to Democracy.* Translated by Mark Oakley. 1996. New York / Oxford: Berghahn.

Aguilar, Paloma, and Carsten Humlebæk. 2002. Collective Memory and National Identity in the Spanish Democracy. The Legacies of Francoism and the Civil War. In *History and Memory* 14.1–2:121–64.

Aldaraca, Bridget. 1982. *El ángel del hogar*: The Cult of Domesticity in Nineteenth-Century Spain. In *Theory and Practice of Feminist Literary Criticism.* Edited by Gabriela Mora and Karen S. Van Hooft, 62–87. Ypsilanti, MI: Bilingual.

Alexander, Jeffrey C. 2004. Toward a Theory of Cultural Trauma. In Alexander, et al. 2004, 1–30.

Alexander, Jeffrey C. et al., eds. 2004. *Cultural Trauma and Collective Identity.* Berkeley: University of California Press.

Alonso, Santos. 2003. *La novela española en el fin de siglo, 1975–2001.* Madrid: Mare Nostrum.

Álvarez Junco, José. 2004. *Mater Dolorosa: La idea de España en el siglo XIX.* 2001. Madrid: Taurus.

Álvarez Lázaro, Pedro. 1985. *Masonería y librepensamiento en la España de la Restauración. (Aproximación histórica)*. Madrid: Publicaciones de la Universidad Pontificia Comillas.

———. 1998. *La masonería, escuela de formación del ciudadano. La educación interna de los masones españoles en el último tercio de siglo XIX.* 2nd ed. Series Instituto de Investigación sobre liberalismo, krausismo y masonería, 13. Madrid: Publicaciones de la Universidad Pontificia Comillas.

Alvear, Inmaculada. 1996. Escritoras teatrales españolas del siglo XIX. In *Autoras en la Historia del Teatro Español. (1500–1994).* Vol. 1, *Siglos XVII–XVIII–XIX.* Directed by Juan Antonio Hormigón, 607–17. Madrid: ADE.

Anderson, Andrew. 2005. *El veintisiete en tela de juicio: Examen de la historiografía generacional y replanteamiento de la vanguardia histórica española.* Madrid: Gredos.

Anderson, Benedict. 1991. *Imagined Communities: Reflections on the Origin and Spread of Nationalism.* 1983. Revised edition. London: Verso.

Anderson, Malcolm. 1996. *Frontiers: Territory and State Formation in the Modern World.* Cambridge: Polity.

Andrews, Malcolm. 1999. *Landscape and Western Art.* Oxford: Oxford University Press.

Anes, Gonzalo, and Álvarez de Castrillón. 2000. La economía: España en el cambio de siglo. In *España: Cambio de siglo* 2000, 167–92.

Aranguren, José Luis. 1981. *Moral y sociedad. La moral española en el siglo XIX: Introducción a la moral social española del siglo XIX.* Madrid: Taurus.

Arkinstall, Christine. 2006. Configuring the Nation in Fin-de-Siècle Spain: Rosario de Acuña's *La voz de la Patria. Hispanic Review* 74.3 (Summer 2006): 301–18.

Artola, Miguel. 2001. *La burguesía revolucionaria (1808–1874).* 1990. Madrid: Alianza.

Astell, Mary. 1996. *Reflections upon Marriage.* In *Astell. Political Writings,* 1–80. Edited by Patricia Springborg. Cambridge: Cambridge University Press.

Bachelard, Gaston. 1958. *The Poetics of Space.* Translated by Maria Jolas. Foreword by Etienne Gilson. Boston: Beacon. Original edition, Presses Universitaires de France.

Bahamonde, Ángel, and Jesús A. Martínez. 2001. *Historia de España: Siglo XIX.* Madrid: Cátedra.

Bahamonde, Ángel, and J. Toro Mérida. 1978. *Burguesía, especulación y cuestión social en el Madrid del siglo XIX.* Madrid: Siglo XXI.

Bakhtin, Mikhail. 1984. *Rabelais and His World.* Translated by Hélène Iswolsky. 1965. Bloomington: Indiana University Press.

Baudrillard, Jean. 1981. *For a Critique of the Political Economy of the Sign.* Translated and introduction by Charles Levin. St. Louis, MO: Telos Press.

Bauman, Zygmunt. 1987. *Legislators and Interpreters: On Modernity, Post-Modernity and Intellectuals.* Oxford: Polity.

Bell, Shannon. 1994. *Reading, Writing, and Rewriting the Prostitute Body.* Bloomington: Indiana University Press.

Bellver, Catherine G. 2001. Rosa Chacel: Masking the Authoritative Voice. In *Absence and Presence: Spanish Women Poets of the Twenties and Thirties,* 120–42. Lewisburg: Bucknell University Press.

Bengoa, María. 2002. *La poeta Ángela Figuera (1902–1984).* Bilbao: BBK.

Benstock, Shari. 1989. Expatriate Modernism. In *Women's Writing in Exile.* Edited by Mary Lynn Broe and Angela Ingram, 20–40. Chapel Hill: University of North Carolina Press.

Bernal Muñoz, José Luis. 1996. *¿Invento o realidad? La generación española de 1898.* Prologue by Pío Caro Baroja. Valencia: Pre-Textos.

Bhabha, Homi K. 1990a. DissemiNation: Time, Narrative, and the Margins of the Modern Nation. In Bhabha 1990b, 291–322.

———. ed. 1990b. *Nation and Narration.* London: Routledge.

———. 1994. Frontlines/Borderposts. In *Displacements. Cultural Identities in Question.* Edited by Angelika Bammer, 269–72. Bloomington: Indiana University Press.

Bieder, Maryellen. 1995. Gender and Language: The Womanly Woman and Manly Writing. In Charnon-Deutsch and Labanyi 1995, 98–119.

———. 1998. Emilia Pardo Bazán y la emergencia del discurso feminista. In *Breve historia feminista de la literatura española (en lengua castellana).* Vol. 5, *La literatura escrita por mujer: Desde el siglo XIX hasta la actualidad.* Edited by Iris M. Zavala, 75–110. Barcelona: Anthropos.

Bolado, José. 1985. Prólogo. In *Rosario de Acuña. El Padre Juan,* XI–XXXIX. Gijón: Ateneo-Casino Obrero de Gijón.

———. 1992a. Biografía de Rosario de Acuña. In Bolado 1992b, 7–42.

———. ed. 1992b. *Rosario de Acuña. Artículos y cuentos.* Gijón: Ateneo Obrero de Gijón.

———. 2000a. *Gijón: El cuerpo de los vientos. Cuatro literatos gijoneses.* Prologue by José Esteban. Gijón: Gran Enciclopedia Asturiana / Ayuntamiento de Gijón.

———. 2000b. Rosario de Acuña y Villanueva. In Bolado 2000a, 31–80.

———. 2007. Introducción. Rosario de Acuña. Escritora y vida aventurada. In Acuña 2007a, 19–463.

Bordons, Teresa, and Susan Kirkpatrick. 1992. Chacel's *Teresa* and Ortega's Canon. In *Anales de la Literatura Española Contemporánea* 17:283–99.

Bosch, Rafael. 1962. La poesía de Ángela Figuera y el tema de la maternidad. *Ínsula* 186:5–6.

Boyd, Carolyn P. 1997. *Historia Patria. Politics, History, and National Identity in Spain, 1875–1975.* Princeton, NJ: Princeton University Press.

Brennan, Teresa, and Carole Pateman. 1998. "Mere Auxiliaries to the Commonwealth": Women and the Origins of Liberalism. In Phillips 1998, 93–115.

Brennan, Timothy. 1990. The National Longing For Form. In Bhabha 1990b, 44–70.

Bretz, Mary Lee. 2001. *Encounters Across Borders. The Changing Visions of Spanish Modernism, 1890–1930.* Lewisburg: Bucknell University Press.

Brihuega, Jaime. 1981. *Las vanguardias artísticas en España: 1909–1936.* Madrid: Istmo.

Brison, Susan. 1999. Trauma Narratives and the Remaking of the Self. In *Acts of Memory: Cultural Recall in the Present.* Edited by Mieke Bal, Jonathan Crewe, and Leo Spitzer, 39–54. Hanover: University Press of New England.

Butt, John. 1980. The Generation of 98. A Critical Fallacy? *Forum for Modern Language Studies* 16:136–55.

———. 1993. Modernismo and *Modernism.* In Cardwell and McGuirk 1993, 39–58.

Calderón, Héctor, and José David Saldívar. 1991. Editors' Introduction. Criticism in the Borderlands. In *Criticism in the Borderlands. Studies in Chicano Literature, Culture, and Ideology.* Edited by Calderón and Saldívar, 1–7. Foreword by Roland Hinojosa. Durham, NC: Duke University Press.

Calinescu, Matei. 1987. Reprint. *Five Faces of Modernity.* 1977. Durham, NC: Duke University Press.

Cameron, Duncan. 1972. The Museum: A Temple or the Forum. *Journal of World History* 14.1:189–202.

Capel Martínez, Rosa María. 1986. *El trabajo y la educación de la mujer en España (1900–1930).* Madrid: Ministerio de Cultura / Instituto de la Mujer.

Cardús i Ros, Salvador. 2000. Politics and the Invention of Memory. For a Sociology of the Transition to Democracy in Spain. In Resina 2000a, 17–28.

Cardwell, Richard A., and Bernard McGuirk, eds. 1993. *¿Qué es el modernismo? Nueva encuesta, nuevas lecturas.* Boulder, CO: Society of Spanish and Spanish American Studies.

Carr, Raymond. 1982. *Spain 1808–1975.* 2nd ed. 1966. Oxford: Clarendon.

Carulla, Jordi, and Arnau Carulla. 1997. *La guerra civil en 2000 carteles.* 2 vols. Barcelona: Postermil.

Caruth, Cathy. 1995a. Introduction. In Caruth 1995b, 3–12.

———. ed. 1995b. *Trauma: Explorations in Memory.* Baltimore: Johns Hopkins University Press.

———. 1996. *Unclaimed Experience: Trauma, Narrative, and History.* Baltimore: Johns Hopkins University Press.

Castañón, Luciano. 1986. Aportación a la biografía de Rosario de Acuña. *Boletín del Instituto de Estudios Asturianos* 117, year 40 (January–April):151–71.

Cayuela Fernández, José G. 1999. Proyectos de sociedad y nación: la crisis del concepto de España en el 98. In Sánchez Sánchez and Villena Espinosa 1999, 45–71.

Celaya, Gabriel. 1986. *Itinerario poético.* Madrid: Cátedra.

Chacel, Rosa. 1980. *La confesión.* 1971. Barcelona: Edhasa.

———. 1981. *Barrio de Maravillas.* 1976. Barcelona: Seix Barral.

———. 1982a. *Alcancía (Ida).* Barcelona: Seix Barral.

———. 1982b. *Alcancía (Vuelta).* Barcelona: Seix Barral.

———. 1984. *Acrópolis.* Barcelona: Seix Barral.

———. 1985. *Memorias de Leticia Valle.* 1945. Barcelona: Lumen.

———. 1988. *Ciencias naturales.* Barcelona: Seix Barral.

———. 1989a. *Estación: Ida y vuelta.* Edited by Shirley Mangini. 1930. Madrid: Cátedra.

———. 1989b. *Obra completa.* 4 vols. Vol. 1, *La sinrazón.* Valladolid: Centro de Creación y Estudios Jorge Guillén / Excma. Diputación Provincial de Valladolid.

———. 1993a. Aclaración, no polémica. In Chacel 1993n, 205–18.

———. 1993b. Autobiografía intelectual. In Chacel 1993n, 33–71.

———. 1993c. Comentario tardío sobre Simone de Beauvoir. In Chacel 1993o, 501–29.

———. 1993d. Cómo y por qué de la novela. In Chacel 1993n, 137–54.

———. 1993e. Cultura y pueblo. In Chacel 1993o, 369–76.

———. 1993f. En el Ateneo. In Chacel 1993n, 299–307.

———. 1993g. En el Ateneo (II). In Chacel 1993n, 309–15.

———. 1993h. Génesis de mis novelas. In Chacel 1993n, 101–26.

———. 1993i. Hablando de mí. In Chacel 1993n, 87–93.

———. 1993j. Invitación a la Escuela. In Chacel 1993n, 319–31.

———. 1993k. La mujer en galeras. In Chacel 1993o, 477–500.

———. 1993l. Lo nacional en el arte. In Chacel 1993o, 285–95.

———. 1993m. Madrid en el recuerdo. In Chacel 1993o, 613–18.

———. 1993n. *Obra completa.* 4 vols. Vol. 3, *Artículos 1.* Edited, prologue, and notes by Ana Rodríguez Fischer. Valladolid: Excma. Diputación Provincial de Valladolid / Centro de Estudios Literarios / Fundación Jorge Guillén.

———. 1993o. *Obra completa.* 4 vols. Vol. 4, *Artículos 2.* Edited, prologue, and notes by Ana Rodríguez Fischer. Valladolid: Excma. Diputación Provincial de Valladolid / Centro de Estudios Literarios / Fundación Jorge Guillén.

———. 1993p. Ortega. In Chacel 1993n, 419–32.

———. 1993q. Ortega a otra distancia. In Chacel 1993n, 395–402.

———. 1993r. Pensábamos entonces. In Chacel 1993n, 293–98.

———. 1993s. Réplica a una entrevista. In Chacel 1993n, 219–24.

———. 1993t. Respuesta a la encuesta sobre la "vanguardia." In Chacel 1993n, 229.

———. 1993u. Respuesta a Ortega: La novela no escrita. In Chacel 1993n, 369–93.

———. 1993v. Revisión de un largo camino. In Chacel 1993n, 403–17.

———. 1993w. Sendas perdidas de la generación del 27. In Chacel 1993n, 231–66.

———. 1993x. Sendas recobradas de la generación del 27. In Chacel 1993n, 267–73.

———. 1993y. Un libro, por suerte, nuevo. In Chacel 1993o, 259–69.

———. 1993z. Volviendo al punto de partida. In Chacel 1993n, 275–91.

———. 1994. Presencia II. In Martínez Latre 1994, 13–16.

Chacel, Rosa, and Ana María Moix. 2003. *De mar a mar: Epistolario.* Edited, prologue, and notes by Ana Rodríguez Fischer. Barcelona: Península.

Charnon-Deutsch, Lou. 1994. *Narratives of Desire: Nineteenth-Century Spanish Fiction by Women.* University Park: Pennsylvania State University Press.

Chefdor, Monique, Ricardo Quinones, and Albert Wachtel, eds. 1986. *Modernism: Challenges and Perspectives.* Urbana: University of Illinois Press.

Cirujano Marín, Paloma, Teresa Elorriaga Planes, and Juan Sisinio Pérez Garzón. 1985. *Historiografía y nacionalismo español (1834–1868).* Madrid: Centro de Estudios Históricos / Consejo Superior de Investigaciones Científicas.

Cruz, Jacqueline. 2004. Mujer y política: la paridad inexistente. In Cruz and Zecchi 2004, 73–97.

Cruz, Jacqueline, and Barbara Zecchi, eds. 2004. *La mujer en la España actual: ¿Evolución o involución?* Barcelona: Icaria.

Darío, Rubén. 1985. *Azul: Prosas profanas.* Edited and notes by Andrew P. Debicki and Michael J. Doudoroff. Madrid: Alhambra.

Davies, Catherine. 1998. "Feminine Prose": Rosa Chacel (1898–1994). In *Spanish Women's Writing 1849–1996,* 152–70. London: Athlone.

Derrida, Jacques. 1994. *Specters of Marx: The State of the Debt, the Work of Mourning, and the New International.* New York: Routledge.

Díaz Fernández, José. 1930. *El nuevo romanticismo. Polémica de arte, política y literatura.* Madrid: Zeus.

Dicenta, Joaquín, and Federico Oliver. 1998. *Juan José. Los semidioses.* Madrid: Biblioteca Nueva.

Dietz, Mary G. 1998. Context Is All: Feminism and Theories of Citizenship. In Phillips 1998, 378–400.

Dobón, María Dolores. 1996. *Sociólogos* contra *estetas*: Prehistoria del conflicto entre modernismo y 98. *Hispanic Review* 64.1:57–72.

Donnan, Hastings, and Thomas M. Wilson. 1994. An Anthropology of Frontiers. In *Border Approaches: Anthropological Perspectives on Frontiers*. Edited by Donnan and Wilson, 1–14. Lanham, MD: University Press of America.

———. 1999. *Borders: Frontiers of Identity, Nation and State*. Oxford: Berg.

El Libro de Asturias. 1975. Edited by Graciano García García. 3rd ed. Oviedo: Prensa del Norte.

Elliott, J. H. 1970. *Imperial Spain, 1469–1716*. 1963. Harmondsworth: Penguin.

Elshtain, Jean Bethke. 1992. Sovereignty, Identity, Sacrifice. In *Gendered States. Feminist (Re)Visions of International Relations Theory*. Edited by V. Spike Peterson, 141–54. Boulder, CO: Lynne Rienner.

Enders, Victoria Lorée, and Pamela Beth Radcliff, eds. 1999. *Constructing Spanish Womanhood: Female Identity in Modern Spain*. Albany: State University of New York Press.

Erikson, Kai. 1995. Notes on Trauma and Community. In Caruth 1995b, 183–99.

España: Cambio de siglo. 2000. Madrid: Real Academia de la Historia.

Evans, Jessica. 1999. Introduction: Nation and Representation. In *Representing the Nation: A Reader. Histories, Heritage and Museums*. Edited by David Boswell and Jessica Evans, 1–8. London: Routledge.

Evans, Jo. 1996. *Moving Reflections: Gender, Faith and Aesthetics in the Work of Ángela Figuera Aymerich*. London: Tamesis.

Felipe, León. 1981. *El Hacha. (Elegía española)*. In *Nueva Antología Rota*, 59–76. Madrid: Visor.

———. 1990. *Ganarás la luz*. Edited by José Paulino. 2nd ed. Madrid: Cátedra.

Felman, Shoshana. 2002. *The Juridical Unconscious: Trials and Traumas in the Twentieth Century*. Cambridge, MA: Harvard University Press.

Felman, Shoshana, and Dori Laub. 1992. *Testimony: Crises of Witnessing in Literature, Psychoanalysis, and History*. New York: Routledge.

Felski, Rita. 1995. *The Gender of Modernity*. Cambridge, MA: Harvard University Press.

Fernández Riera, Macrino. 2005. *Rosario de Acuña en Asturias*. Gijón: Trea.

Ferrer Benimeli, José Antonio. 2001. *La masonería*. Madrid: Alianza.

Figuera Aymerich, Ángela. 1986. *Obras completas*. Prologue by Julio Figueras. Introduction and bibliography by Roberta Quance. Madrid: Hiperión.

Foncea Hierro, Isabel. 1999. Barrio de Maravillas, *de Rosa Chacel: Claves y símbolos*. 2 vols. Vol. 1. Málaga: Centro Cultural Generación del 27.

Foster, Hal. 1995. Armour Fou. In Melville and Readings 1995, 215–48.

Freeden, Michael. 2005. *Liberal Languages: Ideological Imaginations and Twentieth-Century Progressive Thought*. Princeton, NJ: Princeton University Press.

Freixas, Laura. 2000. *Literatura y mujeres: Escritoras, público y crítica en la España actual*. Barcelona: Destino.

Fusi Aizpúrua, Juan Pablo. 2001a. El régimen autoritario (1960–1975). In Jover Zamora, Gómez-Ferrer Morant, and Fusi Aizpúrua 2001, 767–99.

———. 2001b. La Segunda República (1931–1936). In Jover Zamora, Gómez-Ferrer Morant, and Fusi Aizpúrua 2001, 671–92.

———. 2001c. La transición democrática (1975–1982). In Jover Zamora, Gómez-Ferrer Morant, and Fusi Aizpúrua 2001, 801–17.

———. 2004. *El malestar de la modernidad: Cuatro estudios sobre historia y cultura.* Madrid: Biblioteca Nueva.

Gabriele, John P., ed. 1999. *Nuevas perspectives sobre el 98.* Frankfurt am Main: Vervuert / Madrid: Iberoamericana.

Gaddis, John Lewis. 2002. *The Landscape of History: How Historians Map the Past.* Oxford: Oxford University Press.

Gajic, Tatjana. 2002. *In Search of a Lost Nation: Intellectual Genealogies and Historical Revisions of the Reform of the Spanish Nation in José Ortega y Gasset, María Zambrano, and Rosa Chacel.* PhD diss., Duke University, 2001. Ann Arbor: University of Michigan. 3030231.

Gallego Méndez, María Teresa. 1983. *Mujer, falange y franquismo.* Madrid: Taurus.

García Posada, Miguel. 1999. *Acelerado sueño: Memoria de los poetas del 27.* Madrid: Espasa-Calpe.

Gates, Henry Louis. 1986a. Editor's Introduction: Writing "Race" and the Difference It Makes. In Gates 1986b, 1–20.

———. ed. 1986b. *"Race," Writing, and Difference.* Chicago: University of Chicago Press.

Geist, Anthony L. 1993. El 27 y la vanguardia: una aproximación ideológica. *Cuadernos Hispanoamericanos* 514–515:53–64.

Geist, Anthony L., and José B. Monleón. 1999a. Introduction. Modernism and Its Margins: Rescripting Hispanic Modernism. In Geist and Monleón 1999b, xvii–xxxv.

———. eds. 1999b. *Modernism and Its Margins: Reinscribing Cultural Modernity from Spain and Latin America.* New York: Garland.

Gellner, Ernest. 1983. *Nations and Nationalism.* Oxford: Basil Blackwell.

Gies, David T., ed. 2004. *The Cambridge History of Spanish Literature.* Cambridge: Cambridge University Press.

Giesen, Bernhard. 2004. The Trauma of Perpetrators: The Holocaust as the Traumatic Reference of German National Identity. In Alexander et al. 2004, 112–54.

Giner de los Ríos, Francisco. 1876. Consideraciones sobre el desarrollo de la literatura moderna. In *Estudios de literatura y arte,* 165–245. Madrid: Victoriano Suárez.

Glenn, Kathleen M. 1991. Narration and Eroticism in Chacel's *Memorias de Leticia Valle* and Nabokov's *Lolita. Monographic Review/Revista Monográfica* 7:84–93.

Gómez Molleda, María Dolores. 1966. *Los reformadores de la España contemporánea.* Prologue by Vicente Palacio Atard. Madrid: C.S.I.C., Escuela de Historia Moderna.

Gómez Pérez, Rafael. 1986. *El franquismo y la iglesia.* Madrid: Rialp.

Gould Levine, Linda, Ellen Engelson Marson, and Gloria Feiman Waldman, eds. 1993. *Spanish Women Writers: A Bio-Bibliographical Source Book.* Westport, CT: Greenwood.

Grado, Mercedes de. 2004. Encrucijada del feminismo español: disyuntiva entre igualdad y diferencia. In Cruz and Zecchi 2004, 25–58.

Granja, José Luis de la, Justo Beramendi, and Pere Anguera. 2001. *La España de los nacionalismos y las autonomías.* Madrid: Síntesis.

Grosz, Elizabeth. 1992. Bodies-Cities. In *Sexuality and Space.* Edited by Beatriz Colomina, 241–53. Princeton, NJ: Princeton Architectural Space.

———. 1995. *Space, Time, and Perversion: Essays on the Politics of Bodies.* New York: Routledge.

Guereña, Jean-Louis. 1999. La sociabilidad en la España contemporánea. In Sánchez Sánchez and Villena Espinosa 1999, 15–43.

Guibernau, Montserrat. 1999. *Nations without States: Political Communities in a Global Age.* Cambridge: Polity.

Gullón, Germán. 1993. Lo moderno en el modernismo. In Cardwell and McGuirk 1993, 87–101.

Halbwachs, Maurice. 1992. *On Collective Memory.* Edited, translated, and introduction by Lewis A. Coser. 1952. Chicago: University of Chicago Press.

Hall, Stuart. 1996. Introduction: Who Needs Identity? In *Questions of Cultural Identity.* Edited by Hall and Paul Du Gay, 1–17. London: Sage.

Harley, J. B. 1988. Maps, Knowledge, Power. In *The Iconography of Landscape: Essays on the Symbolic Representation, Design and Use of Past Environments.* Edited by Denis Cosgrove and Stephen Daniels, 277–312. Cambridge: Cambridge University Press.

Henseler, Christine. 2003. *Contemporary Spanish Women's Narrative and the Publishing Industry.* Urbana: University of Illinois Press.

Heron, Liz, ed. 1983. *Streets of Desire: Women's Fictions of the Twentieth-Century City.* London: Virago.

Herzberger, David K. 1995. *Narrating the Past. Fiction and Historiography in Postwar Spain.* Durham, NC: Duke University Press.

History and Memory. 2002. Special Issue. *Spanish Memories: Images of a Contested Past.* Edited by Raanan Rein. Issue 14, nos. 1–2.

Hobsbawm, Eric. 1997. *Nations and Nationalisms since 1780: Programme, Myth, Reality.* 1990. Cambridge: Cambridge University Press.

Holguín, Sandie. 2002. *Creating Spaniards: Culture and National Identity in Republican Spain.* Madison: University of Wisconsin Press.

Holly, Michael Ann. 1995. Past Looking. In Melville and Readings 1995, 67–89.

Hutton, Patrick H. 1993. *History as an Art of Memory.* Hanover, NH: University Press of New England.

Huyssen, Andreas. 1986. *After the Great Divide. Modernism, Mass Culture, Postmodernism.* Bloomington: Indiana University Press.

Iglesias, Carmen. 2000. Fines de siglo y sentimientos de crisis. Imágenes y realidad. In *España: Cambio de siglo* 2000, 193–224.

Inman Fox, E. 1998. *La invención de España. Nacionalismo liberal e identidad nacional.* 2nd ed. Madrid: Cátedra.

Irigaray, Luce. 1993. The Bodily Encounter with the Mother. In *The Irigaray Reader.* Translated by David Macey. Edited and introduction by Margaret Whitford, 34–46. Oxford: Blackwell.

Jaggar, Alison M. 1983. *Feminist Politics and Human Nature.* Totawa, NJ: Rowman and Littlefield.

Janés, Clara. 1994. Pintura y escultura en la obra de Rosa Chacel. In Martínez Latre 1994, 89–104.

Jato, Mónica. 2004. *El lenguaje bíblico en la poesía de los exilios españoles de 1939.* Kassel: Reichenberger.

Jiménez, Alberto. 1948. *Ocaso y restauración. Ensayo sobre la Universidad española moderna.* Mexico: El Colegio de México.

Jiménez García, Antonio. 1985. *El Krausismo y la Institución Libre de Enseñanza.* Prologue by José Luis Abellán. Madrid: Cincel.

Johnson, Roberta. 1993. *Crossfire: Philosophy and the Novel in Spain, 1900–1934.* Lexington: University of Kentucky Press.

———. 2003. *Gender and Nation in the Spanish Modernist Novel.* Nashville, TN: Vanderbilt University Press.

Jones, Wendy S. 2005. *Consensual Fictions: Women, Liberalism, and the English Novel.* Toronto: University of Toronto Press.

Jordan, Barry. 1990. *Writing and Politics in Franco's Spain.* London: Routledge.

Jover, José María, and Guadalupe Gómez-Ferrer. 2001a. Cultura y civilización: la plenitud de la Edad de Plata. In Jover Zamora, Gómez-Ferrer Morant, and Fusi Aizpúrua 2001, 575–631.

———. 2001b. El desarrollo económico. In Jover Zamora, Gómez-Ferrer Morant, and Fusi Aizpúrua 2001, 285–307.

———. 2001c. La Guerra de la Independencia. In Jover Zamora, Gómez-Ferrer Morant, and Fusi Aizpúrua 2001, 11–43.

———. 2001d. La revolución liberal (1834–1874). In Jover Zamora, Gómez-Ferrer Morant, and Fusi Aizpúrua 2001, 151–202.

———. 2001e. Régimen político. In Jover Zamora, Gómez-Ferrer Morant, and Fusi Aizpúrua 2001, 309–58.

———. 2001f. Sociedad, civilización y cultura. In Jover Zamora, Gómez-Ferrer Morant, and Fusi Aizpúrua 2001, 359–427.

Jover Zamora, José María, Guadalupe Gómez-Ferrer Morant, and Juan Pablo Fusi Aizpúrua. 2001. *España: Sociedad, política y civilización (Siglos XIX–XX).* Madrid: Areté.

Juliá, Santos. 2004. *Historia de las dos Españas.* Madrid: Taurus.

Kenwood, Alun, ed. 1993. *The Spanish Civil War: A Cultural and Historical Reader.* Providence: Berg.

Kirkpatrick. Susan. 1990. La "hermandad lírica" de la década de 1840. In *Escritoras románticas españolas.* Edited by Marina Mayoral, 25–41. Madrid: Fundación Banco Exterior.

———. 1991. *Las románticas: escritoras y subjetividad en España, 1835–1850.* Translated by Amaia Bárcena. Madrid: Cátedra.

———. 1992. Introduction. In Rosa Chacel. *The Maravillas District.* Translated by D. A. Démers, v–xxiii. Lincoln: University of Nebraska Press.

———. 1999. Gender and Modernist Discourse: Emilia Pardo Bazán's *Dulce Dueño.* In Geist and Monleón 1999b, 117–39.

———. 2003. *Mujer, modernismo y vanguardia en España (1898–1931).* Translated by Jacqueline Cruz. Madrid: Cátedra.

Kofman, Eleonore, and Elizabeth Lebas. 1996. Introduction. In Lefebvre 1996, 3–60.

Kristeva, Julia. 1984. *Revolution in Poetic Language.* Translated by Margaret Waller. Introduction by Leon S. Roudiez. 1974. New York: Columbia University Press.

———. 1986. Stabat Mater. In *The Kristeva Reader.* Edited by Toril Moi, 160–86. Oxford: Basil Blackwell.

Kritzman, Lawrence D. 1996. In Remembrance of Things French. In Nora 1996c, ix–xiv.

Labanyi, Jo. 1989. *Myth and History in the Contemporary Spanish Novel.* Cambridge: Cambridge University Press.

———. 2000. History and Hauntology; or, What Does One Do with the Ghosts of the Past? Reflections on Spanish Film and Fiction of the Post-Franco Period. In Resina 2000a, 65–82.

———. 2002. Introduction. In *Constructing Identity in Contemporary Spain. Theoretical Debates and Cultural Practice.* Edited by Labanyi, 1–14. Oxford: Oxford University Press.

Lafuente, Modesto. 1888. *Historia general de España: Desde los tiempos primitivos hasta la muerte de Fernando VII.* Continued by Juan Valera et al. Vol. 8. Barcelona: Montaner y Simon.

———. 1889. *Historia general de España.* Vol. 18. Barcelona: Montaner y Simon.

La Porte, Pablo. 2003. Liberalismo y política colonial en la Restauración: La zona de influencia de España en Marruecos (1898–1931). In Suárez Cortina 2003a, 471–90.

Lauretis, Teresa de. 1989. *Technologies of Gender. Essays on Theory, Film, and Fiction.* Basingstoke: Macmillan. Original edition, Indiana University Press, 1987.

Lázaro, Reyes. 1994. *Indecisiones y seducciones familiares: Rosa Chacel, Ortega y la generación del noventayocho.* PhD diss., University of Massachussets Amherst. Ann Arbor: University of Michigan.

Lechner, Johannes. 1968. *El compromiso en la poesía española del siglo XX. Parte Primera: De la Generación de 1898 a 1939.* Universitaire Pers Leiden.

———. 1975. *El compromiso en la poesía española del siglo XX. Parte Segunda: De 1939–1974.* Universitaire Pers Leiden.

Lefebvre, Henri. 1993. Reprint. *The Production of Space.* Translated by Donald Nicholson-Smith. 1974. Oxford: Blackwell. Original edition, Paris: Anthropos, 1974.

———. 1996. *Writings on Cities.* Translated and edited by Eleonore Kofman and Elizabeth Lebas. Oxford: Blackwell.

Lerner, Gerda. 1997. *Why History Matters: Life and Thought.* New York: Oxford University Press.

Lewis, Bernard. 1975. *History: Remembered, Recovered, Invented.* Princeton, NJ: Princeton University Press.

Llera, Luis de. 1991. *Ortega y la edad de plata de la literatura española (1914–1936).* Roma: Bulzoni.

Llobera, Josep R. 2004. *Foundations of National Identity: From Catalonia to Europe.* New York: Berghahn.

López de Abiada, José Manuel, Hans-Jörg Neuschäfer, and Augusta López Bernasocchi, eds. 2001. *Entre el ocio y el negocio: Industria editorial y literatura en la España de los 90.* Madrid: Verbum.

López Sáenz, María Carmen. 1994. La influencia de la estética orteguiana en Rosa Chacel. In Martínez Latre 1994, 107–20.

Machado, Antonio. 1977. *Poesías completas.* Prologue by Manuel Alvar. 3rd ed. Madrid: Espasa-Calpe.

Mainer, José-Carlos. 1983. *La Edad de Plata (1902–1939). Ensayo de interpretación de un proceso cultural.* 2nd ed. Madrid: Cátedra.

———. 2001. Estado de la cultura y cultura de Estado en la España de hoy (o el Leviatán benévolo). In López de Abiada, Neuschäfer, and López Bernasocchi 2001, 157–78.

———. 2004. Spanish Literature between the Franco and Post-Franco Eras. In Gies 2004, 687–93.

Mangini, Shirley. 1987. Women and Spanish Modernism: The Case of Rosa Chacel. *Anales de la Literatura Española Contemporánea* 12.1–2:17–28.

———. 1993. Rosa Chacel. In Gould Levine, Engelson Marson, and Feiman Waldman 1993, 131–40.

———. 1998. Woman, Eros and Culture: The Essays of Rosa Chacel. In *Spanish Women Writers and the Essay.* Edited by Kathleen M. Glenn and Mercedes Mazquiarán de Rodríguez, 127–43. Columbia: University of Missouri Press.

———. 2001. *Las modernas de Madrid: Las grandes intelectuales españolas de la vanguardia.* Barcelona: Península.

Marías, Julián. 1992. *Understanding Spain.* Translated by Frances M. López-Morillas. 1990. Ann Arbor: University of Michigan Press.

Mar-Molinero, Clare, and Ángel Smith, eds. 1996. *Nationalism and the Nation in the Iberian Peninsula: Competing and Conflicting Identities.* Oxford: Berg.

Martín, Miguel. 1973. *El colonialismo español en Marruecos (1860–1956).* Paris: Ruedo ibérico.

Martín Alcoff, Linda. 2003. Introduction. In Martín Alcoff and Mendieta 2003, 1–8.

Martín Alcoff, Linda, and Eduardo Mendieta, eds. 2003. *Identities. Race, Class, Gender, and Nationality.* Edited by Martín Alcoff and Eduardo Mendieta. Oxford: Blackwell.

Martín Nogales, José Luis. 2001. Literatura y mercado en la España de los 90. In López de Abiada, Neuschäfer, and López Bernasocchi 2001, 179–94.

Martínez, María Elena. 2004. The Black Blood of New Spain: *Limpieza de Sangre*, Racial Violence, and Gendered Power in Early Colonial Mexico. *The William and Mary Quarterly* 61.3 (July):1–55.

Martínez Latre, María Pilar, ed. 1994. *Actas del Congreso en homenaje a Rosa Chacel.* Logroño: Universidad de la Rioja.

Maydeu, Javier Aparicio. 2002. De los demasiados libros y sus consecuencias. *Quimera* 223:27–29.

Melville, Stephen, and Bill Readings, eds. 1995. *Vision and Textuality.* Durham, NC: Duke University Press.

Memoria viva del 27. 1993. *Generación del 27. Cuadernos Hispanoamericanos* 514–515:11–22.

Miller, Nancy K., and Jason Tougaw, eds. 2002. Introduction: Extremities. In *Extremities. Trauma, Testimony, and Community,* 1–21. Urbana: University of Illinois Press.

Miró, Emilio. 1987. Algunas poetas españolas entre 1926 y 1960. In *Literatura y vida cotidiana. Actas de las Cuartas Jornadas de Investigación Interdisciplinaria.* Edited by María Ángeles Durán and José Antonio Rey, 307–21. Universidad Autónoma de Madrid / Universidad de Zaragoza.

Mitchell, W.J.T. 1994. Introduction. In *Landscape and Power.* Edited by Mitchell, 1–4. Chicago: University of Chicago Press.

Moix, Ana María. 1994. El Cervantes se quedó sin Rosa. *Cambio 16* 1,185 (August 8): 64–65.

Monleón, José B. 1995a. *Del franquismo a la posmodernidad: cultura española 1975–1990.* Madrid: Akal.

———. 1995b. El largo camino de la transición. In Monleón 1995a, 5–17.

Moore, Henrietta L. 1994. *A Passion for Difference: Essays in Anthropology and Gender.* Bloomington: Indiana University Press.

Moral Ruiz, Carmen del. 1998. *El 98.* Madrid: Acento.

Morales Moya, Antonio. 2001. En torno al nacionalismo español actual. In *Nacionalismos e imagen de España.* Edited by Morales Moya, 187–96. Madrid: Sociedad Estatal España Nuevo Milenio.

Newberry, Wilma. 1988. Rosa Chacel's *Barrio de Maravillas*: The Role of the Arts and the Problem of Spain. *Hispanic Journal* 9.2:37–44.

Nora, Pierre. 1996a. General Introduction: Between Memory and History. In Nora 1996c, 1–20.

———. 1996b. Generation. In Nora 1996c, 499–531.

———. ed. 1996c. *Realms of Memory. The Construction of the French Past.* Vol. 1, *Conflicts and Divisions.* Edited and foreword by Lawrence D. Kritzman. Translated by Arthur Goldhammer. 1992. New York: Columbia University Press.

———. 1998. The Era of Commemoration. In *Realms of Memory. The Construction of the French Past.* Vol. 3, *Symbols.* Edited by Nora. Translated by Arthur Goldhammer, 609–37. 1992. New York: Columbia University Press.

Obligado, Clara. 2003. Estética de la exclusión. In *En sus propias palabras: escritoras españolas ante el mercado literario.* Edited by Christine Henseler, 75–96. Madrid: Torremozas.

Okin, Susan Moller. 1998. Gender, the Public, and the Private. In Phillips 1998, 116–41.

Ortega y Gasset, José. 1981a. Diálogo sobre el arte nuevo. In Ortega y Gasset 1981c, 131–37.

———. 1981b. *España invertebrada: Bosquejo de algunos pensamientos históricos.* 1922. Madrid: Revista de Occidente in Alianza.

———. 1981c. *La deshumanización del arte y otros ensayos de estética.* 1925. Madrid: Revista de Occidente.

———. 1981d. Prólogo a la segunda edición. In Ortega y Gasset 1981b, 11–17.

———. 1981e. Sobre el punto de vista en las artes. In Ortega y Gasset 1981c, 139–57.

Ortiz Albear, Natividad. 2005. *Las mujeres en la masonería.* Málaga: Universidad de Málaga.

Otero, Blas de. 1992. *Expresión y reunión: A modo de antología.* Introduction and notes by Sabina de la Cruz. 1981. Madrid: Alianza.

Palacio, Daniel. 1992. Rosario de Acuña: pionera del "Tourismo." In *Rosario de Acuña: Homenaje* 1992, 11–12.

Papastergiadis, Nikos. 1997. Tracing Hybridity in Theory. In *Debating Cultural Hybridity. Multi-Cultural Identities and the Politics of Anti-Racism.* Edited by Pnina Werbner and Tariq Modood, 257–81. London: Zed.

Pardo Bazán, Emilia. 2004. *Memorias de un solterón.* Edited by María Ángeles Ayala. Madrid: Cátedra.

Parkinson Zamora, Lois. 1993. *Writing the Apocalypse: Historical Vision in Contemporary U.S. and Latin American Fiction.* 1989. Cambridge: Cambridge University Press.

Pateman, Carole. 1988. *The Sexual Contract.* Stanford, CA: Stanford University Press.

Payeras, María. 2002. *El linaje de Eva: Tres escritoras españolas de postguerra. Ángela Figuera, Celia Viñas y Gloria Fuertes.* Madrid: SIAL.

Pérez, Janet. 1996. *Modern and Contemporary Spanish Women Poets.* New York: Twayne.

Pérez, Joseph. 2001. *Los comuneros.* Madrid: La Esfera de los Libros.

Pérez Díaz, Víctor M. 1993. *The Return of Civil Society: The Emergence of Democratic Spain.* Cambridge, MA: Harvard University Press.

Pérez Galdós, Benito. 1973. *Zaragoza. Episodios nacionales.* Vol. 1. Barcelona: Círculo de Lectores.

———. 1984. *Doña Perfecta.* Edited by Rodolfo Cardona. Madrid: Cátedra.

———. 1998. *Electra.* Introduction by Elena Catena. Madrid: Biblioteca Nueva.

———. 2003. *La familia de León Roch.* Edited by Íñigo Sánchez Llama. Madrid: Cátedra.

Pérez-Manso, Elvira María. 1991. Rosario de Acuña y Villanueva. In *Escritoras asturianas del siglo XX: Entre el compromiso y la tradición.* Prologue by Manuel F. Avello, 48–134. Principado de Asturias.

Perry, Mary Elizabeth. 1999. The Politics of Race, Ethnicity, and Gender in the Making of the Spanish State. In *Culture and the State in Spain, 1550–1850.* Edited by Tom Lewis and Francisco J. Sánchez, 34–54. New York: Garland.

Perry, Nicholas, and Loreto Echeverría. 1988. *Under the Heel of Mary*. London: Routledge.

Phillips, Anne, ed. 1998. *Feminism and Politics*. Oxford: Oxford University Press.

Pijoán, José. 1927. *Mi Don Francisco Giner*. San José de Costa Rica: Repertorio Americano.

Pollock, Griselda. 1988. *Vision and Difference: Femininity, Feminism and the Histories of Art*. London: Routledge.

———. 1995. Beholding Art History: Vision, Place and Power. In Melville and Readings 1995, 38–66.

———. 1999. *Differencing the Canon: Feminist Desire and the Writing of Art's Histories*. London: Routledge.

Poole, Ross. 2003. National Identity and Citizenship. In Martín Alcoff and Mendieta 2003, 271–80.

Porlan, Alberto. 1984. *La sinrazón de Rosa Chacel*. Series De palabra 5. Madrid: Anjana.

Preston, Paul. 1995. *Franco: A Biography*. 1993. London: Fontana.

Quance, Roberta. 1986. En la casa paterna. In *Ángela Figuera Ayermich: Obras completas*. Edited and introduction by Quance, 11–22. Madrid: Hiperión.

Quevedo, Francisco de. 1980. Salmo XVII. In *Poesía lírica del Siglo de Oro*. Edited by Elías L. Rivers, 318. Madrid: Cátedra.

Radcliff, Pamela Beth. 1996. *From Mobilization to Civil War: The Politics of Polarization in the Spanish City of Gijón, 1900–1937*. Cambridge: Cambridge University Press.

Ramos Palomo, María Dolores. 1999. Mujer, asociacionismo y sociabilidad en la coyuntura de 1898: Las afinidades con el fin de siglo europeo. In Sánchez Sánchez and Villena Espinosa 1999, 73–99.

Requena Hidalgo, Cora. 2002. *Rosa Chacel (1898–1994)*. Madrid: Ediciones del Orto.

Resina, Joan Ramon, ed. 2000a. *Disremembering the Dictatorship: The Politics of Memory in the Spanish Transition to Democracy*. Amsterdam: Rodopi.

———. 2000b. Short of Memory: The Reclamation of the Past since the Spanish Transition to Democracy. In Resina 2000a, 83–125.

Richards, Michael. 1996. Civil War, Violence and the Construction of Francoism. In *The Republic Besieged. Civil War in Spain, 1936–1939*. Edited by Paul Preston and Ann L. MacKenzie, 197–239. Edinburgh: Edinburgh University Press.

———. 1998. *A Time of Silence: Civil War and the Culture of Repression in Franco's Spain, 1936–1945*. Cambridge: Cambridge University Press.

———. 2002. From War Culture to Civil Society: Francoism, Social Change and Memories of the Spanish Civil War. In *History and Memory* 14.1–2:93–120.

Ricoeur, Paul. 2004. *History, Memory, Forgetting*. Translated by Kathleen Blamey and David Pellauer. Chicago: University of Chicago Press.

Ringrose, David R. 1996. *Spain, Europe, and the "Spanish Miracle," 1700–1900*. Cambridge: Cambridge University Press.

Rodríguez Fischer, Ana. 1988. El tiempo abarcado. In *Rosa Chacel. Premio Nacional*, 9–23.

———. 1993. Introducción. In Chacel, *Barrio de Maravillas* 1993. Edited, introduction and notes by Rodríguez Fischer, 7–45. Madrid: Castalia / Instituto de la Mujer.

———. 1999. Introducción crítica. In *Prosa española de vanguardia.* Edited and introduction by Rodríguez Fischer, 9–73. Madrid: Castalia.

Rodríguez Puértolas, Julio. 1987. *Literatura fascista española.* Vol. 2, *Antología.* Madrid: Akal.

———. 1995. Democracia, literatura y poder. In Monleón 1995a, 267–77.

Romero Salvadó, Francisco J. 1996. The Failure of the Liberal Project of the Spanish Nation-State, 1909–1923. In Mar-Molinero and Smith 1996, 119–31.

———. 1999. *Spain 1914–1918: Between War and Revolution.* London: Routledge.

Rosa Chacel. Premio Nacional de las Letras Españolas. 1988. Madrid: Biblioteca Nacional.

Rosario de Acuña en la Escuela. 1933. Madrid: De Lamo Hermanos.

Rosario de Acuña: Homenaje. 1992. Gijón: Ateneo Obrero de Gijón.

Ross, Marlon B. 1988. Romantic Quest and Conquest: Troping Masculine Power in the Crisis of Poetic Identity. In *Romanticism and Feminism.* Edited by Anne K. Mellor, 26–51. Bloomington: Indiana University Press.

Ruiz Ramón, Francisco. 1980. *Historia del teatro español: Siglo XX.* 4th ed. Madrid: Cátedra.

Salaün, Serge. 1985. *La poesía de la guerra de España.* Madrid: Castalia.

Salcedo, Emilio. 1983. *Rosa Chacel.* Valladolid: Obra Cultural de la Caja de Ahorros Popular.

Sánchez Sánchez, Isidro, and Rafael Villena Espinosa, eds. 1999. *Sociabilidad fin de siglo: Espacios asociativos en torno a 1898.* Cuenca: Ediciones de la Universidad de Castilla-La Mancha.

Scanlon, Geraldine M. 1986. *La polémica feminista en la España contemporánea (1868–1974).* Translated by Rafael Mazarrasa. Madrid: Akal.

Scarry, Elaine. 1985. *The Body in Pain: The Making and Unmaking of the World.* New York: Oxford University Press.

Schammah Gesser, Silvina. 2006. What to Do with a Distressing Past: The Spanish Civil War in Commemorative Exhibitions and Catalogues. Abstract presented at the conference on War Without Limits, Bristol University, July 19.

Sen, Amartya. 2006. *Identity and Violence: The Illusion of Destiny.* New York: W. W. Norton.

Shaw, Donald L. 1975. *The Generation of 1898 in Spain.* London: Ernest Benn.

Showalter, Elaine. 1990. *Sexual Anarchy: Gender and Culture at the Fin-de-Siècle.* New York: Viking.

Simón Palmer, María del Carmen. 1989. Introducción. In Acuña 1989c, 7–35.

———. 1993. Rosario de Acuña (1851–1923). Translated by Myrsa Landrón. In Gould Levine, Engelson Marson, and Feiman Waldman 1993, 1–11.

Smith, Anthony D. 1996a. Anthony D. Smith's Opening Statement. Nations and Their Pasts. In *Nations and Nationalism* 2.3:358–65.

———. 1996b. Memory and Modernity: Reflections on Ernest Gellner's Theory of Nationalism. In *Nations and Nationalism* 2.3:371–88.

Smith, Theresa Ann. 2006. *The Emerging Female Citizen: Gender and Enlightenment in Spain.* Berkeley: University of California Press.

Soufas, Christopher. 1998. Tradition as an Ideological Weapon: The Critical Redefinition of Modernity and Modernism in Early 20th-Century Spanish Literature. *Anales de la Literatura Española Contemporánea* 23:465–77.

Stallybrass, Peter, and Allon White. 1986. *The Politics and Poetics of Transgression.* London: Methuen.

Stein, Gertrude. 1993. Sacred Emily. In *Geography and Plays,* 178–88. Introduction by Cyrena N. Pondrom. Madison: University of Wisconsin Press.

Steinberg, Leo. 1996. Ad Bynum. In *The Sexuality of Christ in Renaissance Art and in Modern Oblivion,* 364–89. 2nd ed. Chicago: University of Chicago Press.

Stratton, Suzanne L. 1994. *The Immaculate Conception in Spanish Art.* Cambridge: Cambridge University Press.

Suárez Cortina, Manuel, ed. 2003a. *Las máscaras de la libertad. El liberalismo español, 1808–1950.* Madrid: Marcial Pons.

———. 2003b. Republicanismo y nuevo liberalismo en la España del Novecientos. In Suárez Cortina 2003a, 327–58.

Subirats, Eduardo. 1985. *La crisis de las vanguardias y la cultura moderna.* 2nd ed. Madrid: Libertarias.

Teresa de Ávila. 1989. *La vida. Las moradas.* Edited by Antonio Comas. Introduction and notes by Rosa Navarro Durán. Barcelona: Planeta.

Theweleit, Klaus. 1987. *Male Fantasies.* Vol. 1, *Women, Floods, Bodies, History.* Foreword by Barbara Ehrenreich. Translated by Stephen Conway, with Erica Carter and Chris Turner. Cambridge: Polity. Original edition, Marburg: Roter Stern, 1977.

Tone, John Lawrence. 1999. Spanish Women in the Resistance to Napoleon, 1808–1814. In Enders and Radcliff 1999, 259–82.

Torre, Guillermo de. 1974. *Historia de las literaturas de vanguardia.* 2 vols. 3rd ed. Madrid: Guadarrama.

Tranche, Rafael R., and Vicente Sánchez-Biosca. 2002. *NO-DO. El tiempo y la memoria.* 6th ed. 2000. Madrid: Cátedra / Filmoteca Española.

Tusell, Javier. 1999. *España, una angustia nacional.* Madrid: Espasa.

Ugarte, Michael. 1994. The Generational Fallacy and Spanish Women Writing in Madrid at the Turn of the Century. In *Siglo XX/20th Century* 12:261–76.

———. 1996. *Madrid 1900. The Capital as Cradle of Literature and Culture.* University Park: Pennsylvania State University Press.

Unamuno, Miguel de. 1986. *En torno al casticismo.* 1902. Madrid: Alianza.

Uriarte, Edurne. 2003. *España, patriotismo y nación.* Madrid: Espasa.

Vázquez Ramil, Raquel. 2001. *La Institución Libre de Enseñanza y la educación de la mujer en España: La Residencia de Señoritas (1915–1936).* Betanzos: LUGAMI.

Voet, Rian. 1998. *Feminism and Citizenship.* London: Sage.

Vogel, Ursula. 1986. Rationalism and Romanticism: Two Strategies for Women's Liberation. In *Feminism and Political Theory*. Edited by Judith Evans et al., 17–46. London: Sage.

Walker, Lynne. 2002. Home making: An Architectural Perspective. *Signs* 27.1.3 (Spring): 823–35.

Walker Bynum, Caroline. 1982. *Jesus as Mother. Studies in the Spirituality of the High Middle Ages.* Berkeley: University of California Press.

Wallach Scott, Joan. 1988. *Gender and the Politics of History*. New York: Columbia University Press.

Warner, Marina. 1985. *Alone of All Her Sex: The Myth and Cult of the Virgin Mary*. 1976. London: Pan.

White, Sarah L. 1999. Liberty, Honor, Order: Gender and Political Discourse in Nineteenth-Century Spain. In Enders and Radcliff 1999, 233–57.

Wilcox, John C. 1993. Ángela Figuera Aymerich (1902–1984). In Gould Levine, Engelson Marson, and Feiman Waldman 1993, 181–93.

———. 1997. *Women Poets of Spain, 1860–1990: Toward a Gynocentric Vision*. Urbana: University of Illinois Press.

Williams, Raymond. 1973. *The Country and the City*. London: Chatto and Windus.

———. 1985. *Towards 2000*. 1983. Harmondsworth: Penguin.

———. 1989. *The Politics of Modernism: Against the New Conformists*. Edited and introduction by Tony Pinkney. London: Verso.

Wilson, Elizabeth. 1991. *The Sphinx in the City*. London: Virago.

Wolff, Janet. 1990. *Feminine Sentences: Essays on Women and Culture*. Cambridge: Polity.

Wright, Eleanor. 1986. *The Poetry of Protest under Franco*. London: Tamesis.

Young, Iris Marion. 1998. Polity and Group Difference: A Critique of the Ideal of Universal Citizenship. In Phillips 1998, 401–29.

Zabala Aguirre, José Ramón. 1994. *Ángela Figuera: Una poesía en la encrucijada*. Prologue by José Ángel Ascunce. San Sebastián: Universidad de Deusto.

Zaplana, Esther. 2005. Rewriting the *Patria*: War, Militarism and the Feminine *Habitus* in the Writings of Rosario de Acuña, Carmen de Burgos and Emilia Pardo Bazán. In *Bulletin of Spanish Studies* 82.1:37–58.

Zavala, Iris. 1972. *Románticos y socialistas: Prensa española del XIX*. Madrid: Siglo Veintiuno.

Index